# DOUBLE IDENTITY

## The Chinese in Modern Thailand

泰國華僑之雙重身份

# Double Identity

## The Chinese in Modern Thailand

*by*

RICHARD J. COUGHLIN

*Assistant Professor, Department of Sociology and Southeast Asia Studies, Yale University*

HONG KONG UNIVERSITY PRESS
OXFORD UNIVERSITY PRESS
1960

*Printed in April 1960, 2,000 copies*

THE OXFORD UNIVERSITY PRESS, AMEN HOUSE, LONDON, E.C.4
AND 417 FIFTH AVENUE, NEW YORK 16, ARE THE EXCLUSIVE
AGENTS FOR ALL COUNTRIES EXCEPT ASIA EAST OF BURMA

香 港 印
*Printed in Hong Kong by*
CATHAY PRESS
*153 Island Road at Aberdeen*

# CONTENTS


| | | |
|---|---|---|
| | PREFACE ... ... ... ... ... ... | vii |
| I. | DIMENSIONS OF THE PROBLEM ... ... ... | 1 |
| II. | IMMIGRATION AND ITS CONTROL ... ... ... | 13 |
| | Trends and volume, *p. 14*. Sources of immigration, *18*. Reasons for emigrating, *20*. Sex composition, *22*. Control of immigration, *24*. Summary, *29*. | |
| III. | CHINESE COMMUNITY LIFE ... ... ... ... | 32 |
| | Surname associations, *p. 38*. Regional or dialect associations, *40*. Occupational and business associations, *47*. Benevolent and charitable associations, *55*. Functions of associations, *60*. | |
| IV. | HOME AND FAMILY LIFE ... ... ... ... | 67 |
| | The Chinese home, *p. 68*. Marriage and intermarriage, *74*. Ethnic prejudice, *80*. Source of changes, *86*. | |
| V. | TEMPLES, SPIRITS AND FESTIVALS ... ... ... | 92 |
| | Temples and their religious groups, *p. 93*. House spirits and activities, *101*. Religious syncretism, *104*. Festivals and holidays, *106*. | |
| VI. | ECONOMIC ORGANIZATION AND INTERESTS ... ... | 116 |
| | Occupational patterns, *p. 116*. The Chinese in Business, *121*. Government restrictions on the Chinese, *127*. Effect of restrictions, *135*. Land ownership and residence restrictions, *138*. | |
| VII. | CHINESE SCHOOLS AND EDUCATION ... ... ... | 144 |
| | Rise and decline of Chinese education, *p. 145*. Changes in Chinese schools, *153*. Persistence of Chinese schools, *157*. Future prospects, *164*. | |
| VIII. | CITIZENSHIP AND POLITICAL INTERESTS ... ... | 169 |
| | Citizenship by birth, *p. 170*. Citizenship by naturalization, *173*. Rights as citizens, *177*. Chinese political interests, *181*. | |
| IX. | RETROSPECT AND PROSPECTS ... ... ... | 188 |
| | Misconceptions, *p. 188*. Three Spheres of Influence, *190*. The Assimilation question, *192*. Values: Chinese and Thai, *197*. Rapprochement, *199*. Western influence, *202*. China's march South, *203*. | |
| | NOTES ... ... ... ... ... ... | 207 |
| | REFERENCES ... ... ... ... ... ... | 211 |
| | INDEX ... ... ... ... ... ... | 213 |

## TABLES

1. Chinese Aliens in Thailand, based on Census from 1919 to 1947 ... ... ... ... ... ... 17

2. Declared Occupations of Incoming Male Chinese Aliens ... ... ... ... ... ... 21

3. Sex Composition of the Chinese Alien Population ... 23

4. Population Changes of the Chinese Aliens ... ... 24

5. Persons of Chinese Race by Sex ... ... ... 77

6. Numbers of Chinese and Thai Monks and Monasteries 97

7. Occupational Categories ... ... ... ... 119

8. Chinese Schools in Thailand and in Bangkok Province 147

9. Teachers in Registered Chinese Schools: Thai *vs* Chinese ... ... ... ... ... ... 153

10. Thailand's Budget for Education and Aid to Private Schools ... ... ... ... ... ... 162

11. Chinese Applications for Thai Citizenship and Naturalization ... ... ... ... ... 176

## MAPS

Thailand ... ... ... ... ... ... xii

Provinces and Ports of Chinese Emigration ... .. xiii

# PREFACE

THE initial field research on which this book rests was undertaken in Thailand during 1951 and 1952 in order to test, in an Oriental cultural context, certain Western-derived theories relating to the contact of cultures and the assimilation of immigrants; the result of that research appeared in 1953 as the author's doctoral dissertation in Sociology at Yale University, entitled *The Chinese in Bangkok, A Study of Cultural Persistence*. When preparing my dissertation for publication I saw two choices: either to present the material in theoretical and conceptual terms for an audience of professional social scientists, or to write a book which by content and organization would be useful to a wider range of intelligent readers. I chose the latter course for what I regard as good reasons. There is no paucity of publications—books, monographs, articles, newspaper accounts—on the overseas Chinese in Southeast Asia, for this is a strategically located, economically powerful minority whose importance is enhanced now by kith and kin ties with Communist China, a major imperialist force in contemporary Asia. But in recent years the published material, with a few notable exceptions, has seemed either highly specialized and analytical, written like my dissertation by and for academicians, valuable as contributions to knowledge certainly, but remote so far as the general reader is concerned; or, if not heavy, the published accounts have appeared to me one-dimensional and excessively thin; they are rewarding neither so far as new facts are concerned nor the imaginative combination of old facts. It was to fill the gap between the professional tomes and popular literature, and to flesh out the portrait of the overseas Chinese, that this book was written in its present form. Readers who want a theoretical and conceptual orientation for a further understanding of this rich culture contact situation are referred to my dissertation mentioned above. In it will be found the voluminous detail demanded in such studies, only part of which was selected and much of which was briefly summarized for this book. Although both the dissertation and this book are products essentially of my own personal research efforts in Thailand, whenever pertinent other published materials are employed. This book has been broadened, therefore, by points of view other than my own; it has benefited moreover from successive evaluations of the situation

I have made during several visits to Thailand between 1957 and 1959.

The major focus of the book is the contemporary group-life of the Chinese, their community structure, principal institutions and interests. The account carries the Chinese from their origins in China and subsequent emigration, to their possible role today *vis-à-vis* Communist China. An analysis is made of the developments occurring in familial, educational, economic, religious, political and other institutional aspects of overseas Chinese life; and an effort is made to identify the sources of change, within the context of an evolving Chinese community and a Thai society, both of which are increasingly sensitive to Westernizing pressures and trends. The body of social science theory regarding immigration and the subsequent establishment of minority communities is derived very largely from studies of Western societies. The Chinese in Thailand offer an example of a minority in an Asian setting, and the analysis of their adjustment provides not only the perspective of an Eastern experience but understanding as well of similarly situated minorities in other pre-industrial countries elsewhere in the world. The outstanding fact about the Chinese in Thailand is not their stubborn retention of Chinese cultural forms, but their ability to participate successfully, without evidence of social or psychological disorganization or feelings of marginality, as dual members of their own community and of Thai society as well. I have plotted here the extent of this dualism and called attention to the factors leading to its persistence or decline. When useful, historical influences are discussed, but this is essentially a sociological treatise rather than a history of the overseas Chinese.

The period covered is the last half century for the most part, with heavy emphasis on the past three decades. This is the period of serious Thai concern with the Chinese minority when restrictive laws designed to limit its power were promulgated. This is the period of greatest change, so far as the minority is concerned, and therefore the most significant period in the lives of those now composing the Chinese community.

It is easy to become partisan about a minority people on the defensive. But the Chinese in Thailand are not an oppressed group and their only hope for a peaceful future is to seek a closer identification with the national interests of Thailand. This I have tried to say, fairly and objectively. At the same time I have resisted a temptation, undoubtedly felt by all Asian specialists, to avoid criticisms of government policies or discussion of sensitive indigenous cultural patterns for fear that future study and research in the area will be jeopardized. By characterizing the Chinese minority as a 'problem' I am simply repeating local practice, and no derogatory value judgment is intended. Certainly the burden for resolving any difficulties that exist regarding the Chinese rests heavily on both Thai shoulders and those of the overseas Chinese.

In writing this book I reduced or eliminated impediments to readability and comprehension. So far as possible jargon and a specialized vocabulary have been avoided. Foot-notes are minimal and are used only when an explanation or addenda seemed essential. References to sources, quotes or referred to are given in the body of the text, with the author's name followed by the publication date of the cited study and the page reference, as (Landon 1939: 212). Moreover, I have retained generally accepted local spellings and transliterations of Chinese and Thai names, falling back on the Wade-Giles system for Chinese terms only when given no choice. This is not going to please the specialists but it will help the general reader. However, I have been consistent in using the word 'Thai' rather than the more popular term 'Siamese', and for this I have no excuse than to note that the Siamese call themselves Thai.

For those readers who need an informational orientation for Thailand, beyond that given in the text, the following brief description is presented. Thailand lies in tropical, monsoon Asia, south of China (but lacking a common border with that nation) and tucked between Burma on the west, the old Indo-China on the east, and Malaya to the south. It is a country of about 200,000 square miles, roughly the size of France but considerably larger than Japan. The Thai see four geographical regions in their country: the mountainous north notable for its teak forests, tribal minorities, and an industrious peasantry; a dry and barren plateau of the northeast bordered by a mountain range; the extensive central plain, drained by the Chao Phraya River and with Bangkok at its lower edge, containing the great rice-growing area of Thailand; and the long, narrow peninsula reaching southward to the Malayan border important as the Kingdom's rubber and tin producing region. The 1947 census gave the total population as about 17,500,000; it is now (1959) estimated to be 23,000,000, and is growing at a rate of 3 per cent per annum; yet this is an under-populated country compared with other parts of Asia, with only about 18 per cent of the total area under cultivation. Thailand's main exports—rice, rubber, teak, and tin—mirror the non-industrial and agricultural state of the economy and the rural nature of the country.] The capital city of Bangkok, with a population now well over one million (counting the neighbouring suburb of Thonburi) is of pre-eminent social and cultural importance as the Kingdom's only true metropolis; other urban centres are simply market towns, not one of which probably exceeds 50,000 in population. For further details about the country's economy readers are referred to James Ingram's excellent *Economic Change in Thailand since 1850* (Stanford University Press, 1955), and for information about the development of the present constitutional monarchy to D. G. E. Hall's stolid *History of Southeast Asia* (Macmillan, 1955). A good up-to-date study of political, economic, and social features of Thai society is *Thailand* published in 1958 by HRAF Press, New Haven, Connecticut. Cornell University's Southeast Asia Program issued in 1956 as its Data Paper No. 20 a *Bibliography of Thailand;* this is recommended for studies beyond those listed as references for this book.

Many persons have been helpful in preparing this study. The chronological order of contributors would certainly begin with Kenneth Landon who in a discussion during the winter of 1950 urged the Chinese in Thailand as a likely topic for further study; he is not responsible, of course, for the results here produced. I am grateful for the invaluable guidance provided by Professors Maurice R. Davie and Stephen W. Reed of the Sociology faculty of Yale University during my initial field-work and preparation of the dissertation on which this book is based. Among those of greatest assistance in Thailand were a number of government officials, diplomats, teachers, business men, and ordinary citizens whom space does not permit me to mention individually; they can be assured of the depth of my appreciation for their help as friends. The preparation of this book, interrupted in 1955, was able to go forward again thanks entirely to Dr Graham Clark of the Presbyterian Hospital of New York; although never quoted, he has affected all I have seen since that time. Henri Vetch, Publisher of the University of Hong Kong, has been a most patient and knowledgeable editor and friend; it is he who added the final touches before publication.

I should like to thank Mr Er Siak Hong of Bangkok for introductions into the Chinese community, Dr William Gedney and Mom Rajawongse Tanaumsri Devakul for assistance with the translations of Thai laws, Miss Linda Soo for typing parts of the manuscript in Hong Kong, and Mr Robert L. Williams, Research Associate in Cartography of Yale University for preparing the maps. I am appreciative of the grants given by the Social Science Research Council and the United States Education (Fulbright) Foundation to finance my original research.

My wife, Margaret Morgan Coughlin, from beginning to end, has made the contribution that counts for most.

RICHARD J. COUGHLIN

*New Haven, Connecticut*
*December 1959*

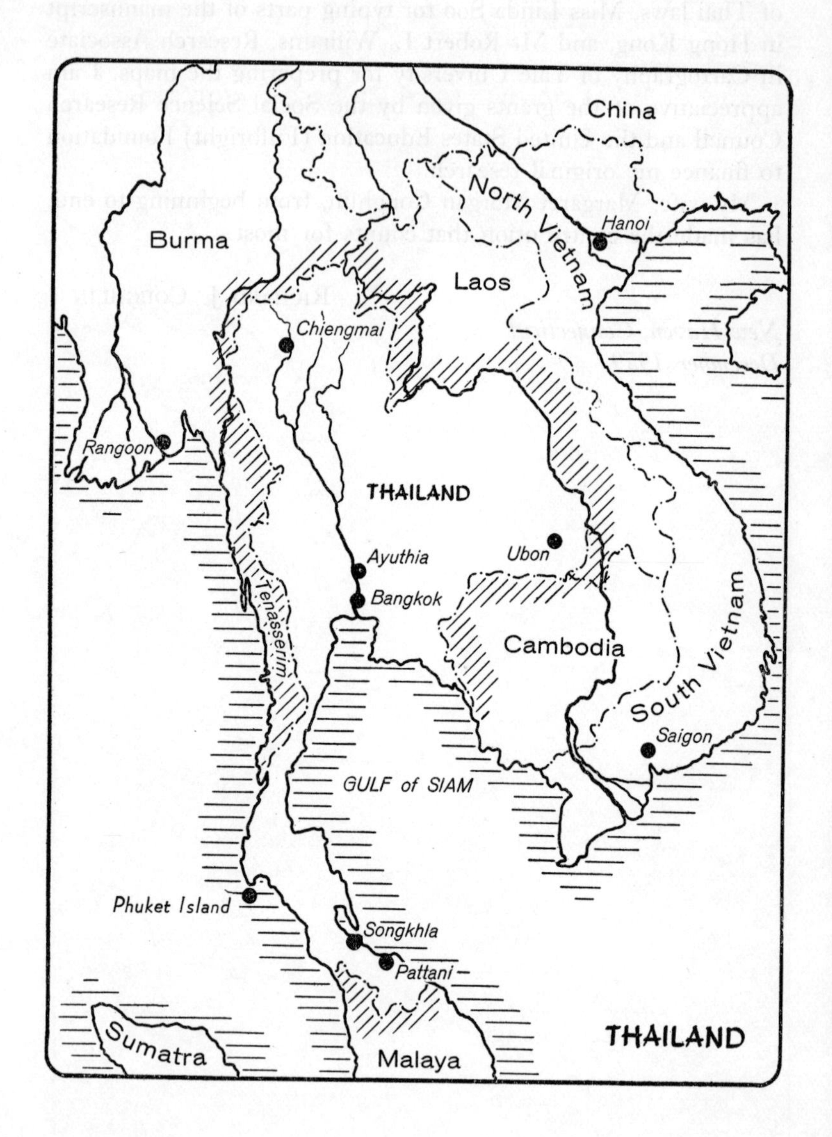
China
North Vietnam
Hanoi
Burma
Laos
Chiengmai
Rangoon
THAILAND
Ubon
Ayuthia
Bangkok
Tenasserim
Cambodia
South Vietnam
Saigon
GULF of SIAM
Phuket Island
Songkhla
Pattani
Sumatra
Malaya
THAILAND

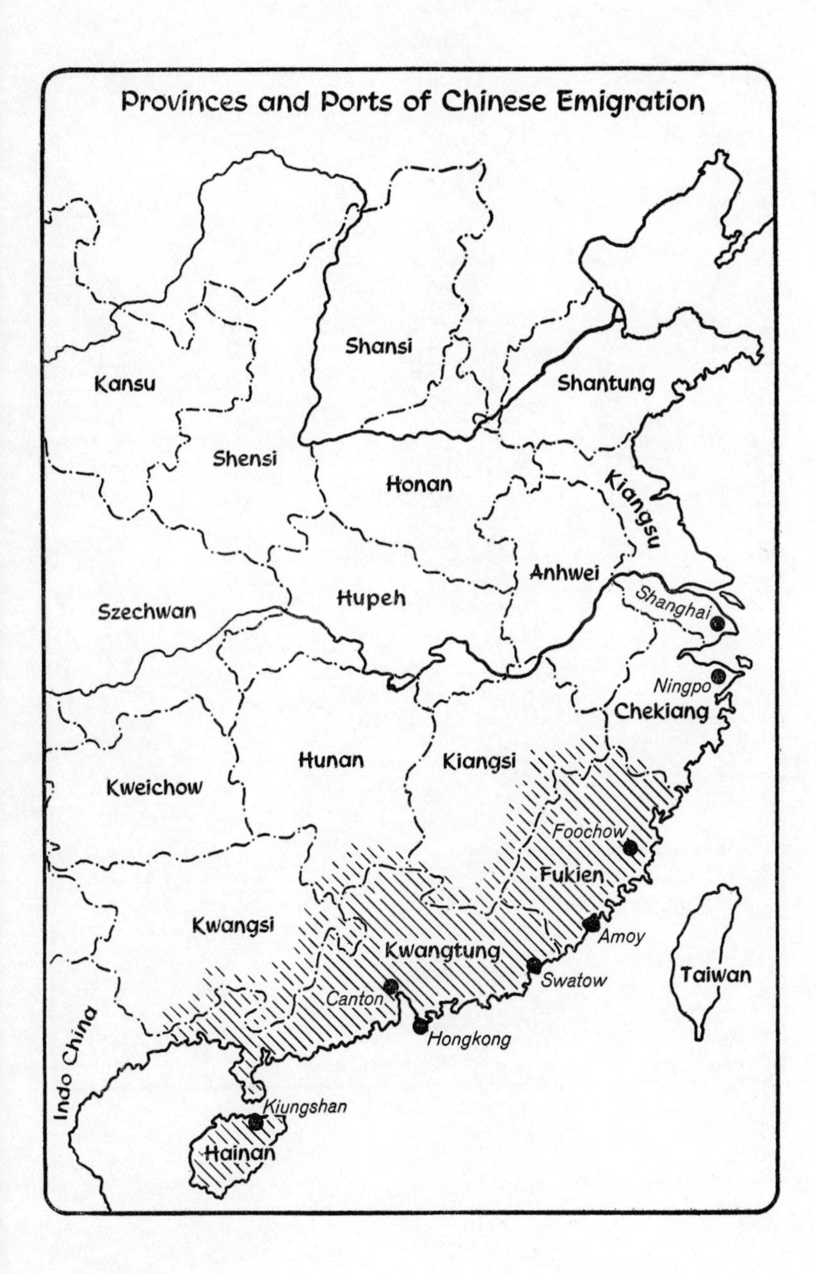
Provinces and Ports of Chinese Emigration
Shansi
Kansu
Shantung
Shensi
Honan
Kiangsu
Anhwei
Szechwan
Hupeh
Shanghai
Ningpo
Chekiang
Hunan
Kiangsi
Kweichow
Foochow
Fukien
Kwangsi
Amoy
Kwangtung
Swatow
Taiwan
Canton
Hongkong
Indo China
Kiungshan
Hainan

CHAPTER I

# DIMENSIONS OF THE PROBLEM

ONE of the most serious concerns of the Thai government for the past forty years or so has been the presence within the national society of an economically powerful minority group whose way of life is alien, and in some respects incompatible, to the Thai way of life. How to assimilate this minority, or at least to reduce its influence nationally, is a question which has troubled a succession of Thai monarchs and prime ministers. To speak of the Chinese minority as constituting a problem is only to recognize this concern felt in varying degrees by all Thai political leaders. Yet, the Chinese living in Thailand are peaceful and self-disciplined, a thrifty and very industrious people who have made significant contributions to their adopted land—to what extent, then, can they be regarded as a 'problem'?

Any ten-day visitor to Thailand cannot help but become aware of one dimension of the 'Chinese problem', his own casual observations providing some measure of its proportions. He will find daily life in the capital of Bangkok dominated by the Chinese: the central business area solidly filled from one street corner to another with Chinese shops and houses, pushing out along arterial roads into neighbourhoods still predominantly Thai. The capital seems now half Chinese and considering the fervent energy of this minority, one can imagine the not far-distant future when, like Singapore, it may become a Chinese city. Outside the capital the Chinese are less numerous but still conspicuous as merchants and traders. In every town, as in the capital, a cluster of Chinese shops forms the main business area. In most of these centres the only accommodations for travellers are provided by Chinese restaurants and hotels, so that a knowledge of Chinese is almost as useful as Thai. Everywhere in the Kingdom one finds the Thai peasant growing rice—this is the product on which the country's economy depends—and everywhere the Chinese dominate the transportation, milling and marketing of this crop. In two other major export industries, tin and rubber production, Chinese supply the bulk of the labour force, and in some of the smaller enterprises, the capital and management as well. They form the backbone of the non-agricultural labour force of the country and as such play a key role in the young labour organizations of the Kingdom. But they are pre-eminently small businessmen and traders, and virtually any article bought or sold in Thailand passes through the hands of one or more Chinese middlemen. Whether one sees the Chinese in Bangkok, or in Chiengmai, or Ubon, or Songkhla, one finds a hardy, enterprising, energetic people exploiting to the fullest extent the commercial opportunities around them.

While the Chinese problem has many dimensions, it is first of all an economic problem, and it is precisely this aspect which looms largest for the Thai. As they see it, the Chinese, welcomed into the Kingdom years ago by a generous government, have since that time subtly undermined the livelihood of the Thai people themselves. They have driven the latter from various skilled crafts, monopolized new occupations, and through a combination of commercial know-how and chicanery have gained a stranglehold over the trade and commerce of the entire Kingdom. The Thai see the Chinese as exploiting unmercifully their advantageous economic position: the Thai are obliged to pay high prices to the Chinese for the very necessities of life, and on the other hand are forced to accept the lowest price for the rice they grow. Through deliberate profiteering, according to standard Thai thinking, this minority has driven up living costs, hitting especially hard government employees on fixed salaries. It is also charged that profits made by the Chinese go out of the country in the form of remittances to China, which means a continuous and gigantic draining away of the Kingdom's wealth. To protect their favoured economic position, one hears, the Chinese have not hesitated to bribe officials, which in turn has undermined the efficiency and morale of the public service. Efforts to protect the economic interests of the Thai people through legislation have been only partially effective, again because of Chinese adeptness at evasion and dissimulation.

Some of these complaints are valid, as this study will show, but often one is reminded of anti-Semitism in the West, and like this latter phenomenon much of the animosity against the Chinese seems based on a partial consideration of the facts. Indeed Western anti-Semitism may well have been involved at the outset in Thailand's reaction toward the Chinese—one still hears educated Thai speak of the overseas Chinese as 'the Jews of the Orient'.

The charge of economic exploitation is so widely heard that it deserves our special attention. Reluctant as many Thai leaders are to admit it, the Chinese are by no means an entirely mischievous element in the country. They provide essential services and in so doing have contributed to the economic development of Thailand. It is indeed doubtful that the country could have achieved her present position as the world's leading exporter of rice and an important source of tin, rubber, teak, wolfram and shellac without the labour and the middleman services of the Chinese. Far from deliberately crowding out Thai workers, until recent times the Chinese have simply filled occupations the Thai themselves were unwilling to enter.

A further qualification must be mentioned. The economic position of the Chinese in Thailand today may only too easily be exaggerated. While it is true that they are overwhelmingly concentrated in trade and commerce, two other groups in the population dominate important segments of the economy. The first of these are Thai women who have a secure position as market sellers, itinerant hawkers of foodstuffs, and proprietors of small shops specializing in dressmaking, hairdressing, and other services for women. Thai women practically run the fresh food markets of the Kingdom, and in any market, whether in the cities or the rural areas, they vastly outnumber Chinese sellers. In these open-air markets a curious ethnic division is apparent: the Thai women sell fresh vegetables, fruit and fish, while the Chinese are the meat retailers, the sellers of notions and cheap manufactured goods. Despite the fact that street hawking of foodstuffs and market selling are occupations favoured by Chinese immigrants, Thai women have never been dislodged from these callings. Only in the northeastern part of Thailand, where in some places Vietnamese women have taken up these occupations, have Thai women been replaced to some extent. There is no reason to expect Thai women to replace Chinese traders, although women do show a marked initiative and interest in commerce, but their continued presence in commercial activities, often in competition with the Chinese, is proof that the latter do not exercise the monopoly over internal trade which is often attributed to them.

The second group firmly entrenched in commerce are Western business men, mainly Europeans. Through the establishment of export-import companies, banks and shipping companies, they have a thorough control over trade and shipping with Europe and the United States, the collection of local products like tin, teak, wolfram and shellac for export, and the financing of commercial transactions. Although Westerners are numerically insignificant—perhaps 3,000 in all—their institutions are among the largest business enterprises in Thailand, and the most financially powerful. Landon (1941: 141) examined the ethnic affiliation of trading firms in the *Directory for Bangkok and Siam* for 1933 and estimated that of the 235 firms listed, 112 were Western, 61 were Chinese and 62 were of other nationality; of the 299 firms in the 1940 Directory, 103 were Western, 98 were Chinese, and 98 were of other nationality; the largest business houses, he writes, were Western. Recently the author asked an officer of a British bank in Bangkok to make an analysis of the nationality of the owners of the 50 leading commercial firms (exclusive of banks) on the basis of confidential information in his files. He reported that 29 of these 50 top companies were Western-owned, only four were Chinese, and 17 were owned by other nationalities (Indians and Near Eastern principally).

Although both Chinese and Westerners are engaged in commerce, there is little competition thus far between them. Rather a symbiotic relationship has developed, with European companies, like the Bombay Burmah Trading Corporation or the Danish East Asiatic Company, bringing Western manufactured products to Thailand, but depending upon Chinese retail shops and itinerant traders to distribute these goods to buyers among the indigeneous population. The Western companies are wholesalers only, the Chinese are the retailers. The arrangement is sensible and profitable. Western companies, long established and well known, have direct access to European and American manufacturers and usually exclusive franchises for the import of certain brands—Omega watches, Chevrolet trucks and so on. On arrival in Bangkok these goods are usually consigned to Chinese wholesalers and jobbers who undertake the task of finding suitable retail outlets. Western banks provide the necessary financing for these commercial transactions.

Here and there, however, some larger Chinese establishments stand by themselves, without direct dependence on Western institutions, the forerunners perhaps of a new kind of Chinese business endeavour. These include a few wealthy rice and rubber exporting firms, three or four influential Chinese banks (branches of larger institutions located in Hong Kong or Singapore), and a growing number of insurance firms dominated by Chinese capital and business leadership. The development of these larger enterprises indicates that the Chinese, now firmly established in retail trade, are gradually enlarging the commercial areas they dominate. But there is little reason to expect that they will easily or quickly gain a complete control over Thailand's trade and commerce.

The Chinese problem has also a demographic dimension. The Chinese form the largest minority in the country, and by all evidences their numbers are increasing despite rigorous limitations on the entry of additional immigrants. Yet one of the curious anomalies of the situation in Thailand is that we have no clear idea how many Chinese are actually in the country.

There are today an estimated ten to fifteen million Chinese living in Southeast Asia and of this number anywhere from half a million to over three million are said to be in Thailand. If only persons possessing Chinese nationality, i.e. Chinese aliens, are counted, then according to the 1947 census 476,582 Chinese resided in the Kingdom, or 2·5 per cent of the total population. Evidence indicates a much larger number of Chinese in the country.[1] Inasmuch as the Chinese minority is a *culture* group, it seems more realistic to count as Chinese any person who is *culturally* Chinese, that is, who speaks Chinese habitually, wears Chinese dress, and in general 'looks' Chinese, or who identifies himself with Chinese, whatever his actual nationality may be. The difficulty here is that no count, official or otherwise, has ever been taken of these persons, and the estimates one finds in the published literature are largely guesses. One writer (CHEN Su-ching 1945:52) declared half the people of Thailand to be Chinese—almost ten million therefore in the current population—but this we can dismiss as a gross exaggeration. The Chinese Nationalist Government in its *China Handbook* for 1955–56 claims a total of 3,690,000 Chinese in Thailand, which is closer to the consensus of other estimators.

Southeast Asian specialists generally agree that there are from 2·3 to 3 million Chinese in Thailand (Skinner 1950: 3; Purcell 1951: 104; Thompson 1955: 44; Skinner 1957: 183).[2] Although based again on subjective impressions, these estimates appear reasonable, which means that 16 per cent of the population, or one person in every six or seven in Thailand, is Chinese, by nationality or cultural affiliation. In this study the broader definition of 'Chinese' will be used, unless otherwise specified, to mean these persons who are culturally Chinese and who regard themselves as members of the Chinese community in Thailand.

Probably half the Chinese in Thailand live in Bangkok or nearby in the Chao Phraya River delta of the Central Plains. A second major concentration occurs in the Kra Isthmus region of southern Thailand where the tin and rubber industries are centred. Every town and large village has Chinese residents, and while no province is without some Chinese, those in the extreme western part of the Kingdom, in the north, and the northeast, which are removed from railroads and main roads, are very lightly settled.

These demographic facts contribute their bit to Thai awareness of the Chinese problem. Being a highly concentrated minority, the Chinese are conspicuous, and seem to form an even larger group than they actually do. Their concentration in Bangkok is a continual reminder to government leaders that the Kingdom is threatened with not only economic but social and political domination by the Chinese. This may well be an unrealistic fear, yet it cannot be denied that the tendency of this minority to concentrate in certain areas, to form numerically powerful communities, in short to dominate the landscape has helped it to resist assimilative influences.

The Chinese minority in Thailand does not form a homogeneous group, although the basis for unity is developing steadily. The most pronounced differences stem from their identification with various 'dialect' or speech groups. Almost the entire Chinese immigrant population of Thailand—and indeed throughout Southeast Asia generally—comes from South China, particularly from the provinces of Kwangtung and Fukien. The people themselves in this part of China are divided into speech groups, each occupying a fairly well-defined region of China. The Chinese population of Thailand is represented by the following major divisions:

1. *Teochiu* (or Tiochiu, Twechew, Chaochow, etc.). This speech group in China is centred in the cities of Swatow and Chaochow (hence the name given to this group), and the surrounding rural areas of the Han River delta in northeastern Kwangtung Province. In Southeast Asia they are sometimes referred to as the 'Swatow people'.

2. *Hakka.* Unlike the Teochiu this speech group in China is concentrated in no urban centre of its own. Hakka-speaking people occupy a band of country stretching east and west from Fukien to Kwangsi and compressed between the two parallel mountain ranges running to the north of Kwangtung Province. However, Hakka farming villages are scattered through South China, around the British Crown Colony of Hong Kong and on Hainan Island.

3. *Hainanese* (or Hailam). This group forms the major population (but not the aboriginal inhabitants) of Hainan Island, which is part of Kwangtung Province. The Hainanese in Southeast Asia appear to have originated in two rural districts in the northeastern part of the Island.

4. *Cantonese.* The most numerous language group in South China (estimated at more than 30 million), is the Cantonese; it forms the major population of Kwangtung and parts of southeastern Kwangsi Province. The city of Canton is the centre of settlement.

5. *Hokkien* (or Fukienese). The Hokkien speech group in China occupies the southern section of Fukien Province with the city of Amoy as its centre. Spoken Hokkien is similar to Teochiu (Swatow) but it differs so considerably from the speech of other Fukienese that it can be regarded as a distinct language.

In addition to these groups, there are a smaller number of immigrants from Taiwan, and from the Shanghai and Ningpo areas of China.

The size of each dialect group is not known with certainty and again we must place reliance on estimates. Of the total Chinese population in Thailand the Teochiu people are estimated to constitute about 56%, Hakka 16%, Hainanese 12%, Cantonese 7%, Hokkien also 7% and Taiwanese and others together about 2% (Skinner 1957:212). The Fukienese are the oldest group in Thailand and are concentrated now in the southern provinces where the early immigrants came to work tin mines. Teochiu people have their heaviest concentration in the Bangkok area whence they have been moving out in numbers to other parts of the Kingdom, particularly to the south.

The so-called 'dialects' spoken by these groups are in actuality distinct languages; they are mutually unintelligible, and differ from one another in both pronunciation and vocabulary.[3] A Cantonese cannot understand a Teochiu, nor a Hakka a Hainanese. Within each speech group there are further sub-divisions comparable to village or locality differences; these alone are true dialects.

Spoken language is the most obvious divisive factor within the Chinese community in Thailand. The average Chinese thinks of himself primarily in terms of his speech group; he is a Teochiu, or Cantonese, or Hakka, etc. Each dialect group is very cohesive, the fact that most immigrants originate in a few villages or rural districts of China contributes to these ties. The dialect associations, which are among the most influential Chinese organizations in Thailand, help to perpetuate the ethnocentric sentiments of each language group. To some extent these groups are characterized by distinctive occupations. Thus the Teochiu compose the majority of the large wholesalers; the Cantonese form a high proportion of the mechanics and carpenters; the Hainanese are chiefly engaged in domestic service and form the staff of many European households, clubs and Chinese restaurants. These distinctions are by no means absolute or rigid, however.

[By virtue of their numbers and their wealth, the Teochiu occupy a dominant commercial position in the Chinese community and, therefore, are occasionally resented by other dialect groups.] The Cantonese, who have a high proportion of doctors and dentists, tend to look down upon the Teochiu as parvenus, uncouth but rich peasants. Teochiu women are said to occupy a more inferior position than women in the other dialect groups. [Yet while differences are recognized, there is no overt hostility among the various dialect groups.] In urban centres, they mix together in business and in residential areas, and they mingle without hesitation in the institutions and activities of the Chinese community. [Some 30 years ago each dialect association maintained its own schools in which its dialect was the sole medium of instruction. Schools are still run or supported by these associations, but now Mandarin *(kuo-yü)*, the national language of China, is the medium of instruction for all.] [Although there seems to be an understandable preference for marriage within one's group, 'dialectual exogamy' is not uncommon. Whatever their language differences, the Chinese in Thailand are generally alike in physical appearance, dress and religion.]

In addition, to the dialect groups, there are significant differences among the overseas Chinese in social and economic standard of living. While the wealthy Chinese merchant is most conspicuous, probably a good proportion of the overseas Chinese eke out a bare subsistence. It would be premature to speak of class difference among the Chinese minority in Thailand, but in certain places an incipient class structure seems to be emerging along occupational, economic and dialectual lines—in southern Thailand, for example, in towns like Phuket, and Songkhla, the settled Fukienese group, representing wealth and influence in local politics, holds itself aloof from the poorer group of Teochiu. Finally, the political split that has formed between Nationalist and Communist Chinese elsewhere is in Thailand a deep and bitter source of difference among the Chinese.

The political and legal dimensions of the Chinese problem might be expected in any country which has evolved only recently from a traditionally autocratic system of government. [Until 1932 the government of Thailand was an absolute monarchy. Apart from the purely advisory functions of a small group of high-ranking royalty and officials, there was no popular participation in the government. In June 1932 a group of Western-educated intellectuals backed by Army officers overthrew this government and established a constitutional monarchy under which the King was stripped of his former powers, a parliament created with all Thai citizens 21 years and over given the right to vote, and a cabinet form of government, similar to that in the United Kingdom, established. This constitutional government under three different kings has ruled the country to the present time.

Outwardly this government is democratic, but in practice it remains autocratic; the king as the repository of power has been merely replaced by a handful of military men who since the Revolution have held tight the reins of government while practicing their own brand of 'guided democracy'. Half of the National Assembly is still appointed, and sufficient influence maintained in the other half to enable the group in power to control parliament. With the promise of self-government largely nullified, and parliament subservient to the whims and prejudices of ultra-nationalists, legislation has frequently been anti-foreign and specifically anti-Chinese.

Not elections but *coups d'état* provide the principal dynamic for political change; in the 26 years since the 1932 Revolution there have been 13 coups and attempted coups. Since World War II especially, struggles for power between various individuals supported by factions in the armed forces have led to one coup after another, each one increasingly destructive of property and civic liberties, each one a further impediment to Thailand's slow march toward democracy. By and large, the people are politically apathetic or inexperienced, while among the politically sophisticated one finds an undercurrent of cynicism and disillusionment not greatly different from that reported for large American cities ruled by political machines.

Such a situation has kept the Chinese out of politics and, so far as the government is concerned, simplified the onerous task of communication directives and the like to the entire group. At the same time, however, it has encouraged the massing of talent and money behind purely Chinese activities and institutions and has thus contributed to the perpetuation of a distinctly Chinese way of life. Moreover, many Chinese business men find they can buy protection and privileges from venal politicians, and have done so, thereby weakening the whole structure of responsible government.

The denial of full rights, particularly in the political sphere, is often justified on the ground of security. Because of cultural affinities between the overseas Chinese and their homeland, and the understandable pride the former take in achievements of China, the Chinese minority in Thailand may be more susceptible to Chinese Communist infiltration and subversion than other peoples in the Kingdom. Under these circumstances, is it reasonable, ask many Thais, to give them the same rights and political opportunities which might be used to throw Thailand into the Communist camp? This is a real fear and to some extent a real danger, although internal security and Communism provide an all too easy justification for any violation of democratic rights. These are issues, however, on which Thai leaders would want reassurances before amending their present policies toward the Chinese minority.

Finally, the social and cultural dimensions of the Chinese problems cannot be overlooked, for they lie at the very root of the exclusiveness which characterizes both the Chinese and Thai communities. When considering the position of the overseas Chinese in Southeast Asia today, a distinction should be made between the great civilization which arose in China historically and the unschooled peasants who have for the most part emigrated into Southeast Asia in recent times. The overseas Chinese only in a very attenuated sense can be considered the bearers of that great civilization. The typical overseas Chinese, it is true, has often a sense of his own cultural superiority over the alien people among whom he lives. Many of the traditional values regarding the family particularly which are associated with classical China by Western scholars are exemplified by the overseas Chinese. Yet other values are conspicuously absent. The typical Chinese immigrant is more likely than not to be illiterate, uncouth in his manners even by traditional Chinese standards, ignorant about Chinese history, geography, literature, philosophy and the arts; a simple spirit worshipper in his religious beliefs; unappreciative of scholarship, and interested chiefly in getting rich. The acquisition of wealth helps to smooth off the rough corners but it rarely produces a Confucian gentleman and much less a scholar. Undoubtedly, much of the unfavourable reaction to this minority stems from the fact that many imigrants are coarse and rough, often lacking in personal cleanliness (particularly when compared to Southeast Asian peoples), and insanitary about their living conditions.

The Chinese and the Thai are both Mongoloid peoples, and thus racially alike, although some physical differences are recognized. Both people trace their ancient origins to the present territorial area of China; yet despite this historical affinity, any cultural similarities which may have existed between the two peoples were erased centuries ago by the rich infusion into Southeast Asia of Indian cultural influences, particularly Theravada Buddhism, which transformed Thai culture and society. Consequently, the Thai and the Chinese today differ in language, literature, music, drama, religion, family organization, and in the values and activities relating to these aspects of culture. Such cultural differences as these cannot but encourage separation rather than the integration of the two peoples (Coughlin 1955).

Yet the very fact of contact over a period of time has inevitably produced changes among the overseas Chinese. Like Chinese everywhere they have a well-ingrained cultural pattern of adaptability and flexibility. Culturally and socially this minority in Thailand has learned to accept Thai ways without, however, losing its attachment to Things Chinese. The question is whether these changes represent simply protective coloration or true identification with Thai society. It is the seemingly opportunistic and vacillating quality of their cultural and social dualism which has made the Chinese, in the opinion of many responsible Thai, only summer patriots and fair-weather citizens.

In the following chapters we shall treat in detail the major influences which have contributed to the development of this dualism, paying particular attention to those overseas institutions and related values which give the Chinese community a separatist character. The central interest throughout will be those conditions affecting the integration of the Chinese and Thai people and leading to the perpetuation or the elimination of the Chinese 'problem'. The present status and future position of this minority has significance beyond Thailand, for two reasons. As the only independent country of Southeast Asia during the colonial period, Thailand began earlier and has gone further in limiting the activities of its Chinese minority. In the other countries of this region, the colonial powers protected and encouraged minority interests, and under colonialism these groups flourished. With independence has often come a hard intransigence on the part of the new national leaders toward the so-called 'foreign' minorities, mainly the overseas Chinese. For South Vietnam, Cambodia, Laos, Burma, Malaya, the Philippines, and Indonesia seeking ways and means to handle a suddenly difficult internal problem, the policies and devices of Thailand provide a ready example, all the more instructive because it is an Asian example. The Chinese in Thailand are representative in broad outline of Chinese minorities elsewhere in Southeast Asia where their situation has in general the same dimensions. Thailand therefore should provide insights into similar problems for the other countries of the region.

But further than this, our enquiry may also help to understand a type of immigrant adjustment which thus far has received little attention in studies of assimilation. We refer specifically to societies, like that of Thailand, characterized traditionally by a two-fold division of the population into peasantry and officialdom, with little indigenous development of trade and commerce beyond dealings in local agricultural produce and domestic handicrafts. With the penetration of industrialized nations and the resulting modernization, these societies offer new and increasing opportunities for commercial expansion, principally in the realm of retail trade. Go-betweens are needed to funnel imported consumer goods through wholesale and retail outlets to the mass of the population. An immigrant group may take advantage of this need far more readily than the indigenous people whose social goals continue to be realized within the framework of the traditional class and occupational structure. An immigrant group may thereby work itself into privileged economic and social positions and successfully resist integration; further economic development simply reinforces its strong position. The Chinese in Thailand are illustrative of such a group, though other groups exist in similarly underdeveloped countries of Southeast Asia, South America, the West Indies and the Near East.

CHAPTER II

# IMMIGRATION AND ITS CONTROL

OUT of the long sea coast that comprises South China, several million Chinese have emigrated to Southeast Asia since the beginning of this century. The two provinces of Kwangtung and Fukien have supplied the majority of these emigrants, many coming in particular from Hainan Island, a part of Kwangtung Province.

Seen in broadest perspective, this great movement has probably been one of the larger human migrations of the present century, a slow but relentless overflow of exceedingly populous provinces. To the principals concerned, however, it has the character of a simple, localized movement. The individual Chinese in Thailand, for example, does not ordinarily think of himself as a native of one or the other province. Rather he describes himself as a member of a certain dialect group, and often the immigrant names the specific village from which he has come. This great migration has temporarily at least run its course—travel from Mainland China is beset with difficulties, and Chinese immigrants are no longer as welcome in Thailand as formerly. Whether this is only a lull remains to be seen, but even this respite is one of the more hopeful features of the Chinese problem in Thailand.

By contrast with the situation in some other countries of Southeast Asia, where detailed and accurate immigration statistics have long been compiled, information about Chinese immigration to Thailand is incomplete and often misleading. A number of difficulties stand in the way of obtaining a clear historical picture of Chinese immigration to Thailand. Statistics by nationality or race collected for the Port of Bangkok, available only since 1918–19, show the total numbers of persons of Chinese nationality entering and departing, but no distinction is made between immigrants and non-immigrants (persons in transit to another country, for instance) and no attempt is made in these statistics to separate those who made several trips to Thailand from those who arrived or departed only once. Thus a Bangkok business man who makes five trips to Hong Kong will be counted as an entering Chinese each time he returns to Thailand. Only since 1921–1922 have Chinese women been counted separately from men, and consequently to determine the extent of Chinese female immigration before 1921 is virtually impossible. Official statistics fail to take into account, of course, any illegal entry, or forced immigration of Chinese by the Japanese military during World War II.

The national censuses of 1919, 1929, 1937, and 1947, provide a more accurate count of the Chinese population in Thailand and by inference reflect the extent of Chinese immigration. Prior to 1919 one must rely for the most part on the informal and impressionistic observations of visitors to Thailand, supplemented to a limited extent by official counts for purposes of taxation.

All these sources, official and otherwise, although varying greatly in reliability and accuracy, do present a consistent picture of a continuing stream of Chinese immigration. We have no reason to doubt these various reports as indicative of trends in Chinese immigration, even though they are not probably accurate as to specific details.

### TRENDS AND VOLUME

Chinese immigration to Thailand is not a new phenomenon, although in the course of the last century the characteristics and the volume of this immigration have changed markedly.

The first published European accounts about the Thai Kingdom in the seventeenth century mentioned the presence at the capital of several thousand Chinese artisans and merchants, the latter engaged in trade between Thailand and other Oriental countries. At the close of the seventeenth century, some 3,000 Chinese were said to be living at Ayuthia, then the capital. By the middle of the nineteenth century several thousand Chinese immigrants each year were reportedly entering the Kingdom, and travellers to Thailand began to comment upon their presence. H. S. Hallett, an Englishman who visited the Kingdom in 1884, declared that 'the Chinamen in Siam seem to be ubiquitous. Half the population of the Menam delta — the Bangkok area — is Chinese and very few of the people are without some trace of Chinese blood in them' (Hallett 1890: 460). He went on to say that the Chinese formed one-third of the total population, probably in the neighbourhood of 9 million. Obviously this was a wild guess. A government-sponsored publication gave a more reasonable estimate (Carter 1904:111). Using poll-tax returns, the Chinese alien population of Bangkok in 1900 was estimated at 85,500 in a total urban population of 500,000. By 1903, using the same method of calculation, the number of Chinese aliens in Bangkok had risen to 100,000. Given the importance of the capital, certainly more than half the Chinese population was concentrated there or in the near vicinity. A good guess would place the total Chinese population in the entire country at about 170,000 at the turn of the century. The Chinese came, then as now, from the maritime regions of South China.

Large scale Chinese immigration to Thailand and to other areas of Southeast Asia had already begun by this time. A combination of factors, both in China and in Southeast Asia, caused the increase.

Until the middle of the nineteenth century emigration from China had been prohibited and those who departed illegally were treated as outcasts and were not as a rule allowed to re-enter China. Any who did return ran the risk of flogging, imprisonment and even death. This prohibition to emigration applied not only to persons wishing to settle permanently abroad but often to itinerant merchants as well. It seems to have stemmed, at least in part, from the Chinese attitude of superiority with regard to other peoples. A Chinese who preferred to live among barbarians must likewise be an inferior person. But a more practical reason was the fear of pirates who raided coastal towns and the feeling that people who left China were in league with these pirates. Inasmuch as dissident political elements fled abroad, there was the additional fear that overseas communities were hotbeds of potential intrigue against the Emperor. At this time, too, Western powers were forcing their way into China, and the government entertained the fear that Chinese who had lived many years abroad might be used to advance the designs of these foreign powers. During this period, therefore, emigration from China was minimal.

Following the Opium War with Britain, in 1842, China was forced by several treaties with European powers to accord Westerners the privilege of travel and residence in China. As a consequence Europeans began to recruit Chinese labourers for their rapidly expanding colonial possessions in Southeast Asia. The Chinese government's attitude toward this practice gradually softened, although, while accepting the principle of emigration, it still tried to reduce the unrestricted recruitment of labour. By 1894, the repressive policies of the government regarding emigration were officially abrogated and Chinese diplomatic and consular officers instructed for the first time to protect Chinese residents abroad. Imperial envoys subsequently went out from China to visit Chinese settlements in Southeast Asia in order to strengthen the bonds between these overseas Chinese and the mother country. Thereafter no hindrance was placed in the path of Chinese wishing to emigrate, and no official displeasure was vented on those who returned to China after years of residence abroad.

Yet one must doubt whether the Chinese government could have held back the flood of emigrants to Southeast Asia as Western activities there opened up tremendous new commercial opportunities. The later nineteenth and early twentieth centuries was a period of Western mercantile expansion into the Far East generally. With the advent of Western entrepreneurs and of Western capital the demand for unskilled labour became heavy—coolies were needed for tin mines, for railway construction which proceeded apace in all countries, and later for the burgeoning rubber plantations. As never before or since, during this period Southeast Asia became a land of promise for the poor peasants of South China, and in steadily increasing numbers they streamed out of China to Thailand and other countries of the Nan-Yang 南洋 ('Southern Ocean').

Moreover, under the drive of Western merchants foreign and domestic trade in all countries grew by leaps and bounds, and in this commercial expansion the Chinese benefited no less than the Westerners. Thailand felt the effects of this commercial revolution only after 1855 when the Bowring Treaty between Thailand and Great Britain was signed. From the later seventeenth century Thai monarchs, prompted by fears of subjugation by Western powers, had shut off the Kingdom from commercial intercourse with the West. The treaty which Sir John Bowring negotiated definitely ended this seclusion and threw open the doors to virtually unrestricted trade with the West. Henceforth the character of the Chinese immigrant gradually changed from that of a simple Oriental trader or labourer to an essential middleman between Western importers and exporters on the one hand and the mass of the peasant population on the other. Chinese shopkeepers and itinerant traders funneled the manufactures of the West from European import houses in Bangkok to the indigenous population throughout the Kingdom, and at the same time acted as collection agencies for local products—tin, shellac, rubber—exported to the industries of the West. In the Thai ethos there was lacking then as now a tradition or a liking for trade and commerce. Thai who by dint of ability and education rose above the peasantry sought careers as government officials, not as traders and merchants. It was thus the overseas Chinese who supplied the necessary distribution link between the Western manufacturer and the Thai consumer. Other opportunities opened for the newcomers; they supplied both unskilled labour and craftsmen for the physical expansion of the capital and for roads, railways and canal construction throughout the country. And as rice production rose, new careers opened up for the Chinese as rice traders, moneylenders, barge operators and rice-mill owners. In a steadily swelling stream the Chinese fanned out to towns and villages throughout the Kingdom, and the limitless opportunities opened before them drew fresh waves of immigrants from South China.

By the time of the first full census in 1919 the Chinese were by far the largest minority group in the Kingdom, and as the following statistics indicate, they have increased in numbers until only recent times:

1. CHINESE ALIENS IN THAILAND
BASED ON CENSUS FROM 1919 to 1947

| *Year* | *Total Population* | *Chinese* | *Intercensal Percentage Increase or Decrease* | *Percentage of Total Population* |
|---|---|---|---|---|
| 1919 | 9,207,355 | 260,194 | — | 2·8 |
| 1929 | 11,506,207 | 445,274 | 41·5 | 3·9 |
| 1937 | 14,464,105 | 524,062 | 15·0 | 3·6 |
| 1947 | 17,422,689 | 476,582 | *−9·06* | 2·7 |

SOURCE: *Statistical Year-Book of Thailand*, 1939-1944; 1952.

If we assume that immigrants accounted for the major part of the Chinese minority, as seems reasonable, a comparison of these census statistics shows a net increase by immigration from 1919 to 1929 of 185,000 persons, or a minimum net immigration of 17,000 per year. From 1929 to 1937, the increase was considerably less—79,000 or about 10,000 per year—indicating a much smaller flow of immigrants during the world depression.

In the five-year period of 1937–1941 a net gain, i.e. excess of entrants over outgoers, of some 35,000 Chinese, was recorded at the Port of Bangkok, the major port of legal entry for the Chinese, or an average of 7,000 persons a year. During the principal war years, 1942–1944, the immigration of Chinese was numerically insignificant—officially recorded as only 175 at the Port of Bangkok. However, immigration from China spurted ahead at the end of the

War. In response to an informal query, the Immigration Department reported for the period 1945–1950 a net gain of almost 100,000 Chinese through the Port of Bangkok, or a yearly average of about 16,000 persons. These figures include immigrants newly arriving in Thailand as well as former residents of the Kingdom returning from a temporary stay abroad. In view of the fact that the census shows a net loss of 47,480 in the Chinese alien group between 1937 and 1941, it seems likely that many Chinese entering Thailand after the War were former residents who had left the Kingdom before the War.

The importance of Chinese immigration becomes apparent when it is compared to immigration from other Far Eastern countries. With the possible exception of movement of peoples across the border from contiguous areas of Malaya and Indo-China, which is periodically heavy but usually not for permanent residence, immigration has been almost exclusively Chinese. Both Japan and India have been unimportant as sources of immigrants. Counting all categories of aliens, statistics for the Port of Bangkok show a total net immigration of only 151 Japanese from 1922 through 1937, and a net loss of some 17 Indians during the same period (*Statistical Year-Book* 1939–44: 66). These statistics must be accepted with considerable reserve, like all Thai statistics, yet they are in general agreement with census figures. The census of 1937 showed a total of 514 Japanese and about 13,000 Indians living in Thailand. According to this census, there was in that year a total non-Chinese alien population of about 100,000 persons. If alien peoples from contiguous areas (Malaya, Indo-China, Burma) are excluded from this census count, there was in 1937 a total non-Chinese alien population of only 35,000 persons, as compared to more than half a million alien Chinese.

## SOURCES OF IMMIGRATION

The Thai government collects no data on the origin in China of aliens entering or residing in the Kingdom. However, on the basis of membership in the Chinese dialect associations, which derive from common regional origins in China, it is apparent that the great majority of the Chinese in Thailand have come from the South China provinces of Fukien and Kwangtung, including Hainan Island. Occasionally one meets an immigrant from one of the large cities of South China—Canton, Swatow, Amoy or

Foochow—but these are the exceptions. The great majority of the Chinese immigrants to the Nan-Yang is from rural villages or small country towns in the hinterland of these large metropolises.

No comparable movement into Southeast Asia has taken place from other provinces of China. In 1949, when the eventual success of the Chinese Communists in China became apparent, there was an exodus of Chinese business men from the cities of central and north China threatened by the Communist armies. The refugees who left China at that time fanned out into Hong Kong, Taiwan, and the countries of Southeast Asia. A number made their way to Thailand. In Bangkok where they have settled these refugees are usually referred to as 'Shanghai Chinese' or, more commonly, 'White Chinese', the latter term being used to distinguish them from the 'Red Chinese' of the Communist regime. Whereas the immigrants from South China can be counted in the hundreds of thousands, these newcomers amount to only a few thousand—quantitatively an insignificant group in the mass of the south Chinese. Yet like the European refugees who entered the United States in the immediate prewar years, these White Chinese are a superior group; because of their professional and educational qualifications, their wealth and cosmopolitan outlook, they are a potentially leavening element among the Chinese in Thailand.[1]

The South China Teochiu village, intensively studied by D. H. Kulp (1925), which he called 'Phenix Village', may be taken as typical of the communities from which the older immigrant generation in Thailand come. Phenix village was located on a small tributary of the Han River, some distance inland from the coastal city of Swatow but less than half a mile from a neighbouring village. It covered a small area—about seven hundred feet wide and two thousand feet long—not all of which was occupied by buildings. The majority of the villagers were farmers or members of farm families, and in the accepted Chinese manner they had built their houses together in the village rather than separately upon their land. Around the village proper lay the farm lands and the orange and pomelo groves.

Phenix village contained some 650 persons, but the population of other South China villages might vary from a few hundred to several thousand. In Phenix village were 110 buildings, large and small, of which 30 shops located at the periphery of the village made up the business section. Besides this market area, ancestral halls, village temples, tea-shops, and gambling houses were centres of village activity. Beyond the village on hilly ground were located the family tombs.

From Phenix village dirt paths led out to other settlements. At the time Kulp wrote—the early 1920s—throughout the rural district surrounding the village vehicles were completely absent. Goods were carried on poles over the shoulder. The well-to-do rode in sedan-chairs, and others walked. When possible the river was used for transportation. A trip of several hours by ferry brought the villagers to the largest town and railhead. Few went regularly beyond this point or took note of events that occurred farther away.

The simple regularity of farm life of Phenix village was periodically shattered by disastrous floods from the nearby river. Kulp writes that 'one can readily detect the yellow lines in the rooms of village houses and on the walls of the exteriors that indicate the high water marks of floods'. (Kulp 1925: 26). The cost of these ravages can be surmised from the common village saying: 'To be free from floods for three successive years would be to adorn our hogs with shining rings of gold'. Against these floods and the equally disastrous droughts the villagers had no protection. They lived simply, yet always on the bare edge of subsistence; and when the level of production dropped, many were forced to emigrate to the cities or to the lands of Southeast Asia.

### REASONS FOR EMIGRATING

Economic adversity of one kind or another has thus been the principal reason for emigration. The internal chaos attendant upon the dissolution of the Manchu Empire and the establishment of the Chinese Republic in 1912 stimulated emigration. But natural calamities stand out as the major factor—for example, after a tidal wave swept over an area near Swatow in 1922 scores of families emigrated from the flooded regions to Southeast Asia. The extreme crowding of available land in South China and the precarious existence that many peasants and townspeople led made emigration imperative when population began to outdistance the available food supply, or when their livelihood was otherwise endangered.

The typical Chinese immigrant was pushed by intolerable living conditions at home; but he was also pulled by the attraction of better opportunities overseas. The simple desire for quick gains, for enlargement of business experience, for education, or for adventure have played but a small part in overseas emigration. Religious persecution has not been a cause for emigration, nor has political involvement apparently been a significant factor. Landon (1941: 198) who asked many Chinese why they came to Thailand, writes that 'almost invariably the Chinese so interrogated draws a word picture of privation and hardship in China which has driven him in search of the larger freedom and opportunity which Thailand offered'.

Personal observation and the questioning of immigrant Chinese shows that while many were farmers in China, a good proportion were in other occupations. Some were fishermen or boatmen, a considerable number were artisans—carpenters, basket-makers, masons, tinkers, tailors—others in China had been marginal traders or small merchants. The following data collected from official publications supports the conclusion that the majority of immigrants were small traders or labourers, perhaps in addition to being farmers; it is not uncommon for farmers in China to have some craft or trade whereby they are able to make up for their insufficient agricultural incomes.

2. DECLARED OCCUPATIONS OF INCOMING MALE CHINESE ALIENS

| *Occupations* | *1935–36* | *1936–37* | *1937–38* |
|---|---|---|---|
| General Labourers | 1,782 | 1,911 | 2,731 |
| Professional | 251 | 178 | 1,742 |
| Commercial | 17,100 | 20,095 | 19,510 |
| Officials | 4 | 25 | — |
| Agriculturists | 150 | 109 | 375 |
| Personal and Domestic | 53 | 181 | 2,333 |
| Theatrical | 339 | 106 | 126 |
| Others and not stated | 237 | 277 | 1,527 |
| Total | 19,916 | 22,882 | 28,344 |

SOURCE: *Statistical Year-Book of Siam*, 1935-37

In view of these data the successful economic adjustment of the Chinese immigrant in Thailand is not surprising, for many arrived in the Kingdom with skills or crafts they could immediately utilize or with commercial experience that gave a sound basis for active participation in the business life of the Chinese community. However, one must accept with some reservations the figures on

'Professionals' given in the above compilation, for few doctors, dentists, teachers, or even scholars in the traditional Chinese sense have emigrated overseas.

In general, immigrants have been illiterate, coarse by urban standards, and poor. Most had struggled hard to make a livelihood in China, and they arrived at their destination almost penniless. They had not been recruited by labour contractors as happened frequently in other parts of Southeast Asia, and thus no promised job awaited them.

Yet it would be a mistake to consider these immigrants of the last several decades alone and friendless in an alien land. Even before leaving China, their way had been smoothed by good organization and a spirit of co-operation. The prospective immigrants merely registered with a hotel in any of the cities of South China, and this hotel secured passage for the immigrant and his family if necessary—usually on the open deck of a European coastal steamer—took care of legal documentation, and saw that at their destination the emigrants were welcomed by persons speaking their own dialect, guided safely through immigration inspection, and finally housed at another Chinese hotel until a more permanent residence could be found. In prewar years the trip from Swatow to Bangkok as a deck passenger cost about $25 a person and took only three or four days. An immigrant needed only his sleeping mat and a bundle of clothes to start a new life in Southeast Asia.

Once in Bangkok, the usual port of disembarkation, the immigrant was certain to have helpful hands extended from relatives, friends from his own village in China, or persons speaking his dialect. Through these persons, living quarters, a job, and perhaps sufficient capital to get started as a street hawker would be provided without question. Once past the initial crisis of arrival, however, the immigrant was on his own, dependent upon his own ingenuity, capacity for hard work, and his own physical strength to make his way.

### SEX COMPOSITION

Initial Chinese immigration to Thailand, like the early phases of immigration to all Western countries, was predominantly male. Prior to the Chinese Revolution of 1911 families seldom followed the immigrants overseas; one reason was that the immigrant himself had every intention of returning to China once he had made his fortune overseas. Immigrants often married Thai women, established homes and raised families in the new land, while continuing to support wives and children in China. Eventually many immigrants retired permanently to China, sometimes with their Thai families, sometimes without them. In the latter case a generous monetary settlement might be made on their Thai wives and children, and not infrequently the business so carefully built up by the immigrant during his lifetime was turned over to his Thai descendants.

So few Chinese women followed these early immigrants that in the early part of this century a Chinese woman was a rarity in Bangkok, enough to cause a small sensation when she appeared. The very fact that statistics on the number of Chinese women entering and leaving Thailand have been kept only since 1921 indicates perhaps that until the second decade of this century female immigration was insignificant.

Immigration statistics from 1921 to the present continue to show a preponderance of Chinese males over females, but since these statistics include all Chinese alien travellers—immigrants, temporary visitors, and persons merely in transit—they are of small value in ascertaining with accuracy the extent of female immigration. Again, the census probably provides a more reliable picture of the immigration of women.

The following table gives data on the Chinese male and female population in Thailand derived from the four national censuses:

3. SEX COMPOSITION OF THE CHINESE ALIEN POPULATION

| *Year* | *Total* | *Male* | *Female* | *Numerical Increase or Decrease of Females Since Last Census* |
|---|---|---|---|---|
| 1919 | 260,194 | 205,470 | 54,724 | — |
| 1929 | 445,274 | 313,764 | 131,510 | 76,786 |
| 1937 | 524,062 | 335,524 | 188,538 | 57,028 |
| 1947 | 476,582 | 319,196 | 157,386 | – *31,152* |

SOURCE: *Statistical Year-Book of Thailand*, 1939-44; 1952

Further analysis of these figures in Table 4 show the growing importance of female immigration during the prewar years.

To the influx of immigrant women in the 1920s and 1930s is often attributed the decrease in intermarriage, the establishment of the all-Chinese home, with all the implications of this for the perpetuation of Chinese culture, and the growing emphasis on the

4. POPULATION CHANGES OF THE CHINESE ALIENS

| *Categories* | *1919* | *1929* | *1937* | *1947* |
|---|---|---|---|---|
| Chinese aliens, increase or decrease since previous census | — | 185,080 (+71%) | 78,788 (+18%) | −47,480 (−9%) |
| Chinese alien males, increase or decrease since previous census | — | 108,294 (+53%) | 21,760 (+7%) | −16,328 (−5%) |
| Chinese alien females, increase or decrease since previous census | — | 76,786 (+140%) | 57,028 (+43%) | −31,152 (−17%) |
| Number of Chinese alien females to every 1,000 alien males | 266 | 419 | 562 | 493 |

In the 38-year period between 1919 and 1947 the Chinese alien population increased by 83% while the number of women in this group increased by 188%. Since the end of the War, however, the total alien group has shown a decline and for the first time since 1919 the number of Chinese alien women in the population has fallen since the previous census.

building of schools to carry on Chinese traditions. In short, the Chinese became, in the eyes of many Thai, a separatist minority actively resisting integration. This view of the Chinese as virtually unassimilable in turn encouraged the Thai government to take drastic steps to limit immigration as described below.

We have no reason to expect that the recent decrease in the number of immigrant women indicated in Table 4, has stimulated intermarriage, for the decrease has more than made up by second-generation women in the population. Yet if the immigrant composition of the Chinese population continues to decline, and the Chinese community becomes increasingly second- and third-generation in character, then we can expect a softening of these sharp cultural differences which have hitherto separated the Thai and the Chinese minority. Restrictions on immigration thus become of crucial importance to the further integration of the Chinese.

## CONTROL OF IMMIGRATION

Despite the mounting anti-alien feelings that swept the government after 1932, until 1947 Thailand made no attempt to control directly the numbers of Chinese entering the Kingdom. It is true that the first Immigration Act, passed in B.E. 2470 (1927–28),[2] provided for the eventual restriction of immigration (Landon 1941: 205):

> SECTION 8. The Minister [of the Interior] with the concurrence of the Minister of Commerce and Communication, is empowered to make an order fixing the number of aliens of any nationality or of any category of such aliens that may be admitted into the Kingdom each year . . .

But although this provision was repeated in the Immigration Act of B.E. 2480 (1937–38), not until ten years later were any numerical limitations actually applied.

The first immigration quota system went into effect on May 1, 1947, following the issuance of the necessary regulations by the Ministry of the Interior under the legal authority cited above. Curiously, this first quota system actually favoured the Chinese over all other peoples. Ten thousand persons of Chinese nationality were permitted to enter Thailand each year, while only 200 persons each for all other nationalities were allowed entry. The quota for 1947 was pro-rated by month so that from May to the end of the year only 6,668 Chinese immigrants were actually admitted. However, during 1948 a full quota of 10,000 Chinese immigrants was permitted.

A commentary on the origin of this quota system and the feelings which prompted it is provided by Alexander MacDonald, American editor of the *Bangkok Post* (MacDonald 1949: 204–205):

> Shortly after the *Post* was founded in August 1946 I was talking to Pridi, Premier at that time, one day about the Chinese problem. Although he himself was part Chinese, he feared the great flow of Chinese immigrants into the country as a serious threat to the Kingdom's sovereignty. Some day, by virtue of numbers and economic aggressiveness, they would overwhelm the Siamese in their own land. Something must be done, he said gravely, to stem the flood of the Chinese, who were coming into the Kingdom annually by thousands. I suggested the obvious solution of immigration control, something which Siam had not tried before . . . I described how the system operated in the United States and other places. Offending the Chinese, which he was reluctant to do, could be avoided, I proposed, by setting a quota for them that would be liberal in comparison with the quotas for other nationals. The more he thought about it, the more enthusiastic he became . . .

And a few months later the quota system was established.

In 1948, however, Phibun Songgram, the ultra-nationalist wartime premier, again assumed control of the Thai government. One of his first announcements on taking office was that China's quota would be cut from 10,000 to 200 yearly, or equal to that of all other nationalities. Despite protests from Chinese diplomats and the local community, the Thai government through the issuance of a ministerial regulation fixed immigration quotas for all nationalities at 200 persons yearly. This final severe quota restriction was incorporated into the 1950 Immigration Act in the following terms:

> SECTION 29. The Minister is to announce in the *Royal Gazette* the limitations on numbers of immigrants each year, but not to exceed two hundred persons per year from each country, and for persons without nationality likewise not to exceed two hundred persons annually . . .

Beginning in 1949, therefore, Chinese immigration has been officially limited to only 200 persons yearly, although several thousand refugees (or 'White Chinese') from China have entered the Kingdom for an indefinite period as so-called 'temporary' residents.[3]

It should be noted that while the upper quota limit is set at 200 persons annually, the Ministry of the Interior is provided with the implicit authority to fix a smaller quota at its discretion. Significantly by 1952 the quota for stateless persons which had originally been set at 200 persons was cut to 100 annually.

In accordance with the policy of the Thai government in matters affecting this minority, Chinese as such are nowhere mentioned in either this or previous immigration laws. Yet Chinese aliens normally constitute the overwhelming bulk of immigrants wishing to enter Thailand, and the restrictive effect on them is the same as though the laws had specifically named them.

Under the Immigration Act of 1950 no exemptions or preferences are given to the children, wives, or other relatives of immigrants or present residents of Thailand. Children of whatever age are counted under the quota, with the exception of children born abroad of alien parents on a temporary visit abroad. As the Director of the Immigration Department explained, 'We count all souls, no matter what age'. Teachers and other professional persons, according to information furnished by the Immigration Department in Bangkok are likewise counted as immigrants and charged to the quota.

While numerical limitations on immigration are of recent origin, all immigration laws since that of B.E. 2470 (1927–1928) have excluded certain undesirable classes, namely, persons who are physically or mentally incapable and persons of bad character likely to constitute a danger to the Kingdom. These provisions, like so many other laws and regulations in Thailand, were never strictly enforced except in the most obvious cases. Few Chinese before World War II had any trouble entering Thailand, although some may have had difficulty remaining in the Kingdom. Since 1928 an alien has been required to have in his possession a certain sum of money to be fixed by ministerial regulations (Landon 1941: 205–211). The precise sum was apparently never determined; consequently the regulation was never enforced. If it had been, some of the wealthiest Chinese in Bangkok at the present time would never have been permitted to enter the Kingdom, for they landed virtually penniless. Landon (1941: 207) notes a regulation of 1932–33 excluding all aliens aged 12 years and over unable to read and write Thai or their own language, but there is considerable doubt whether this was ever effectively enforced, and by 1939 even this requirement had been dropped from immigration laws. None of these requirements, despite their potential efficacy, appear to have reduced in any way the volume of Chinese immigration.

Immigration control in Thailand has been closely allied with the collection of revenue, and this latter feature, rather than any numerical limitation, was deemed of greater importance until recent years in the policies of the government. Fees have been levied on two groups: immigrants entering the Kingdom and on aliens already residing there. These two fees may be used as a barometer of Chinese immigration, for as the volume of immigration has fallen and revenues from this source consequently reduced, the fees on alien residents have increased.

Immigrant fees were initially large and they have grown still heavier. The Immigration Amendment Act of B.E. 2474 (1931–1932) required immigrants with their papers in order to pay a 30 baht fee (US$12·00)[4] for a Certificate of Residence, or 40 baht (US$16·00) if their papers were not in order. A year later a Certificate cost 100 baht (US$35·00). The Immigration Act of B.E. 2480 (1937–1938) doubled the fee to 200 baht. By 1950, with immigration of Chinese down to a trickle and the baht greatly devalued, a Certificate of Residence cost 1,000 baht (US$50·00).

These immigration fees were apparently high enough in the 1930's to encourage illegal immigration. As a counter measure the government, through the Registration of Aliens Act of B.E. 2479 (1936–1937), required all aliens residing in Thailand or entering thereafter to obtain Alien Registration Certificates. In police checks of aliens henceforth illegal entrants could be easily caught and deported. At first issued without charge, by 1939 a fee of four baht (US$1·60) a year was being charged for these certificates, and the fee was subsequently increased to 20 baht (US$8·00) per year. In 1952 when the revenue from immigration fees was at its lowest point in years the fee for an Alien Registration Certificate was jumped to 400 baht (US$20·00) a year, to the great consternation of Chinese aliens in Thailand. The increase was unexpected and from the Chinese minority came a storm of protest which did not abate until the government within the year had again dropped the registration fee for aliens to its previous level of 200 baht and had exempted certain classes (those under 15 and over 60, widows, infirms, and those with sons in the Thai armed forces).

Here again it must be emphasized that none of these laws or regulations mentioned the Chinese as such. They applied to all aliens indiscriminately, and the Thai government was, in fact, careful to adhere to this principle in practice, regardless of the nationality or race of the alien. Thus Americans or British aliens were subject to payment of immigration fees on entering the Kingdom and Registration Certificate fees when taking up residence there. Yet the Chinese constituted the major portion of the immigrant total in any year and were, in addition, the largest alien group in the Kingdom. Consequently, these fees fell heaviest on them, and because of this, appeared to be directed at them alone. As we have seen, the bulk of the immigrants seeking entry to Thailand have been poor peasants and labourers, the ones least able to pay the increasingly high fees demanded of immigrants and aliens.

One purpose of these fees presumably is to discourage immigration. Yet whether they have in fact caused a fall in Chinese immigration is open to question. Immigration decreased during the 1930's, it is true, but this may be attributed to poor economic conditions in Thailand at that time. The tremendous spurt in Chinese immigration directly after the end of World War II seems to indicate that these fees have not been an effective curb on immigration. Whether or not they were ever designed to curb immigration, fees have been a lucrative source of revenue for the Thai government, and it is perhaps this factor rather than their direct effect on the volume of Chinese immigration which has caused such fees to be applied.[5]

One further result of these various immigration and registration laws should be noted: their enactment beginning in the 1930s convinced the Chinese that the Thai government had definitely adopted an anti-Chinese policy. Landon writes in this connection (1941: 212):

> The Chinese were not slow to realize that they were no longer so welcome in Thailand as formerly. Being realists they were not impressed by the slogan of the government, invented apparently for foreign consumption, 'Thailand is pro-Thai; it is not anti-anything'. As far as the Chinese are concerned this casuistry means nothing. They know intuitively that the new emphasis on Thailand for the Thai means less of Thailand for the Chinese. They have begun to fear direct oppression and persecution.

It is safe to conclude that these laws, impartial as they were in theory, engendered a hostile atmosphere not conducive to the easy absorption of the Chinese immigrants remaining in Thailand.

Recent events show that immigration restrictions are being increased rather than relaxed. Chinese newspapers continue to report that the present quota of 200 persons annually will be cut, as one newspaper explained, 'in order to prevent too many foreigners coming to Thailand and affecting the Thai people's living'. As noted above, the quota for stateless persons has already been cut in half. In actual fact through a simple stratagem the government has reduced Chinese immigration even below the 200 level. Aliens already residing 'temporarily' are permitted to apply for and receive immigration visas, to be charged against the quota—in 1952, for example, 140 of the 200 immigrants were already residing in Thailand, and 60 additional residents were reported to be applying for the remaining numbers; on February 1 of that year, the government announced that the Chinese quota had already been completely filled. This has been the typical pattern and has practically eliminated all but the legal immigrant. Stricter financial and occupational qualfications which would reduce immigration are constantly being advocated. *Siam Radt*, a Bangkok Thai newspaper, reported in this connection:

> . . . hitherto immigrants with nothing but a sleeping mat and a pillow were allowed entry into our country. Through diligence they were able to build up their property and influence. It was reported on the 28th [of May, 1952] that for better protection of the livelihood of the Thai people, only immigrants conforming to the standard of qualifications fixed by the authorities will be admitted. Priority will be given to applications of alien technicians wishing to immigrate into Thailand. Consideration of applications will cover also the prospective immigrants' standing and the occupations they propose to take up after their arrival.

## SUMMARY

Two fundamental changes can be seen to have occurred in Chinese immigration to Thailand during the past half century, both with implications for the integration of this minority. The first is the substantial drop in numbers of immigrants entering the Kingdom—from many thousands yearly to a few hundred, assuming the general accuracy of official counts. During the same period the number of native Thai people has increased steadily, so that the aliens form now a smaller part of the total population than formerly. This respite in the flow of immigrants has given Thai society a breathing spell, a chance to absorb more effectively the aliens in its midst; it has also meant that the constant refurbishment of alien cultural enclaves has been slowed down markedly. Chinese communities have become increasingly peopled by those who know China only through the eyes and experiences of others, a fact which must inevitably weigh on the side of assimilation.

The second noteworthy change is the increased numbers of Chinese females to the population, so that the original unbalance in sex ratios has been steadily reduced. Of course, immigration alone has not accounted for the balance that now presumably exists, but it has given substantial help. If the coming of women is responsible in large part for the exclusiveness of the Chinese home and other institutions, then we have little reason to expect, now that there are more Chinese women than previously, any immediate levelling of barriers between the Thai and Chinese.

In the survey of Thailand's immigration policies one is impressed by similarities to the policies of Western nations, particularly the United States. Overseas Chinese immigration in Thailand has run a course in a relatively brief time not unlike that which occurred in the United States, from virtual freedom of entry to drastic quota restrictions amounting almost to exclusion. Moreover, the specific legislation enacted by the Thai government was obviously influenced by similar legislation previously enacted in the United States. Thus we find such ideas and techniques as exclusory categories of aliens, literacy tests, and quota restrictions being written into Thai laws. The very concept of immigration laws and regulations is itself an innovation from the West. We can note further that the control of Chinese immigration in Thailand has coincided roughly with the period of the most drastic United States control of its own immigration—there seems to have been a similar 'run of attention' in the two nations, as each sought to cope with similar problems of alien migration.

Thailand's immigration policies have suffered from a number of weaknesses, not all of them unavoidable. The Thai government is confronted with the serious immigration problem of the Chinese, more urgent perhaps than the problem faced by the United States in the early part of this century with regard to European immigration. It has attempted to telescope in less than 25 years immigration programmes which the United States has taken over 75 years to develop. Western-inspired techniques to control immigration in the prewar period were ineffective at times because the measures were not strictly enforced at the inspection level, at other times because government leaders themselves had failed to provide implementing regulations. This experience points up a common difficulty attendant on Westernization: the incomplete diffusion of values on all levels of the receiving society. Another source of confusion has been the fact that many of the Kingdom's most important immigration decisions stem from ministerial regulations, which are not strictly speaking laws but have the force of laws. These immigration regulations are apt to be decided upon by a few high-placed officials guided more by emotional considerations than cold analysis. Understandably the development of Thailand's immigration policies has been haphazard and sometimes contradictory.

But a fundamental question remains to be answered in the future: can Western-derived immigration policies, particularly quota limitations of immigrants, provide a solution for Thailand's peculiar problem? Thus far, Chinese immigration has been kept within the quota limitations, it is true, but events in China since 1948 have greatly reduced the pressure and the facilities for immigration from the Mainland to Southeast Asia. Historically these lands south of China have served to relieve the recurring pressures of China's population, if only in the sea-coast regions of South China. As floods, droughts and famines have intensified the precariousness of livelihood in South China, an irresistible tide of Chinese people have flowed into Southeast Asia. There is reason to believe that this century-old movement cannot be so abruptly terminated, at the desire of the receiving country alone. The pertinent question is whether unilaterally-derived immigration techniques and policies which have served so effectively for world powers like the United States can function as well for small nations like Thailand who live under the shadow of the Chinese colossus. It seems more likely that drastic restrictions in numbers can only be effective if they happen to coincide with the policy of the sending country—as Thailand's restrictions do at this moment, for Communist China herself is permitting very little emigration—or, failing this circumstance, if restrictions are based on international agreements in which the sending and the receiving nations are both partners; in short, in the immigration field something comparable to reciprocal trade and tariff agreements is needed. The acceptance of this, even in principle, may be the next major development in Thailand's immigration policy.

CHAPTER III

# CHINESE COMMUNITY LIFE

THE phenomenal commercial success of the Chinese in Thailand, and indeed throughout Southeast Asia, has no single or simple explanation. Certainly this success is partly attributable to such personal qualities as perseverance, capacity for hard work, and business acumen, but one of the most important factors has been the tight social and economic organization developed by overseas Chinese communities. Such communities in Southeast Asia appear remarkably self-sufficient and to many observers seem to form alien societies within the host society. They have proved unusually effective, on the one hand, for encouraging mutual aid and co-operation among heterogeneous linguistic and socio-economic groups and, on the other, for providing protection from hostile or competitive individuals and governments. Better than most people the Chinese have learned the dictum that 'in unity there is strength'. Their organizational cohesion furnishes much of the answer not only to the economic well-being of the Chinese as a group but also to the persistence of their cultural patterns and values in an alien and sometimes unfriendly social environment.

The centre of Chinese life in Thailand is the Chinese community in Bangkok, specially an area made up of four urban districts (Bangrok, Pratumwan, Pomprap, Sampangtuwan) which together contain 75 per cent of the city's Chinese population. This is not simply an exotic 'Chinatown' set off from the main stream of urban life, such as one finds in New York or San Francisco. Rather, with their extraordinary concentration of retail and wholesale business houses, shops, banks, markets and factories, these Chinese districts constitute the economic nucleus of the city and indeed, of the nation. At the hub of a great population concentration, the Chinese community has become the locus of all commercial recreation and public entertainment. Here are located the largest and best Chinese restaurants, theatres and movie houses, gambling halls, opium dens, brothels, and public dance halls. This is a community of interest as well, for the wealth accumulated by the successful business man is used in part to support a multiplicity of ethnic organizations: trade guilds, a powerful Chinese Chamber of

Commerce, dialect associations, benevolent and charitable organizations, surname associations, religious groups for both men and women, sports associations and social clubs. To a lesser extent similar organizations are found in virtually every town in Thailand, but those in Bangkok are the dominant organizations, the largest in terms of membership, and the most effective in providing essential services to the individual.

The Chinese community in Bangkok has no overall political or administrative organization. No mayor, community council, or formally constituted group of elders directs community life. The Thai government claims full political and administrative control over the Chinese districts, and only occasionally does it delegate any of its powers to any individual or group. On the whole, the four districts comprising the Chinese community are treated no differently from any other parts of Bangkok so far as the enforcement of law and order are concerned. Whatever control the Chinese do exercise over their affairs comes simply by an informal, mutual agreement among themselves; it has no legal authority.

This is not meant to imply that the Chinese associations mentioned below are illegal organizations which operate clandestinely. On the contrary, unless otherwise noted, all the associations mentioned in this study are licit organizations whose activities are entirely open to official inspection. On the whole these organizations are recognized as stabilizing agencies for the Chinese population, and the Thai government has encouraged their benevolent and intermediary functions. In 1951, for example, when the Chinese Chamber of Commerce was torn by an internal dispute, high government officials pressed the Chinese to reconcile their differences so as to 'assume the responsibilities of directing the Chinese community'.

Rather than create one encompassing organization, therefore, the Chinese in Bangkok have formed a large number of separate associations which tie together individuals with similar interests: familial, economic, social, religious. Each of these associations is a distinct unit, each one pursues its own goals, but taken in their totality these associations direct the life of the community. The associations control business competition, regulate prices, mediate disputes, provide a system of social security, and act as intermediaries between the individual and the Thai government. They provide the Chinese population with schools, community centres, hospitals, clinics, temples, cemeteries and recreational facilities. In doing this the associations sometimes act in concert, but most often they carry out individual plans and projects, not infrequently duplicating each other's work. Looked at broadly, however, they all fit together into a smoothly running mechanism, albeit a mechanism composed of a great many separate gears.

Before describing the specific associations, it will be useful to consider some general features common to all. The personnel of the typical Chinese association comprises three distinct categories of persons. There are, first, the body of members who may range from a few score in the case of certain social clubs to several thousand in the dialect associations. Membership is generally of two kinds: personal and business. That is, an individual may join the association himself, or he may enroll the shop or business he owns as a member. In the latter case, the name of the business rather than the owner's name is placed on the rolls. In a business membership all persons who own or have a share in the business are considered members of the association. Thus the membership list of an organization like the Chinese Chamber of Commerce is apt to be misleading, for the number of persons who actively participate is much larger than the simple membership list would indicate. The typical large association also has a leadership group—usually composed of a President or Chairman, a Board of Directors, and various committees—which is elected by the combined membership every two years. These officials direct but do not actually run the association. For the latter task a permanent staff headed by a manager is employed, and this group continues in office regardless of changes in leadership. In addition to its day-to-day tasks, the permanent staff has responsibility for preparing an annual report which describes the association's activities, lists contributions and benefactors, and gives publicity to the officials of the association. These reports are published and distributed to members. The annual report of a large association is a heavy volume handsomely printed in several colours and replete with photographs of officers and benefactors. These reports are fascinating social documents; but to the man in the street, they give evidence of the vitality of the Chinese community spirit and the continuing concern of wealthy and influential Chinese with the well-being of even the poorest immigrant.

The typical Chinese association owns a building where meetings are held and sometimes other structures (schools, temples, clinics, etc.) as well. The larger associations boast imposing headquarters of brick and concrete, several stories high, with large meeting halls, numerous conference rooms, and fairly well-equipped offices. Yet the atmosphere of these headquarters is sometimes deceptively sleepy. A casual visitor finds them silent and virtually empty, like a church on weekdays, with only two or three employees present. Only occasionally do these associations become centres of community life. During the day individual Chinese drop in, but there are few social gatherings apart from the regular meetings held once a month or so. Many of the most important activities are carried on informally outside the headquarters proper, such as providing bail bonds, mediating in disputes, burying indigent Chinese, or unsnarling an alien's registration difficulties. These essential services as much as the desire for congeniality and the sharing of reminiscenses about the homeland hold the associations together. Problems requiring action are met as they arise, and until they arise the organization simply waits. With their operations so amorphous it is easy to see why the full importance of these Chinese associations as the very backbone of the Chinese community has so long escaped the attention of observers.

All the Chinese associations which will be described below were brought to or developed within Thailand by the Chinese. They have no counterparts in Thai society. In many instances, as will be shown later, they are similar in their institutional structure to associations found in the villages and towns of South China, whence these people came. In every case the mutual-aid function remains unchanged, and the activities of certain community institutions are almost identical with village institutions of China. However, new activities and functions, ones not undertaken by the village organizations, have been added in Thailand; and frequently membership is based on different qualifications. In no case has a village institution been transplanted intact and unchanged. Some community institutions which have arisen in response to the demands of urban, commercial life are new, so far as Chinese immigrants are concerned. The Chamber of Commerce is a case in point.

There is one outstanding difference between these associations and those found in the villages of South China. In China, family and kin groups were predominant, and in fact other groups tended to be relatively unimportant. Just the reverse is true in Bangkok. Here, family and kin groups are numerous but exert small influence on the direction of community affairs. The real locus of power lies with business groups and the regional or dialect associations, both of which are formed on non-kin lines.

Chinese associations in Bangkok may be separated into two categories: legal associations registered with the police which operate publicly; and illegal, i.e. unregistered, associations which must be informal in nature or unobtrusive in their operations. Truly secret associations are few in number and are usually formed among the Chinese to attain some political end oriented toward the mother country. They are normally not important in the social structure of the Chinese community, although their development at times has contributed to disunity. Among the permanent associations four major types are of paramount importance in maintaining a closely knit, co-operative community. These are the surname associations; the dialect associations based on place of origin in China; the various occupational, professional and business associations; and finally the benevolent and charitable organizations. None of these can be fully appreciated without a brief summary of a Chinese village organization which seems to stand as the model for many associations found in Thailand.

In the villages of South China the common-descent group called the *tsu* 族 occupied a controlling position in the life of the individual peasant and in community affairs. The tsu, usually translated as 'clan', is composed of persons and families tracing their descent along the male line from one male ancestor. A typical tsu might number several thousand persons and hundreds of families, usually living in one locality. All tsu members bear the same surname and consider themselves related by blood. Tsu bonds were particularly well developed in the two emigrant provinces of Kwangtung and Fukien. For example, in the village in Kwangtung Province studied by Kulp, all 650 persons, with the exception of a few merchants from outside, traced their relationship back nineteen generations to a single man who had founded the clan. All bore the same surname and regarded themselves as blood relatives (Kulp 1925).

In these villages the centre of tsu activities was the ancestral hall where the memorial tablets of deceased tsu members were kept, from the original founder of the clan onwards. At regular intervals during the year, and in the full presence of all male members of the tsu, highly formalized rites were conducted to honour the founder and the other ancestors. The religious importance of these rites and of the ancestor group itself can scarcely be overemphasized; but the ancestral hall had more than religious significance in these villages. It symbolized the corporate personality of the tsu and its authority over living members, and provided the setting for judicial, social, and philanthropic services.

Local governments traditionally acknowledged the authority of tsu elders over their groups. Virtually all offences, with the exception only of the failure to pay taxes, were considered to be against the tsu, and subject therefore to tsu authority rather than any outside agency. The elders constituted an informal tribunal which strictly enforced law and order, seeing that a wrongdoer's family paid compensation or offered apologies, as custom demanded, and that the wrongdoer himself was punished. Intractable villagers were not permitted to participate in the ancestor rites, and were sometimes driven out of the community and their names struck from the tsu genealogy. Quarrels were likewise resolved. Disputants were brought to the ancestral hall and in the august presence of their ancestors and the village elders were made to compose their differences. So effective was the tsu in preserving order that in these villages formal police organizations and courts were ordinarily unnecessary.

The tsu acting through the ancestral hall also assumed social service and mutual aid responsibilities. Because of its ownership of land the tsu often became a very wealthy institution, exceeding by far individuals and families in this respect. Olga Lang in her study of South China found that 50 to 70 per cent of the cultivated land in Kwangtung Province was owned by clans, and in some villages clan ownership of this land rose to 90 per cent (Lang 1946: 174). Income from such property was used for a number of philanthropic and educational purposes. Loans and other help were given to tsu members in need. The tsu might also pay maternity benefits, distribute free medicine, provide medical treatment, and pay the burial expenses of those in need. Sometimes surplus monies were divided among all families with persons aged 59 years and over receiving double shares as a sort of old-age pension. In addition, the tsu often provided free education in schools conducted in the ancestral hall, and later assisted worthy scholars to obtain higher education at outside schools and universities. The burden of making a livelihood was the full responsibility of the individual families, and in times of crisis that family was the first line of protection. But immediately behind this line stood the tsu, and only in times of exceedingly grave disasters would recourse to outside help be necessary.

The peasant who leaves his village in South China to make his fortune in the Nan-Yang remains a part of his clan, whether he lives or dies. Yet in the practical terms of control and protection he is estranged from this powerful and all-sufficient group. Among the Chinese in Thailand there is thus a weakening of the traditional bonds with the clan in China. The immigrant often finds but few relatives beyond his immediate household group in Thailand, and he must rely on organizations different from the tsu for protective and mutual-aid services.

### SURNAME ASSOCIATIONS

One such organization of the Chinese in Bangkok is the 'surname association', a kind of quasi-kinship organization formed by persons bearing the same family name. Although these associations take on some of the characteristics of the tsu, they should not be confused with the latter. The outstanding differences between the tsu organization and the typical surname association in Bangkok are the following:

*a.* While the tsu counted as members persons with the same surname tracing their origin from one male ancestor, a surname association in Bangkok is composed of persons bearing the same surname and originating in one dialect region of China. For example, Chinese with the surname *Ch'en* and coming from any part of Hainan Island have formed the *Ch'en Chia She*, or Ch'en Family Association. Cantonese persons with *Ling* as their surname have formed another such association. Members of these associations need not be related, and most members are actually not blood relatives.

*b.* In China the tsu's ancestral hall had a predominant religious function in that it was the repository of the sacred ancestor tablets and the site for the solemn rites for the ancestors. The Bangkok surname associations have no ancestor tablets whatsoever. At the most they simply display pictures or plaques to honour individuals both living and dead who donated especially large sums to build the association's meeting hall. Full membership meetings are held only once a year, and this day depends on the availability of members and the demands of their businesses, rather than a sacred calendar. During the year the associations have a social rather than a religious character. At the one annual meeting a memorial service is conducted, patterned in general on the traditional ancestor rites, but otherwise the building provides a meeting place for members, their relatives, friends, and business colleagues, and a convenient place to hold wedding and birthday parties. The typical association building in Bangkok is a large, two-storied structure with several spacious rooms suitable for gatherings. Furnishings are sparse—bare tables and hard chairs and on the walls pictures of generous members. Some associations may provide a ping-pong table for the young people and for the older members a reading-room with local Chinese newspapers.

*c.* Tsu leaders in China were commonly the elders of the clan. Officers of the surname associations are usually successful business men chosen with more regard to wealth and enthusiasm than age. The President of one large club, for example, is an insurance executive only 45 years old, considerably younger than several less honoured members of this association.

*d.* The traditional tsu performed a variety of social welfare, educational and protective services. Only some of these are carried over to the surname associations in Bangkok. These associations only occasionally sponsor schools, and appear not at all interested in assisting worthy scholars to obtain a higher education. No medical services are provided, and rather than distributing income and surpluses, members are constantly being approached for contributions. However, these surname associations often maintain a large common burial site or memorial at a Chinese cemetery in Bangkok for burial of members too poor to afford an individual grave, and where memorial services are held on certain Chinese festival days, normally Ch'ing-ming and Chung-yüan. The association also extends help to any indigent persons of the same surname and dialect group, even though they may not actually belong to the association. It collects money from members to support various Chinese community activities—schools, hospitals and temples. When called upon the association officers will mediate in disputes between association members or between member families and outsiders.

Members of these associations in Bangkok declare that they are not designed to replace the tsu organization of China, nor to weaken the ties of members with their kin groups there. They merely provide the opportunity for Chinese to gather together, to renew friendships, and to remind second- and third-generation youths of their cultural and family ties with China. Individual associations have memberships of several hundred persons, drawn from all over Thailand. Few women participate in any of their activities.

A second type of surname association formed by the Chinese may be called an 'informal surname club'. This is a similar institution with a loose organization and no established headquarters. Meetings are held at the homes of members and once or twice a year the group foregathers at a restaurant for a dinner meeting. These informal groups are not registered with the police as required by law, and are in a sense illegal, although their activities, similar to those of the formal surname associations, are in no way contrary to law and order. Membership in a typical organization is fairly small—usually less than 100 persons—and is entirely male. While there are relatively few formal surname associations in Bangkok, there are a large number of these informal clubs. At the Cantonese cemetery may be seen a memorial containing plaques for several scores of different families, each of which is probably represented by an informal surname organization within the Cantonese dialect group.

The surname associations are not key organizations within the Chinese community. They are primarily immigrant institutions; the second and succeeding generations appear to take but little interest in their activities. For this reason these associations are gradually declining in membership, and the buildings of some are already being put to other uses. The leaders have importance chiefly within their own groups, not in the community as a whole.

## REGIONAL OR DIALECT ASSOCIATIONS

Each of the major dialect groups—the Teochiu, Hakka, Cantonese, Hainanese and Hokkien—has formed an association for persons speaking that dialect as a native language. These are among the most influential organizations in the Chinese community because of the large membership lists—several thousand in the case of some—and the even greater numbers who, although not formal members, can be counted on to support their own dialect associations.

These groups have a great variety of activities. Most maintain cemeteries—these are probably the oldest establishments of the Chinese in Thailand. Early in their histories all associations built Chinese temples (open of course to everyone). In more recent years many dialect associations have established clinics and hospitals which serve the entire population, Chinese and non-Chinese. During the last few decades the associations have become increasingly concerned with the founding of Chinese schools. Originally the language of instruction in such schools was the dialect of the sponsoring association; but for the last 25 years or so Mandarin *(kuo-yü)*, the national language of China, has become the common medium of instruction. These schools today admit children from all dialect groups.

Such activities derive from a sincere desire to satisfy real needs of the Chinese minority and partly from a frank effort to make money. Schools, hospitals, and even temples can be very profitable enterprises, often enriching sponsoring organizations. Consequently association leaders have little trouble in raising funds for proposed building programmes and expansion of their services. An active association wins praise from the community and enhances the prestige of its leaders.

Because of the size and wealth of its membership, the Teochiu Association *(Ch'ao-chou hui-kuan)*, formally organized only about 30 years ago, is the largest and most powerful of the dialect associations. It has a total membership of about 7,000, more than half of whom reside in the Bangkok area. Located just outside the city is the Teochiu Association cemetery, the largest Chinese cemetery in the whole of Thailand, with space for several thousand graves and extensive godown (warehouse) facilities for the storage of coffins and the remains of persons to be returned to China eventually for burial. The association controls primary schools and formerly ran a large secondary school as well; the latter was closed, as were all Chinese secondary schools, by the Thai government in 1948. In 1950 it opened a small but well-equipped medical clinic on Western lines with the full time services of a doctor (orginally a Thai) and several Thai and Chinese nurses. In addition to these facilities in Bangkok, the Association maintains a branch office in Swatow to help Teochiu people returning to China from Thailand.

Within the Teochiu group and forming subdivisions of it are eight smaller district associations whose members come from specific districts in the Teochiu region of China. These smaller organizations are independent but normally act in conjunction with the parent association in matters affecting the Chinese community, thus enabling the numerically dominant Teochiu dialect group to exercise control over other important organizations such as the Chinese Chamber of Commerce and the benevolent associations. The Chao-Yang Association, one such district organization, has been particularly energetic—it has already constructed an exquisite replica of an old country ancestral hall (the only one of its kind in Bangkok) and a small sports arena and stadium.

The Hakka Association *(Hakka hui-kuan)*, considered by many Chinese to be the live-wire among the dialect organizations, concentrates its activities in one large building in a densely populated Chinese section. Here are the association headquarters, a primary school, and a temple. The Hakka Association also maintains its own cemetery, and in recent years it has built a clinic and hospital and opened a second primary school (Ching Da No. 2).

This association, like others in the community, keeps a bulletin board on which items of interest to members are posted. We can get a fair idea of the Association's orientation by examining a typical listing on this board. The first thing to be noted is that all notices are in Chinese, none in Thai. Given prominent display is a list of some ten new members who joined the association in the past month. Below this one finds a detailed bookkeeping record of the Association's income and expenditures during the past year—all such associations take pride in opening their accounts to public view. The bulletin board also will contain, in all probability, several acknowledgements of contributions, in each case listing the name of the donor and the amount given. In a typical listing seen by the author, the largest contribution was 1,000 baht; made at the request of the donor's father, it represented the money which was being set aside for the father's funeral—a simpler funeral in order to help the Association. Such contributions show the high place that the dialect associations hold among the rank and file of the Chinese community.

The Cantonese Association *(Kwang Chao hui-kuan)* is the oldest dialect association in Bangkok, having been founded some 75 years ago. It occupies a compound adjacent to the main Chinese business section on which has been built a temple (now seldom used), and a clinic hospital. On the outskirts of Bangkok the association maintains a large cemetery with warehouse facilities for storing remains awaiting return to China. Nearby is the large Cantonese primary school; formerly the Association operated a secondary school also. The Secretary of the Cantonese Association when asked to name the requirements for association membership, listed the following: (i) a person must be Cantonese or of Cantonese parentage; (ii) he must be sponsored by two established members of the Association; (iii) he must pay his dues regularly. Other dialect associations have similar membership requirements. According to the secretary, the association had about 1,700 active members, virtually all of whom were men. Each member paid dues of 24 baht (US$1·20) per year, or if a business member, yearly dues of 48 baht. He emphasized, however, that no Cantonese would be denied assistance by the Association merely because he was not an active paying member.

The Hainan Association *(Hainan hui-kuan)*, recently organized under this name but incorporating Hainanese organizations more than 70 years old, maintains a cemetery, three temples, a primary school, and a newly constructed headquarters building. This association and the organizations from which it derived consistently supported Nationalist China. To counter this influence a dissident group of Hainanese with its own school banded together after the war. The school was later closed down by the Thai authorities. In recent years the dissident group has declined in influence but feelings between the two groups continues to be bitter. This dichotomy between pro-Communists and pro-Nationalists is found in every dialect association, but the Hainan Association is the only one thus far to suffer a schism of such serious proportions. Perhaps because of this the Hainanese have not been so influential in community affairs as their numbers in the population would warrant.

The Hokkien Association *(Fu-chien hui-kuan)*, one of the smaller and weaker organizations in Bangkok, has less than 1,000 members but gains importance as the representative of the wealthy Hokkien population of south Thailand. The latter have interests in the lucrative tin mines and rubber plantations of that area and in the prosperous exporting firms in Bangkok. Despite the wealth it represents, the Association itself is not wealthy or powerful. Founded about 1900, the Hokkien Association today maintains a headquarters and runs a separate primary school; it practically supports a nearby temple and has one of the oldest Chinese graveyards in Bangkok. Before World War II, the association ran a secondary school which it would reopen at once if the government permitted.

The remaining regional associations, the *Taiwan hui-kuan* and the *Chiang-Che hui-kuan* (*Chiang* for Kiangsu Province, *Che* for Chekiang Province)—composed of persons from the Shanghai and

Ningpo area—are much smaller organizations and have relatively little influence in the Chinese community.

Membership in all these regional and dialect associations is predominantly male. A few older women belong, the wives of well-established members, but they do not assume active roles in the running of the associations. Officers are always men.

Socially the dialect associations offer opportunities for sharing news and reminiscences about the home districts and indulging in recreation—card playing, mahjong—with friends who speak the same dialect. Yet these activities by themselves can scarcely account for the strength of the dialect associations among the Chinese and their persistence as active organizations in some instances for more than half a century. The place of the dialect association can be better evaluated if it is seen, first, as a typical immigrant institution providing general social welfare services to ease the shock of the immigrant's initial adjustment; and, secondly, as a local variation of protective and mutual-aid institutions found in China, specifically the tsu and its ancestral hall organization mentioned earlier.

A Chinese immigrant arriving in Bangkok is assured of ready assistance from his dialect group, and this help is offered without question by people who speak his own language and know his needs. Through them, he is put in contact with relatives or persons from his own village in China. They see that he is housed and given work. Later the association stands always ready to give help when needed—to offer advice on sending remittances to China, to provide interpreters when dealing with officials, and to intercede when the immigrant runs afoul of the government's red tape. Like the prototype institutions of China, the dialect association provides educational and medical facilities—more elaborate in fact than anything available in the rude villages of South China, and a continuing system of protective services in times of crisis or misfortune. In Thailand the individual Chinese who needs a loan, a job, or help of any kind will ordinarily appeal to his relatives first as he would in China. When these are unable to help, he can usually get assistance from his dialect association. While the type of problem brought to the attention of the dialect association may differ from problems faced in China, the fact remains that the association stands ready to help the individual Chinese in precisely the same manner and with the same spirit as he would expect from his clan group in China. Furthermore, just as everyone with the same surname and family origin was considered a member of the clan in China and therefore entitled to assistance from other members, so in Thailand all persons of a certain dialect group are considered *ipso facto* members of the dialect association and thereby entitled to its full assistance.

Like the ancestral hall in China, the association provides mediation facilities when quarrels develop, a service which helps in no small measure to preserve the unity and stability of the Chinese community. Here is a newspaper account of a resolution of a dispute by the Hakka Association:

> One hundred and twenty shirt-tailoring workers of 30 local shops stopped working yesterday demanding better treatment. As both parties are Hakka people, the Hakka Association has stepped out to mediate between them. After a talk with both sides yesterday afternoon, no agreement was reached as the representatives of the capital side said that they were not in a position to accept the three items of the request of the opposite party and that further decision would have to be made after consultation. The three items are: (i) to cancel the fees demanded for workers' meals; (ii) to raise their pay; (iii) the capital side cannot fire workers without any reason.

An announcement two days later reported that this dispute had been satisfactorily settled by the Association.

Usually the problems brought to the association's attention concern business affairs—disputes between employees and employers, between business partners, or between a bankrupt merchant and his creditors. Disputes between relatives or close family members are too personal usually to be given unwelcome publicity. Airing of such troubles lowers the family's standing in the community, and most Chinese will do everything in their power to avoid this.

Unlike the powerful tsu organization in China, the dialect associations have no formal means of enforcing their decisions in mediation and must rely almost entirely on the goodwill of the parties concerned. Before the association can act in any dispute both parties must request its assistance. A meeting is then held in the association headquarters attended by the association leaders, the disputants, and some of their friends or relatives. The dispute is discussed informally and friendly pressure is put on both sides to compromise. Appeals are made to be 'a good Chinese', or a good Cantonese, or Hakka, and not give the Chinese community a bad name. Usually this method works, for, although neither party is forced to accept such advice, often the association leaders are wealthy and influential business men whose opinions carry considerable weight. The most that might be done if a member remains uncooperative is to oust him from the association, but this seems to be very rarely done.

Many dialect associations, as noted above, help to support Chinese temples, but they themselves engage in no religious activities comparable to those of the ancestral halls of China. One of the essential services of the various dialect associations in Thailand is to provide a place for burial and facilities for storage of the remains of deceased members. This of course is a function which the ancestral hall in China had no reason to assume. The ideal for Chinese immigrants who die abroad is to be returned to their homeland for burial. Chinese cemeteries in Bangkok are designed with this in view. Relatively small for the large Chinese population, their space is used for the most part for temporary graves only, which are opened after a few years and the bones removed. If the remains are to be returned to China for re-burial, they are placed in a small tin or wood box directly, or are partially cremated and the ashes placed in a similar box. These boxes are then stored in godowns located within the cemetery until they can be taken to China by a relative. Godowns in the Teochiu Cemetery which the author inspected in 1951 were filled from floor to roof with some 10,000 of these boxes. The Cantonese Cemetery at the time was storing more than 6,000 boxes of remains. If the family of the deceased is indigent, the bones, together with those of thousands of others in like circumstances, are cremated and the ashes placed in a large communal crypt. The more wealthy of the traditional Chinese families avoid burial entirely; coffins are simply stored in the cemetery's godowns until they can be returned to China. In 1951 the Teochiu Cemetery godowns contained about 200 such coffins, the Cantonese Cemetery but four, a commentary perhaps on the relative wealth and size of the two dialect groups. Each box or coffin in these godowns is labelled with the name of the deceased, the date of death, the cemetery's registration number, and the village or the locality in China to which the remains will be sent. In prewar years about 100 coffins yearly were returned to China for burial. The small boxes of remains—about the size of a shoe box—are usually sent back as passengers' luggage, and since they are not manifested, no count is kept by the steamship companies. Chinese shipping firms report that since the war almost no coffins and relatively few boxes of remains have been taken to China.

The dialect association cemeteries in Bangkok are built of necessity on extremely flat land, for there are no hills in or near the city. The graves are arranged in regular rows as in Western cemeteries to obtain the maximum use of the land and without the traditional regard for *feng-shui*.[1] Moreover, the land is low-lying and often waterlogged. These features have probably helped to induce Chinese to return relatives' remains to China for interment in a more favourable place.

### OCCUPATIONAL AND BUSINESS ASSOCIATIONS

Covering practically every type of economic activity in which Chinese are engaged, the occupational and business associations of the Chinese community make a fundamental separation between capital and labour. Chinese managers and employers generally are represented by trade guilds and the Chinese Chamber of Commerce, which will be described shortly. Chinese labour—chiefly coolies working on lighters and in rice-mills—have been represented by a variety of organizations, some formed by Chinese themselves, others sponsored by the Thai government. In November 1958, when Marshal Sarit took over full control of the government, all labour organizations were ordered dissolved. By that time four different labour associations had appeared. The most significant of these, so far as the Chinese community was concerned, was the Central Labour Union (CLU).

The Central Labour Union was formed in the early postwar period from a small nucleus of quasi-benevolent associations, the only kind of labour organizations up to that time permitted by law in Thailand. Recognized by the government in 1947, the CLU from the outset accepted all workers who wished to join, both Thai and Chinese; actually, however, it was almost completely Chinese, both in its rank and file and its leaders. At its height the CLU claimed a membership of 75,000 but observers believe it had only half that number. Its main strength came from Chinese rice-mill coolies, but it also included a body of tram workers in Bangkok, many of whom, as operators of vehicles, were required by law to be Thai citizens.

In 1948 the Thai government came under the control again of the war-time premier, Phibun Songgram, who at once threw his support behind an effort to separate Thai and Chinese workers. Thus the Thai Labour Union was formed for Thai workers exclusively as a rival to the Central Labour Union. Thai workers were urged to leave the older union and join the new Thai Labour Union (or the Thai National Trade Union Congress, as it was called after 1951). In 1952, the government ordered the dissolution of the Central Labour Union, on the ground that the CLU was dominated by Chinese and run by Communists, and therefore could not adequately represent the interests of Thai labour. The CLU was indeed affiliated with the World Federation of Trade Unions (WFTU), a recognized Communist organization, and undoubtedly included Communists among its members and officers. Despite the stiffening of government support and, after 1952 a virtual monopoly of the field, the TNTUC never became a strong nor an active union, despite its claims to contain 60 federated unions, mainly in Bangkok and the industrialized suburb of Thonburi.

Two other labour organizations of significance for the Chinese community appeared in the postwar period. In 1954 an organization called the Free Workers Association (FWA) was registered with the government as a labour union. The FWA opened its ranks to both Thai and Chinese workers, and because of heavy backing from influential politicians, it flourished for a time. However its strength was political rather than organizational, and when the Phibun Songgram group was ousted by a *coup d'état* in 1957 the Free Workers Association virtually collapsed.

A more substantive and entirely Chinese organization was the Overseas Chinese Labour Union (OCLU), probably the oldest labour organization in Thailand, having been formed initially in 1907 as the Association of Industry and Commerce; in 1924 the name was changed to the Overseas Chinese Labour Union. Strongly pro-Kuomingtang, the OCLU helped organize opposition to the Japanese in the prewar period; it went underground during the War, but re-appeared in 1946 and later affiliated with the Free Workers Association mentioned above. The OCLU was never large nor influential; at the time it joined the Free Workers Association the OCLU claimed only 100 dues paying members. It was principally a Chinese workers beneficent society rather than an active labour union, furnishing benefits to members in case of sickness, old age, death and disaster.

None of these organizations, nor their officers, held a high place in the social structure of the Chinese community. This is understandable in the case of those organizations dominated by the Thai government, namely, the Thai National Trade Union Congress and the Free Workers Association, which were more political than social in their interests. Yet the thoroughly Chinese organizations, the Central Labour Union and the Overseas Chinese Labour Union, were also of minor importance locally, possibly because they did not represent much wealth and therefore had limited influence. Their low position may be inferred from the fact that their officers were rarely asked to participate in joint association meetings called to discuss community-wide problems. As noted above, the Central Labour Union was suspected of being dominated by Communists, but the latter did not show any unwillingness to co-operate fully with Chinese business interests. The importance of these organizations in the community should not be minimized, however. They were stabilizing influences since they helped to prevent festering disputes. Prolonged strikes among the Chinese are exceedingly rare, thanks to the willingness of both management and labour to compromise their differences. Much of the labour peace which characterizes the Chinese community can also be attributed to the benevolent policies of employers. Workers are often furnished with housing and rice, guaranteed a continuing wage during illness, given free medical care, and usually paid a year-end bonus calculated on the profits of the business. In addition, good wages are paid—in 1952 a rice-mill coolie was earning more each day than a government clerk.

On the capital side, more than 30 different trade guilds *(kung-hui)* flourish among Chinese merchants and professional men in Bangkok, such as the Chinese Rice Merchants Associations, the Chinese Press Guild, the Vegetable Merchants Association, the Chinese Physicians Association, and so on. These trade guilds are principally business groupings, and their activities ordinarily are confined to the commercial field. Their importance lies in the assistance they render in the economic adjustment of the Chinese immigrants and in the continuing services of an economic nature they perform for members—circulating trade information, advising on economic trends and policies, hindering the development of unwanted competition. They also serve as a buffer between the lone merchant and the Thai government.

Membership in these trade guilds is entirely Chinese, either immigrants or their immediate descendants. To become a member of a trade guild, one has first to be engaged in a particular type of business or profession; and secondly, one must be approved by the leaders of that particular guild. Both these provisions work to exclude Thai. An individual cannot ordinarily become a goldsmith, or vegetable merchant, or printer, or take up any of the other occupations represented by these guilds without first learning the trade. This apprenticeship system is controlled by Chinese organizations, open normally to other Chinese whatever their dialect group affiliation, but closed to outsiders, i.e. the Thai and the newly-arrived 'White Chinese' from Shanghai.

The trade guilds which are often wealthy can exert considerable influence and their officers are respected leaders of the community.

### *Chinese Chamber of Commerce*

The largest business association from point of view of membership, and probably the most influential Chinese organization in Thailand, is the Bangkok Chinese Chamber of Commerce.[2] In 1950 the Chamber had over 5,000 members, both individuals and firms, ranging from proprietors of small shops to the most influential and wealthy merchants in Thailand. Membership is open to any person or business upon payment of a moderate fee. There is no evidence that the leadership of the Chamber would deliberately bar any person or business—Thai, Western or whatever—who might wish to join the Chamber. Actually, however, the membership is almost entirely Chinese, as the organization activities demonstrate. Notices and publications are printed in Chinese, and meetings are conducted in Chinese. Thus a non-Chinese would find it almost impossible to participate effectively in the organization or to derive much benefit from membership.

The ostensible function of the Chinese Chamber of Commerce is to promote Chinese business interests, and this it does in a number of ways. First of all, the Chamber together with the trade guilds seeks to combat adverse legislation and government policies. It does this quietly and often indirectly, working through influential government officials with whom the Chamber's officers are acquainted. The following items selected from Bangkok's Thai press show how in one instance adverse legislation was successfully thwarted. The newspaper *Prachathipatai* reported on November 11, 1952:

> The bill governing aerated water taxation will definitely be submitted to the National Assembly shortly. It was reported that last Sunday evening influential merchants in the aerated water trade entertained a number of assemblymen to dinner, during which the business men pointed out that the various taxes now imposed are already very onerous to the business community, so that the bill for imposing taxes on aerated water should advisably be dropped.

On November 13, *Siam Radh* reported:

> The government has proposed an aerated water bill aimed at obtaining a tax revenue of some 12 million baht annually. However, it appears that the majority of pro-government assemblymen are not in favour of the bill. This is because aerated water manufacturers are at present already paying increased taxes connected with their business. . . .

On November 20, *Thai Mai* reported in part:

> A meeting of the government sponsored aerated water bill was held for the the third time in the afternoon of the 18th instant. Opposing the measure were Nai Pethai Amatavakul (Bangkok) who asserted that the Premier had disapproved of the bill on the ground that most of the aerated water factory owners are mostly Thai nationals. Nai Thiem Na Songkla (Rajburi) who declared that farmers and planters should be allowed to buy aerated water to assuage their thirst at not too exorbitant prices, Nai Sanguan Sirisawang (Chiengmai) who argued that aerated water taxes would add to the high living cost of the people. It was Nai Yat Waidi who moved for the meeting to turn down the bill . . . Nai Somsakdi queried why aerated water should be enjoying tax exemption while on the other hand rice, as a staple food item, is being taxed.

This newspaper attributed the delay in considering and submitting the bill to the fact, as reported in the *Prachathipatai* item cited above, that Chinese merchants had invited members of the National Assembly to a banquet, during which the merchants 'distributed pamphlets to the guests explaining their stand in regard to the bill'. Whether something else was distributed by the merchants can perhaps be inferred. Not long after this episode some of the highest ranking personalities in the ruling military clique acquired substantial positions and financial interests in world famous American-style soft drink companies set up in Bangkok. One newspaper man summed up the *coup d'état* of 1957, when Marshal Sarit ousted General Phao and Phibun, as the 'Triumph of Coca-Cola over Seven-Up'.

While the Chamber and other associations are not always able to defeat so easily all adverse legislation proposed by the government, they have succeeded in many instances in tempering their effect on the Chinese. For this service they have earned the whole-hearted respect of the entire community, but, on the other hand, have stimulated a rising hostility among many Thai who resent the economic power of the Chinese.

The Chamber also issues certificates of origin for goods exported from Thailand by Chinese firms, and these are recognized in all the parts of Southeast Asia. For a time the Chamber published a paper of financial and commercial news. It now furnishes trade information to merchants and provides a reading room at its headquarters where newspapers and trade journals may be consulted. All these commercial services are useful to Thailand's Chinese.

Yet the principal community services of the Chamber of Commerce, the ones which have made it the outstanding Chinese association, go beyond these purely business activities. Before and immediately after World War II it actively promoted Chinese education in Thailand by running the largest Chinese secondary school in the country until the government banned such schools; the Chamber is today a powerful advocate of Chinese schooling. One of the Chamber's main jobs is acting as an intermediary between the Chinese minority and the Thai government. Specifically this means that the Chamber through its officers intercedes for individuals and groups who get in difficulties with the government. During the last several years the Chinese language press has reported appeals to the Chamber for the following services: to obtain bail money, to secure food, clothing, and medical supplies for Chinese held in jail or awaiting deportation; to intervene with police officials who refused to return certain important documents to a Chinese after ordering him to produce them; to provide legal advice for a Chinese arrested for tax evasion—but perhaps the special nature of these requests can best be illustrated by direct quotations from Bangkok's Thai and Chinese newspapers:

> In view of the proposal of the Interior Ministry to ban from Bangkok streets horse carriages, drays and rickshaws in 1953, over one thousand Chinese rickshaw pullers are reported to have submitted a joint petition to the Interior Ministry for leniency in making gradual abolition of rickshaws over a period of some five years. The total number of rickshaws should be reduced by 25 per cent each year, it was suggested.
>
> The petitioners have also approached the Chinese Chamber of Commerce for intercession with Police General Phao Sriyanod, Interior Minister and Director-General of the Police Department. (*Kiattisak*, December 22, 1952)
>
> Some 200 Chinese tenants on the Suksamran Lane opposite the Chinese Embassy, who were evicted by landlords, appealed to Chinese Chamber of Commerce Chairman Chang Lan-ch'en to help in solving the problem. (*Hsin-pao*, January 28, 1958)
>
> Representatives of the Chula Land fire victims called on Chamber of Commerce Chairman Chang Lan-ch'en on July 13, asking the latter to approach the authorities for a permission to rebuild their shelters in the fire-ravaged area. Chang was understood to have promised to render assistance in this regard. (*Chung-yüan wan-pao*, July 15, 1958)
>
> In response to the request of the Chinese scrap-iron dealers, Chamber of Commerce Chairman Chang Lan-ch'en will soon seek a permission from the Finance Minister for having scrap-iron exempted from export duty. (*Shih-chieh*, May 14, 1958)
>
> Twenty-four Chinese watch shops again urge Chamber of Commerce Chairman Chang Lan-ch'en to help solve their retroactive tax problem. (*Chung-yüan*, May 29, 1958)

All such requests received a sympathetic and effective response. At times of urgent personal need, the resources of the entire community are drawn upon. For example, an appeal in 1951 from deportees lodged in jail was channelled by the Chamber to associations, schools, and newspapers in the community and the response was electric. On one of the author's visit to the Chamber during this period he found its large offices almost filled with piles of blankets, food, clothing and medicines, all contributed by the Chinese community. The Chamber later supervised the distribution of these goods to the deportees.

When action by the Government is required, as in the scrap dealers' appeal cited above, the Chairman of the Chamber personally calls on the proper authorities and seeks by persuasion and personal influence to obtain what is needed. The highest officials of the Chamber are usually Sino-Thai of considerable wealth and recognized social standing in Thai as well as Chinese circles. Fluent in Thai and entirely conversant with Thai cultural patterns, personally friendly with high officials, they make effective intermediaries.

When other matters of community-wide concern arise—the closing of Chinese schools, increases in taxation—the Chamber takes the initiative in calling together representatives of the major dialect groups, the trade guilds, and the benevolent associations to decide on a proper course of community action *vis-à-vis* the government. At such time the Chamber acts as the spokesman for the entire Chinese minority. In 1952 when the alien registration fee was suddenly jumped from 20 to 400 baht the Chairman of the Chamber of Commerce was delegated by these other associations to intercede with the highest authorities for reduction in the fee.

The Thai government itself recognizes the commanding position of the Chinese Chamber of Commerce as the spokesman for the Chinese in Thailand, and has approached the Chamber's officers for help on problems concerning the Chinese community. Thus, when the government sought to induce Chinese immigrants with defective or false identification papers to re-register, it worked through the Chamber of Commerce, allowing the latter organization to distribute the forms to applicants and to carry on the registration at its own offices rather than at police stations. In 1951 at the request of the Thai government the Chamber of Commerce acted as the go-between in negotiations with the Chinese Communist Government for the deportation of Chinese from Thailand to the China Mainland. The Thai government had not recognized the Chinese Communist regime and there were consequently no formal channels of communication between them.

The Chamber of Commerce has historical precedence for its present role as the representative of the Chinese minority in Thailand. Prior to 1946, despite repeated requests, Thailand consistently declined to recognize the Chinese government, motivated probably by the realization that if diplomatic relations were established, and a Chinese Embassy opened in Bangkok, Thailand could no longer deal unilaterally with its Chinese minority. During this time the Chinese Chamber of Commerce, as the leader of Chinese business interests in Thailand, performed necessary consular tasks of assistance to business men—particularly the issuance of certificates of origin needed by shippers—and gradually assumed its present role as spokesman for the Chinese community.

Following World War II Thailand was forced by peace negotiations with the victorious Allies to recognize the Chinese Nationalist Government and to permit the opening in Thailand of diplomatic and consular offices. With the opening of the Chinese Nationalist Embassy in Bangkok in 1946 the Chamber of Commerce relinquished for a time its former consular duties and some of its protective services.

However, upon the subsequent decline of the Chinese Nationalist Government's fortunes, and with it the usefulness and prestige of its Embassy in Bangkok, the Chamber once more assumed much of its former role as the representative of Thailand's Chinese population. The Thai government is presumably happy to by-pass the Chinese Embassy, and to resume its more advantageous position *vis-à-vis* the Chinese minority. The Chinese for their part raise few objections, seeking help from any quarter that is effective. The Chinese Nationalist Embassy itself acknowledged the power of the Chamber, and the Ambassador in Bangkok has given the highest priority to improving relations with the Chamber so as to secure its support on important issues.

The Chinese Nationalist Embassy would like to be the spokesman for the Chinese minority but it operates under serious handicaps. Many Chinese who normally would be pro-Nationalist are bitter over the loss of China to the Communists, as they put it, because of dissolute living and brazen corruption. Unfortunately, for almost ten years after the war, the Nationalists refused to send anyone higher than a *chargé d'affairs* to Bangkok, a decision which hurt the interests of the Chinese more than it upset the Thai. Moreover, the vast majority of the Chinese in Thailand come from the Chinese Mainland, not Formosa, and they want an organization which can assist them in travel to and communication with the Mainland where their relatives still live. The Chinese Nationalist Embassy obviously cannot do this, but the Chamber of Commerce can.

As one might expect, the Chinese Chamber of Commerce in Bangkok is a dynamic organization which shows no signs of weakening. However, like some other associations of the Chinese in these postwar years, the Chamber has split over the question of Communism. For a brief period in 1951 pro-Nationalist officers, including the Chairman of the Chamber, withdrew from the organization following a dispute with pro-Communist elements. Quarrels like this have led to serious and prolonged schisms in other associations. However, a measure of the Chamber's importance is furnished by the fact that all Chinese, pro-Nationalists as well as pro-Communists, and Chinese leaders as well as Thai officials, urged reconciliation. The dispute was quickly and successfully resolved and the Chamber enabled to continue its work.

### BENEVOLENT AND CHARITABLE ASSOCIATIONS

All the Chinese associations mentioned above have benevolent functions in that they stand ready to furnish assistance to the victims of unusual misfortunes and of catastrophe. However, to meet the day-to-day needs as well as any extraordinary crisis of the Chinese in Thailand, there are organizations whose purpose is solely and entirely charitable.

The largest of these is the *Sian Lua Hua Ch'iao Pao Teh Shang T'ang* (Siamese Overseas Chinese Repay Virtue Benevolent Association), which conducts or supervises practically all of the benevolent and charitable work in the Chinese community. The 'Poh-tek' Association, as it is popularly called in Thailand, operates on an annual budget which approaches one and one-half million baht (US$75,000). These funds are derived mainly from donations (approximately 66 per cent are unsolicited) and from the nominal dues—two baht each month—of several thousand members. As would be expected, the Association is supported almost entirely by the Chinese rather than by the Thai.

The Poh Tek Association was founded about 1910 to help Chinese financially unable to help themselves. During its existence the Association has devoted its main efforts to furnishing medicines, medical treatment, and hospitalization for the sick, arranging for the burial of indigent Chinese in its own cemetery plot, and giving immediate food and shelter to victims of fires, floods and other disasters. A summary of its expenditures in 1950, as given in its annual report, shows that the Association gave clothes, medicines, and supplemental food to 46 Chinese deportees held by the Immigration Department in Bangkok; assisted up-country people made homeless by a fire; donated money to the School for the Blind in Bangkok (a Thai and Western institution); constructed an addition to its hospital and equipped the hospital's operating and dining-rooms; and—hardly an act of charity—sent a present to the King on his coronation.

After any large fire in Bangkok, the Poh Tek Association is the first on the scene with large tubs of rice, hot tea, and vegetables, all distributed to refugees without charge or restraint. Even bowls and chopsticks are provided. At one large conflagration in 1952 which swept through several city blocks, people were being fed by the Association before the fire itself was brought under control. Although several thousand persons were made homeless, losing as well their means of livelihood, so thoroughly was relief provided by the Poh Tek and other associations that the next day one could see nothing unusual about the community, no homeless refugees, no begging for aid, no apparent interruption of work except in the now empty, fire-swept area. For days following such a disaster, the Association, if necessary, continues to distribute food and to arrange for temporary shelter for refugees.

Although these associations were established in the first place to help the overseas Chinese, assistance is given to all in need, regardless of nationality. The following item quoted from a Chinese newspaper in Bangkok shows the spirit behind this benevolence:

> This morning at nine, the Chinese Charity Organization sent some officials to give common drugs, food stuffs, and daily necessities to the persons held by the Immigration Department. Altogether there were 24 persons of which 17 were Chinese, 6 Indians, and 1 French Indochinese. All these people were treated alike and each person received 30 baht in cash as well as other useful things. (*Chung-yüan wan-pao,* June 14, 1952.)

Benevolent organizations and charitable individuals who offer assistance to the needy and helpless receive the highest praise of the Chinese press, a good indication of the value attached to the concept of mutual aid in the Chinese community. By contrast, their work is scarcely noticed in Thai newspapers, although assistance, particularly in times of a fire or flood, is extended to all, Thai and Chinese alike.

The running of the Hua-ch'iao (Overseas Chinese) Hospital is the most important single activity of the Poh Tek Association, with an estimated two-thirds of the Association's funds normally going to the support of this institution. The second-largest Chinese hospital in Bangkok, it is of fairly recent origin, having been initiated in 1938 as an out-patient clinic offering Western medical[3] treatment only. In 1945 a maternity hospital was added—now described by the hospital's manager as the largest maternity hospital in Thailand. This hospital now has a staff of about 100 nurses (graduate and student) and several doctors. The Hua-ch'iao Hospital is not primarily a charity hospital. Of the 107 beds in 1951, only 21 were for charity patients, although this number would be increased on demand. The Poh Tek Association apparently guarantees any deficits of the hospital and furnishes funds for new construction and equipment.

The largest and oldest Chinese hospital in Bangkok—and in the whole of Thailand—is the T'ien-hua Hospital, which was founded about 1900. For many years T'ien-hua Hospital offered Chinese medical treatment only, but about 1950 the practice of Western medicine was instituted. In its out-patient department either Chinese or Western medical treatment can be obtained (although the Chinese section seems to be far better developed and much more popular). All its services are free with the exception of Western medical injections in the out-patient department. While both men and women may use the out-patient clinic, the in-patient department accepts only males. In the ten-year period 1941–50, the hospital treated an average of about 2,000 in-patients a year and gave free medicine to an average of 10,000 out-patients yearly, according to the 1950 annual report of this institution.

This hospital was founded originally and has been controlled since by the major dialect associations of Bangkok through a Board of Directors which is composed of representatives from these organizations. In 1950 the hospital's expenditures amounted to more than one million baht (US$50,000), which was more than adequately covered by voluntary contributions and donations. A monthly record is kept of voluntary contributions, and when these fall below expenditures, the dialect associations together make up the deficit. Public recognition, community good-will, and some fame can be gained by donating money to this and other organizations in the Chinese community. The names of all contributors are printed in the annual report issued by the hospital. Those who have given 10,000 baht or more are especially honoured by having their pictures printed in the report. In addition, the upper walls of the old-fashioned, high-ceiling office and waiting room of the hospital are hung with large framed photographs of persons who have made especially generous donations.

These are the customary ways by which the Chinese community recognizes beneficence. The reports of the Poh Tek Associations, for example, lists all contributions, large and small alike, pointing out for special mention those who have given large sums. All Chinese hospitals and charitable associations, and even some dialect associations, honour benefactors by hanging their framed pictures in conspicuous places on the premises. This form of recognition shows the part that charity plays in attaining social prominence in the community. Philanthropy too is one of the few ways in which Chinese can win the favourable attention of the Thai government. A wealthy Chinese tin-mine owner in Phuket, South Thailand, showed the author the dazzling Thai decoration presented him 20 years ago following his gift of X-ray equipment (said to have cost $100,000) to a government hospital in Bangkok. Such beneficence seems to have been more common years ago than now, yet one still reads of a Chinese being decorated by the King for donations of money or equipment to a Thai hospital or other institution, and the decorations thus received are highly prized by the Chinese. It is pertinent to note that one rarely finds a woman among the large contributors to these benevolent and charitable organizations, additional proof that among the Chinese in Thailand men control the family finances and reap the rewards of philanthropy.

The Hakka Public Hospital, run by the Hakka Dialect Association, is the only other major Chinese hospital in Bangkok. Founded in 1940 as a clinic offering Chinese medical treatment only, it was enlarged in 1950 to include a maternity hospital as well. This hospital is considerably smaller than either the Hua-ch'iao or the T'ien-hua Hospitals and, unlike these two institutions, has no free beds. All services and medicines in its Chinese medicine outpatient department are free, however. It is partially self-supporting; the Hakka Association making up any deficit in its budget.

The majority of persons using this hospital are Chinese, although some Indians and Thai also go there. Neither this nor any other

Chinese hospital nor clinic appears to discriminate against non-Chinese; facilities are open to all without regard to dialect group or ethnic affiliation.

It is not at all unusual at any Chinese clinic to see Chinese interpreting for their Thai or Indian friends whom they have brought there for medical treatment. When the standard home remedies have failed often outside assistance is first sought from a clinic recommended by a Chinese neighbour. Chinese medicines are regarded by the Thai as being particularly efficacious, and at the clinics at least they have the additional advantage of being free. In-patient departments of Chinese hospitals are, on the other hand, almost never used by the Thai, and many Thai women are reluctant to enter maternity hospitals—this latter attitude derives not from any valuation of Chinese medical services but from the exceedingly prevalent fear of dangerous spirits popularly believed by the Thai to inhabit such institutions.

In addition to these major benevolent institutions, there are a number of small groups, many informal and temporary, organized by the Chinese solely for the purpose of donating money for a worthy cause. These appear regularly in the lists of contributors to the large benevolent associations and hospitals, usually under some such title as 'Group of Kind Persons'. Few situations arouse the Chinese community as the need to help others, especially Chinese, who have suffered misfortune. Newspapers, schools, and associations throw themselves whole-heartedly into efforts to raise funds for the victims of a disaster. Mutual aid is a traditional part of life in China, particularly in the rural areas, and judging from the vitality, services, and programmes of the benevolent organizations in Thailand—and the success of the relief campaigns conducted periodically through Chinese newspapers—this practice has not weakened in Thailand.

All the various associations described above are inclusive in the sense that those who belong to one may become members of other associations. These are primarily voluntary *interest* groups, and any person normally may belong to any association which serves his particular interests. Many Chinese do in fact belong to several groups at the same time—a dialect association, trade guild, the Chamber of Commerce, and a benevolent association. Thus the tendency of some groups such as the dialect associations to separate the Chinese population is compensated for by other associations which draw their membership from across the whole community.

These associations are exclusive institutions in the sense that membership is almost entirely Chinese. By formal and informal controls they effectively exclude persons from other ethnic groups. To gain a nominal membership in many associations is not difficult—one need only pay a fee, ordinarily fairly low, to become a member of a benevolent association or the Chinese Chamber of Commerce, for example. But to participate actively in the affairs of the association requires first of all that a person speak and read Chinese, usually the Teochiu dialect. All meetings, all discussions, all notices, all publications are in the Chinese language. Often the employees of these associations will profess to speak only Chinese, which is a very effective barrier to outsiders.

### FUNCTIONS OF ASSOCIATIONS

While these associations perform a great variety of services for the individual, their true importance must be sought not only in terms of these services but on a more complex level in their contribution to the social unity and cultural strength of the Chinese minority in Thailand. First and foremost, all organizations provide mutual assistance among the Chinese and in so doing weld the diverse social, linguistic, and economic elements of the community into one self-protective league.

All associations, no matter what their individual character, have mutual-aid functions, not only for their own members but for the general public. Two factors have contributed to the development of these services by Chinese associations. First, there are few social welfare organizations in Thai society from which Chinese might get assistance. Charity and philanthropy are not well developed among the Thai. Giving to monks and to Buddhist temples *(wat)* is an accepted practice, for it brings merit to the donor; but no particular value is attached to community charity or welfare programmes. Until 1947 when the Public Welfare Department (of the Ministry of the Interior) was established, almost no official cognizance was taken of the population's welfare needs.

This is not to say that the Thai government and its affiliated organizations have provided no social welfare services. Government hospitals and clinics have long been open in Bangkok, offering free medical services to the physically and mentally ill, and to mothers and children. The Department of Public Health since its establishment in 1918 has conducted a number of sanitary campaigns, aided in the training of workers, and encouraged the improvement of public health generally. The Siamese Red Cross, and its adjunct, the Junior Red Cross, conducts health training programmes and provide invaluable treatment for mothers and children. These are all community welfare programmes supported by public funds. Yet beyond these fundamental and essential health services, the average Thai as well as the Chinese alien has had to depend on his own resources, individual or family, in times of difficulty. The development of Chinese organizations to provide other essential social welfare services was necessary and, given the propensity of the Chinese to organize, inevitable.

The second factor contributing to the development of mutual-aid services by the Chinese community is the apparent unwillingness of the government to single out the Chinese for special assistance. The improvement of working conditions is a case in point. In the first years of the constitutional government minimum wages were fixed for certain categories of government employees—these were predominantly Thai—and a social insurance system was developed for their protection, but no minimum wages or hours have ever been fixed for employees in private industry or commerce, and the labour of women and children has never been officially regulated. In January 1939 the National Assembly by an overwhelming majority of 62 to 28 turned down a comprehensive labour law designed to cover the whole field of wages, hours, woman and child labour, old-age pensions, and workmen's insurance. The reason for the Assembly's reluctance to help workers, according to Thompson (1947: 23), is germane:

> The crux of the Thai attitude lay in the fact that a large proportion of the country's labouring force was Chinese, and the nationalistic government had no intention of spending large sums for the improvement of their conditions of living and work.

Nor has the government's attitude in this regard changed greatly in the intervening years. In December 1952 a labour bill designed to improve working conditions for all labourers was soundly defeated in the National Assembly by a 102 to 6 vote. Again, in 1954, social security legislation was adopted to provide maternity, child welfare, sickness, invalidism and old age insurance, and costs of cremation for the population. But after two years of study and fruitless debate of implementation procedures, the Council of Ministers in January 1956 decided to postpone implementation indefinitely. With the government unwilling to act on their behalf,

Chinese are thrown back on whatever protective resources they
n themselves muster within their own community and through
eir own associations.

As an outgrowth of their mutual aid services, Chinese associations help to unify the Chinese population in the pursuit of common objectives; they stimulate ethnocentric sentiments among the Chinese. The Chinese minority in Thailand, like all complex societies, shows a great range of economic affluence, from persons of wealth down to those with very little and with little hope of getting much more. If the minority is to maintain its unity over a period of time, two things seem necessary: to devise a way to 'spread the wealth', so that the economic differences are not continually intensified; and to encourage on the part of those with wealth an active interest in groups lower on the economic scale than they. The Chinese associations described here do both these. It is the unusually wealthy merchant who does not contribute substantially to charitable projects of the community's associations, and the majority participate actively in such organizations as the Poh Tek whose membership runs through all economic levels of the community. Significantly, one finds very little 'class' antagonism as such among Thailand's Chinese, and despite the strong influence of communism among workers, no discernible resentment of the man of wealth or position. This is indeed a remarkable achievement, given the economic and other diversity which marks the Chinese minority.

Like those groups formed by European immigrants in the United States, all the Chinese associations assist the immigrant in his initial adjustment and help to ease the disorganizing effect of subsequent misfortunes which he might suffer in the new land. But their functions go far beyond this type of 'travellers' aid' assistance. The associations, taken collectively, provide a continuing system of social insurance not only for the immigrant but for his family as well. In case of unemployment, sickness, death, natural calamity, quarrels and disputes, whether between groups or between individuals, some association provides the required assistance. The individual never stands alone; even when he has no formal membership in the associations which furnish assistance, he is still entitled to receive their help. Moreover, they act as a necessary 'big brother' for the lone individual, shielding him from unjust and arbitrary police action or interceding for him in the event of his detention, arrest, or proposed deportation.

By minimizing the effects of disasters and carrying the individuals and family safely through a period of social and economic crisis, these associations help prevent disorganization both of the individual and of the group. It is noteworthy that the only unresolved disputes among the Chinese are those in areas where the Chinese associations are powerless. These include family conflicts and similar disputes which for personal reasons the Chinese are unwilling to bring to public notice. Disputes between major Chinese political factions—Nationalist and Communists—also are beyond the scope of any legal Chinese associations. On the other hand, conflicts normally found in other societies—between employee and employer, between business competitors, or between business associates—are easily and quickly resolved by the machinery of the Chinese associations, and they rarely disturb the community's equilibrium. It is, as a rule, only when the associations fail to function or function inadequately that one begins to see evidences of confusion and of disorganization.

The Chinese associations also help to mould public opinion and attitudes in the Chinese community, an activity recognized and used by the government to its own advantage on occasion. Thus when seeking to lower retail prices in 1952, the government called in various trade-guild officials and demanded that they make individual merchants reduce prices. The Chinese watch the leading business and dialect associations for cues before taking any concerted action, whether it be plans for a Chinese national celebration or a protest against proposed taxation. Often a Chinese in doubt about some problem or proposed course of action in his own personal affairs will seek out the officers of his dialect association for counsel.

Finally from these Chinese organizations the social and prestige structure of the Chinese community has developed. Positions of authority within the leading associations are awarded like decorations to wealthy and public spirited individuals. Not all associations rank equally high in prestige and power. In the prestige hierarchy the Chinese Chamber of Commerce stands at the top of the list, followed by the larger dialect associations, the benevolent associations, and the trade guilds. Religious, labour and purely social organizations rank low and have little direct influence on community affairs. In general, however, social recognition in the community is achieved largely through the leadership of associations.

A memorial service which the author attended one December day at the Teochiu Cemetery in Bangkok provided an insight into the social leadership pattern of the community. First an explanation of the memorial service is required. Throughout the year Chinese who die indigent are buried by the Poh Tek Association in a special plot at the Teochiu Cemetery. Every three or four years these remains are disinterred to make room for other burials. At this ceremony the remains of more than 1,000 persons were thus exhumed. The remains are cremated, then re-interred in a large elaborately decorated crypt maintained by the benevolent association. Prior to the cremation a memorial service was held at the cemetery, and in its final phase a number of prominent Chinese were called forward to pay their respects to the deceased. The order and manner in which they were called reflected their relative social standing in the Chinese community.

The first person summoned to stand in the centre of the first row before the altar was the Chairman of the Chinese Chamber of Commerce. The next two persons called to stand on either side of him were the Chairman and Vice-Chairman of the Teochiu Dialect Association. Next the Chairmen of the eight regional associations within the Teochiu Dialect Association were called, and they stood in the second row. Those placed in the third and fourth rows before the altar were the several members of the Executive Committee of the Teochiu Dialect Association and the Chairman of the other dialect associations. Each of these men, from the Chairman of the Chamber of Commerce on down, was a business man. All except one had been born in China. As each of these men was called to take his place before the altar, his name and position were announced over a public address system. The remaining persons waiting to participate in the services were next asked to come forward as a group and take places at the rear of the platform. These numbered about 100 in all and included teachers, doctors, dentists, and lawyers as well as business men. Among this group were a few women. Probably Teochiu officers were given unusual prominance, yet Chinese friends with the author at the time agreed that the ceremony provided a miniature 'who's who' of the Chinese community and a yardstick of the relative importance of associations. In this connection it is notable that trade associations as such, surname associations, and religious organizations were not represented nor signally honoured.

Unwittingly perhaps the Thai government, while deploring the in-group sentiments of the Chinese, has actually helped to draw them closer together. Legal strictures, like those on immigration, or arbitrary taxation, like the 1952 increase in the alien registration fee, affect the Chinese as a group, and in seeking relief from these government actions the Chinese throughout Thailand have responded as a unit. Moreover, in treating with the Chinese minority the Thai government has seldom fully exploited the fault lines which already exist. It declines to deal separately with the the heads of the various dialect associations, for example, but has consistently recognized the Chinese Chamber of Commerce as the representative of the entire Chinese community. Undoubtedly this policy has helped to impress on individual Chinese the practical need for unity among the various groups and organizations in their community.

One schism, however, the Thai government has turned to its own advantage: the split between Communist and Kuomintang groups. In the intrusion of these political differences the first major postwar note of disharmony has been introduced among the Chinese. A community-wide split has grown broader and deeper between pro-Communist and pro-Nationalist associations, schools, newspapers and individuals. Leading associations like the Chamber of Commerce have been racked by fights stemming from this division.

All this has engendered intense bitterness and even hatred, to the detriment of community programs. Actions like the closing of Chinese schools which formerly brought the entire Chinese community to its feet are now ignored by influential Chinese associations and individuals if the question of communism is involved. Whether this serious cleavage among the overseas Chinese is a temporary condition which can be smoothed over by compromise, as previous disputes have been, remains to be seen. This schism is only a reflection of the division in the outside world between the Chinese Communists and the Nationalists, and any resolution of the dispute among the Chinese in Thailand must depend, therefore, on the satisfactory settlement of that larger conflict.

Apart from this conflict, the various overseas associations are viable organizations; surname associations appear to face the least favourable future. Second-generation Chinese, drifting away from the maintenance of traditional ties with the homeland, seem least concerned with the activities and interests of these organizations, and some surname associations have already turned to other services, such as the establishment of primary schools, to justify their existence. By contrast, trade and dialect organizations are dynamic and expanding institutions which appeal to both first and second generation. Membership in the trade guilds and the dialect associations continues to be predominantly China-born, but in these organizations second-generation Chinese are taking increasingly active roles.

The monetary support given to Chinese organizations like trade guilds, the Chamber of Commerce, and the benevolent associations can be taken as a reliable sign of vigorous life, for the Chinese are far too practical to put money in any organization that has passed its usefulness. Many associations are expanding their activities. Thus, as mentioned earlier, the Chao-Yang Regional Association, a sub-group within the Teochiu Association, recently built an exceedingly expensive replica of a traditional ancestral hall and even went so far as to bring skilled artisans from China for the construction. This same association has built a basket-ball court and stadium, the most played on court in Bangkok. The Teochiu Association and the Chamber of Commerce would not only re-open their large secondary schools if given permission by the government but would build even larger schools. None of the associations appear to lack funds for the most ambitious programmes, yet most of their monies are raised by popular subscription among the Chinese. These overseas associations in their totality are so influential in prepetuating social distinctions between the Thai and Chinese population groups that their continued vitality as going institutions beyond the immigrant generation can only mean the indefinite postponement of any major move toward a more thorough assimilation of the Chinese minority in Thailand.

CHAPTER IV

# HOME AND FAMILY LIFE

REGIONAL, occupational and economic diversities among the Chinese in Thailand makes it difficult to speak of a typical Chinese family and home. Behaviour common to the Cantonese may be absent among the Hakka. A wealthy family will live in a larger house with more Western conveniences than a poor family, but will also employ servants, live together with a wider range of relatives, and will be more likely to include a concubine among its members. Moreover, families several generations in Thailand are not so closely bound to traditional patterns as newly arrived immigrants, and Chinese families settled among Thai neighbours in the rural areas will be more susceptible to outside acculturative influences than those living cheek-by-jowl with others in Bangkok's Chinese community.

While differences exist, and must be recognized, certain basic similarities run through all families, regardless of past origins and present circumstances. The overseas Chinese family is patriarchal —the husband is unquestionably its head. Descent is traced along the male line and marriages within the kin group are prohibited. The preferred pattern of residence after marriage is with the bridegroom's family, although conditions sometimes force the newly wed to establish a separate residence. Within the family, a person's responsibilities, rights and expectations are clear-cut and depend on generation, age and sex, as indeed they were traditionally in China. Older persons whether relatives or not are treated deferentially by those younger. Parents are especially respected and honoured throughout their lives. On the other hand, women as compared to men hold a definitely inferior position in the family and are restricted in the activities they may engage in outside the home. The overseas Chinese community is a man's world, and few women care to question male superiority. Perhaps the outstanding feature of this family is that the traditional values mentioned above have persisted so well in an alien environment, a tribute not only to the intensity with which these are held, but also to the insulation of the home from influences which might engender radical changes.

The pattern of family life characteristic of the middle-income Chinese shopkeeper in Bangkok may be taken as illustrative of the majority of the Chinese in Thailand. Inasmuch as Bangkok's Chinese community is the primary locus of commercial and organizational interests, there is good reason to expect that its patterns have served as models for the Chinese elsewhere in the Kingdom, and will continue to do so. Indeed, Bangkok may supersede the homeland itself in this respect; already the capital is setting the standard for dress, recreation, language, and other aspects of behaviour among the Chinese in Thailand.

### THE CHINESE HOME

The typical Chinese house in Bangkok, and indeed in virtually all urban centres in Thailand, is a two or three-storey 'row-house' built of unpainted wood or of brick and concrete. Each house is but one compartment or vertical section of a long building which may extend the entire length of the street. Built directly on the ground, each house abuts immediately on the sidewalk, a feature which facilitates its use for business. In Chinese neighbourhoods one solid row of shops and stores line the street on both sides from one intersection to the other, a sight which must constantly and graphically drive home to the average Thai how thoroughly the Chinese dominate Thailand's trade and commerce. One finds almost no parks or playground or open spaces of any kind in Chinese areas. Crowding is intense. A fire in Bangkok in 1952 in a typical Chinese neighbourhood burned out an area about one-half mile square which had contained about 2,000 individual dwellings and almost 20,000 persons.

Interiors of these Chinese houses vary, depending on the social and economic situation of the family, but in general conform to the accompanying sketch. The family shop or business occupies the front part of the ground floor. Behind this one finds an open area for cooking, and the storerooms and toilet. Bedrooms are located on the second and third floors. By Western standards furnishings are sparse: a few tables, wooden chairs or stools, and beds. Floors are of dull red tile or rough concrete, plaster walls are frequently unpainted, and cobwebs may festoon the ceiling and light fixtures. The construction of these houses provides windows only at the front and back, consequently interior rooms are dark, damp, and airless.

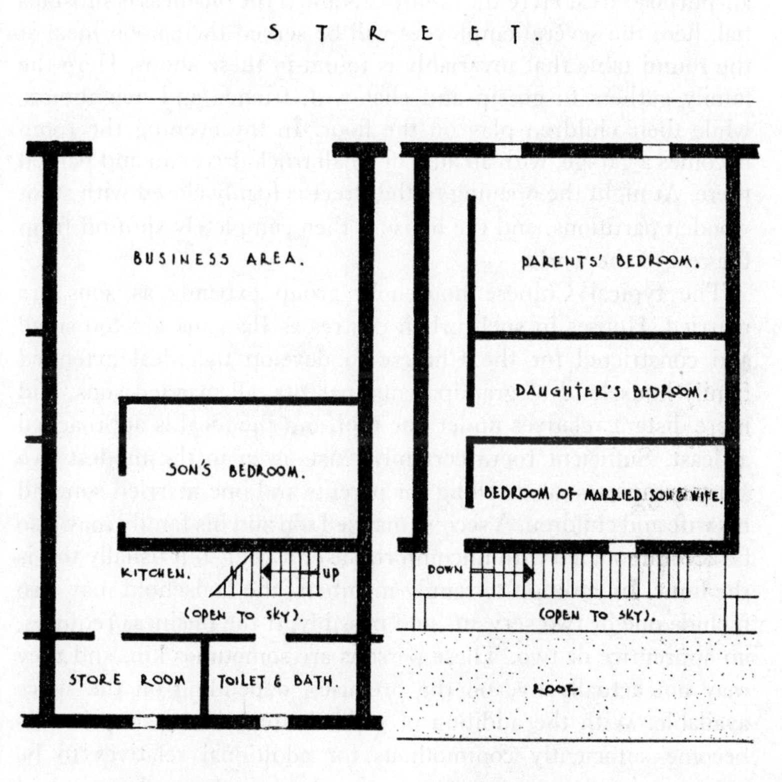


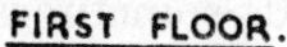

*Floor Plan of Typical Chinese House in Bangkok*

Neighbouring houses to the right and left adjoin this house, with no passage way between houses. Adjoining houses have similar floor plans.

During the day the shop area is the lightest and airiest part of the house because the partitioned wall facing the street is removed entirely, providing a 'door' as wide as the house itself. Few shops have plate-glass windows; only a counter or a low step stands between the shop proper and the sidewalk. The front room is an all-purpose area. Here the family eats and if the business is substantial, here the several employees will be served their noon meal at the round table that invariably is found in these shops. Here the family gathers to gossip and chat with friends and neighbours, while their children play on the floor. In the evening the room becomes a garage, with an auto or small truck driven in and parked there. At night the opening to the street is firmly closed with stout wooden partitions, and the house is then completely shut off from the rest of the world.

The typical Chinese household group expands as sons are married. Houses in such urban centres as Bangkok are too small and constricted for the Chinese to develop the ideal extended family household of grandparents, parents, all married sons, and more distant relatives under one roof, but the ideal is approached at least. Sufficient room certainly exists even in the modest two story compartment dwelling for parents and one married son and his wife and children. A second married son and his family may also be accommodated with uncomfortable crowding, but usually this is the limit. In addition to family members, the household may also include one or two servants and possibly, if the business requires, an apprentice or two. These persons are sometimes kin, and they may not actually live on the premises, depending on the space available. With the addition of a third storey these shop-houses become sufficiently commodious for additional relatives to be accommodated; sometimes an entire apartment may be reserved for a second wife, but this apparently is not common.

Whether the house is large or small, the impression created is of a compact, co-operative, harmonious group, living in a private world of its own which custom and tradition shield from the outside world. The shop inevitably becomes a part of the colourful, noisy street which lies just beyond the threshold, but here the alien world is halted. The family rooms behind are by custom open to kin and close family friends only. All this helps to explain, as we shall see, why the overseas home has been far more successful than other institutions in preserving traditional ways of Chinese life, enabling the Chinese for generation after generation to keep intact the basic values of their culture.

Yet it would not be accurate to describe this minority, even the immigrant generation, as unchanged from their fellows in China. Farmers mainly in the homeland, they become peddlers, artisans and shopkeepers in Thailand. For success in these new economic roles other changes are required. New languages must be learned, principally those two, Thai and Teochiu, most useful in business pursuits. The traditional Chinese style jacket and trousers worn by South China villagers quickly gives way to the Western suit, or, more commonly, a white shirt and khaki trousers. Names may also be changed. Many Chinese business men adopt Thai personal and family names, particularly when dealings with the government are anticipated—an application for an export permit, say, signed with a Chinese name may be rejected out of hand, or inordinately delayed, while the same application with a Thai name will receive better treatment. The new surnames adopted ordinarily incorporate the Chinese family name, thus 'Chang' becomes 'Changtrakul', and 'Hoon' becomes 'Hoonthrarasmi', but this fact is no handicap to their use for all official purposes.

Other changes distinguish the overseas minority from Mainland Chinese. The very tempo of work is altered in response to the new environment. Traditional Chinese festivals are sometimes ignored if they interfere markedly with the conduct of business. Even funeral and memorial services for deceased parents are planned so that business can go on as usual. Chinese schools and business houses readily close for any Thai holiday they consider politic to observe, and on such occasions there are more Thai flags in the Chinese districts of Bangkok than in Thai neighbourhoods. On the other hand a more subtle change also occurs in their attitude toward work. After some years in Thailand immigrants seem to lose part of their earlier drive and industry—'White Chinese' business men from Shanghai (refugees who left China after the Communist victory) complain that the local Chinese are too slow and easy going, precisely the same criticism that the local Chinese make of the Thai. Second-generation youths grumble about working the year round, as many of their fathers do, without frequent holidays. Work for them, as for the Thai, has become simply a means for increased leisure, not an end in itself. All these changes are intimately related to business, with earning a living, or generally to the economic aspect of overseas Chinese life. It is in this sphere they have least in common with those remaining in the rural centres of China.

By contrast with business, however, home and family life among the overseas Chinese has changed but little. Whatever the languages learned and used for business, only the dialect of the parents is spoken in the home, presumably out of deference to the latter, and custom requires that servants, secondary wives and daughters-in-law brought into the family group must learn this dialect. Western clothes may be readily adopted by men for business purposes as the mark of material success and progress, but for family living the traditional Chinese cotton trousers and jacket, unironed and informal, are worn by both men and women. The making of these so-called 'common clothes' continues to be one of the principal tasks of Chinese wives. The changes cited above that occur in names seldom reach as far as the home. Thai personal and family names by which individuals may be officially known are not used within the family group or even among close Chinese friends. Indeed close friends and relatives often know each other only by their Chinese names.

Within the home the traditional relationships are maintained. Filial piety and respect for one's elders are prized virtues still, taught to all children, and expected of all in the community as a matter of course. Children thus submit to their parents' wishes in matters of their education, vocation, courtship and marriage. Within the home the status of women has changed but little. While in the family-run shop the wife will frequently take charge of day-to-day business affairs—many small shopkeepers spend the greater part of their day with friends in coffee-shops and restaurants—yet in the home the woman's position has undergone no such elevation. Here, few opportunities exist for any modifications of her inferior status or of her traditional and accepted duties as housewife and mother.

This contrast between accepted patterns in business and in the homes was well illustrated by a marriage which occurred between a Chinese merchant and a Sino-Thai woman. The merchant in question, proprietor of a small jewelry and gold shop, 'married' a Sino-Thai woman as secondary wife because of her usefulness as a business partner—like many such women she spoke Thai with fluency, had had experience in running a small shop herself, and, of greater weight, had capital to finance an expansion of the company. As a full-fledged business partner, with actually more acumen than her husband, she quickly assumed virtually full control and the shop prospered. Her dominant role in business raised no eyebrows in the community. Her subsequent behaviour in the home did, however. Tradition demands that secondary wives assume an inferior place in the family, subject to the authority of the principal wife. This Sino-Thai wife's efforts to supercede her husband's first wife, an overseas Chinese woman, within the home and in matters affecting the children caused a turmoil among relatives. No one approved such rearrangement of the traditional order, and public opinion was solidly behind the principal wife who opposed the secondary wife's ambitions.

As we have noted above, a newly-wed couple normally takes up residence with the husband's family, the bride thus entering a family group unfamiliar to her and not immediately friendly. As a daughter-in-law she typically assumes menial household chores, much as she would in China, and without protest comes under the domination of an often unsympathetic mother-in-law. She is somewhat isolated within the home—custom frowns on too frequent appearances in public—and is not shown much consideration as a person in this new family until her first child is born; at no time before or after this important event is she accorded the freedom to come and go that the Thai wife is given. Women are so sheltered from change that second-generation girls are said to equal girls from China in the traditional virtues of industry and obedience. The same cannot always be said of young men. There are so many high-living and extravagant sons of wealthy Chinese merchants in Bangkok that a special Teochiu word, *A-sia*, is used to refer to them. No comparable term exists for girls; only rarely do the latter break away from traditional standards set by their parents.

A woman's principal object in life is marriage and the raising of a family, to the exclusion of other interests, and her place is in the home. No woman has ever risen to a position of leadership in the Chinese community. Few Chinese women work outside the home or take part in community organizations. Women are not confined to the home—they do the marketing daily, go to temples and make excursions to Buddhist shrines near Bangkok, they may freely attend movies, festivals and fairs when time permits and they take part in family celebrations outside the home, such as weddings and birthday parties (which are held for persons of advanced age only). But the traditional tasks of cooking, sewing, laundering normally fill the Chinese wife's day. Children become her prime responsibility, from the time they are born through the arrangement of marriage when they come of age. As we shall see in a subsequent chapter, the Chinese home is still the centre for religious activities and women take an important interest in such matters. Most women find their main diversion in simply talking—gossiping—with other women. No woman, who values her reputation and that of her family, will make herself conspicuous in activities or interests outside the home, save perhaps by participating in purely religious associations composed exclusively of women.

Women show the results of their social isolation. Few learn to speak Thai with any fluency, beyond what may be needed for the daily marketing. Normally, they learn no new Chinese dialects. They retain their traditional dress of white shirt-waists and black trousers long after their husbands have begun to wear Western-style clothes. Few immigrant women cut their hair in any modern style and still fewer wave their hair—the only 'pigtails' one sees in Bangkok are worn by Chinese immigrant women. In general, women seem to be a full generation behind their husbands so far as changes in their behaviour and attitudes are concerned, which, considering their close and continuous influence over children, has reduced the rate of change in the home and throughout the Chinese community.

## MARRIAGE AND INTERMARRIAGE

The arrangement of marriage by parents is generally accepted without question among the Chinese minority in Thailand. A young man may indicate his preference for a certain girl, but parents rather than the individuals concerned are ordinarily expected not only to find suitable partners for their children when they reach marriageable age but also to make the initial overtures and the final arrangements. As in China, go-betweens are used for the negotiations—usually older women in the community—and as an initial step the horoscopes of the young people are compared. If for any reason the match cannot be made, disparities in these horoscopes provide a convenient and acceptable excuse. The group from which a spouse is selected includes theoretically the entire Chinese minority in Thailand, excluding those with the same surname, and on occasion marriages are arranged with Chinese from neighbouring countries of Southeast Asia. Infrequently today a bride is brought from China. An attempt is made to arrange the marriage within a person's dialect group, although cross-dialectual marriages are not uncommon and are not strongly disapproved. However, marriages are expected whenever possible to benefit the families concerned. Thus a wealthy family will seek a spouse from a family in a similar social and economic position, preferably situated in complementary business activities, while families occupying lower places in society will try through marriages with families better situated to improve their own life chances.

Marriage with non-Chinese, and this usually means with Thai persons, is openly discouraged. In the past, however, there is reason to believe that intermarriage was fairly common, and many public figures, including every Thai monarch since the middle of the 19th century, were partly Chinese. King Mongkut's maternal grandfather was a Chinese merchant, possibly an immigrant. Queen Saowapa, wife of King Chulalongkorn and mother of King Vajiravudh and King Prajadhipok, was part Chinese on her mother's side. On one occasion King Vajiravudh found on investigation that 90 per cent of his courtiers had 'Chinese blood in their veins' (Landon 1939: 19). The most prominent leader of postwar Thailand, Phibun Songgram—noted incidentally for his anti-Chinese policies—is said to be partly Chinese. The family tree of his arch political opponent, Pridi Phanomyong, also contains a fairly recent Chinese ancestor. The 1932 Revolution is attributed largely to Sino-Thai officials and military men, and many of the members of the first National Assembly set up after the Revolution are said to have been Sino-Thai. Today with the Chinese minority in public disfavour, officials quietly ignore these Chinese connections, but in years past, persons in high positions would boast of them—King Prajadhipok, for example, visiting Chinese schools in 1928 took pains to call attention to his Chinese forbears.[1]

All this indicates that in the recent past intermarriage between Chinese and Thai was not uncommon, and perhaps in the more remote rural areas it may still occur with some frequency. But in urban centres like Bangkok, where the Chinese are concentrated, research by the author shows that intermarriage is a phenomenon of the past. Among a random sample of 145 marriages by offspring of Chinese immigrants, who represented a full range of social and economic levels, the author found no instance in which a Chinese girl had married a non-Chinese, and only two men who had married Thai. One of these was a Chinese youth known to have tuberculosis; he had married a Thai girl only because no Chinese family would have him.

What are the factors which have in recent decades caused a decrease in intermarriage? The answer to this question may also furnish clues as to the probable course of assimilation of the Chinese in the years to come. First, the trend toward a numerical equality between the sexes in the Chinese community helps to explain the decrease in intermarriage. Forty years ago a Chinese woman in Thailand was considered a curiosity both to the Chinese as well as to the Thai—many of the men had not seen such women since their youth in China. Thus, the immigrant had but two choices: to return to China for a bride, or to marry a local Thai woman. The convenience of arranging local marriages, as compared with the expense and difficulty of securing a wife from China, encouraged intermarriage with the Thai. Many immigrants, with wives in China whom they were unable or unwilling to bring to Thailand, readily intermarried with the Thai, setting up as it were two branches of the family, one in China and the other in Thailand. Many prominent Thai leaders today trace their origins to such Sino-Thai unions.

After 1920 Chinese women began to arrive in numbers. The 1919 census reported some 55,000 Chinese alien women in Thailand, while the census of 1937 counted some 188,500 Chinese women—an increase of over 300 per cent in 18 years. Yet numerical equality of the sexes was lacking even in the latter 1930's—Landon (1939: 55) reports for this period that 'most immigrants . . . must marry Thai or Sino-Thai women both because of the shortage of Chinese girls and because of the lesser expense involved'. The 1947 census shows that the sex ratio of the *immigrant generation* at least, is still far from balanced—in that year there were more than two men for every woman in the population (319,196 males to 157,386 females).

Today the situation is vastly different from what these statistics would lead one to expect. There are so many women of marriageable age that spinsters are becoming an accepted feature of the Chinese community. A number of such girls, all daughters of wealthy Chinese merchants living in the oldest Chinese market section of Bangkok, are popularly referred to as the 'Sampang Old Maids'. Nor are they particularly unusual among the Chinese. A girl unmarried by the age of 25 is considered hardly worth making a first wife and can be thought lucky if she is chosen as a concubine. It is not immigrant women but girls born in Thailand of Chinese immigrant parents who have shifted the sex ratio into balance in the Chinese community during the course of the last two decades. These local girls, strictly raised according to traditional standards, are regarded by all as equal to girls born in China, and few parents take the trouble any longer to send their sons to China to be betrothed. All this has not only served to weaken ties with the homeland, but also to make of the Chinese minority a more self-contained and exclusive group.

The census statistics for persons of Chinese 'race' in Thailand give some measure of the change that has taken place with regard to the sex ratio. Presumably second-generation persons as well as immigrants are included in this category—the census provides no explanation, however. As the following tabulation shows, there has been a steady trend toward an equalization of the sex ratio, in addition to a growth in size of this group:

5. PERSONS OF CHINESE RACE BY SEX

| *Year* | *Total* | *Male* | *Female* | *Ratio of Male to Female* |
|---|---|---|---|---|
| 1937 | 618,787 | 409,652 | 209,135 | 1·9 |
| 1947 | 835,931 | 495,188 | 340,743 | 1·4 |

These statistics show that, during this recent ten-year period, almost one and one-half times as many females were added to the Chinese 'racial' population as males (131,608 females to 85,536 males).

Besides the equalization of the sex ratio in the second generation, there are cultural reasons for the high degree of ethnic endogamy. The former intermarriage pattern of 30 and more years ago occurred in the absence of an older Chinese generation, which is present now in Thailand. The situation may be described in this way: those who emigrated from China 30 years ago were separated from their older relatives. Parents remained in China. Thus a Thai woman who married a Chinese immigrant in those times entered a home in which she was the only woman. In short, she was not faced with the problem of adjusting to her mother-in-law or of assuming the traditionally inferior position of a daughter-in-law in the Chinese home. In fact, as Landon (1939: 54) indicates in the following quotation, when these marriages occurred, it was the Chinese husband who made the major adjustment:

> Chinese husbands of non-Chinese wives have home situations which bring them into contact with a different point of view from anything to which they have been accustomed. While their wives may adopt many Chinese ways, the men in these mixed homes are at least aware in an intimate way of other modes of cooking, dressing, speaking, of other ideas of health, education, and religion, and even nationalism, than those to which they themselves have been attached.

But within the last generation a fundamental change has taken place. The young Chinese wife of 20 years ago is now an actual or potential mother-in-law. A girl entering the Chinese home now comes not only as a wife but as a daughter-in-law as well, and she must accept the inferior status and menial role of the daughter-in-law in a Chinese home. This is a position which a Thai woman would be reluctant to accept; reasons will become apparent if the two groups are but briefly compared.

There are some obvious cultural differences between the two ethnic groups—language, food preferences and eating habits, dress, religion, to mention but a few which make it undesirable from the Chinese point of view to bring an alien wife into the home. A generation or so ago, the Chinese husband and his Thai wife living by themselves might well have come to some mutual understanding that would surmount these difficulties. But today the young second-generation youth on being married must live with his parents, and this domestic situation has tipped the scales against any Thai wife. It is noteworthy that in almost every case of intermarriage one hears about now, the couple lives apart from the husband's parents and family.

In addition to the gross cultural differences, Chinese values with regard to the family itself are in many respects strikingly different from those held by the Thai, whether rural or urban, and these more subtle differences contribute to the continued social separation of the two peoples. While the Chinese regard the family as the very keystone of society, and see it as extending back into time for innumerable generations, the Thai have little sense of lineage, no feeling for ancestry, and little interest in or knowledge of kin beyond immediate living relatives. The use of family names provide an illustration of this disinterest: family names were introduced into Thailand only some fifty years ago, and then by government decree, not in response to any felt need on the part of the people. While formally accepted, they are used very little today either socially or personally—indeed children may be quite unaware of their family name, a condition almost incomprehensible to the Chinese. While the Chinese follow whenever possible a patrilocal residence pattern, the Thai have a strong preference for matrilocal residence after marriage, and to the Thai way of thinking it is the husband, not the wife, who should make the adjustment to a strange family. In contrast to the Chinese family's tight organization with definite status for each person and clear-cut rules and obligations governing relationships between family members, the Thai family is a loosely structured organization with considerable permissiveness toward variations in individual behaviour and deviations from the accepted rules (Embrée 1950). Thus elopements, which circumvent family arrangement of marriage, are an accepted and fairly common feature of Thai society. The Thai, like the Chinese, recognize the pre-eminence of men in the family and in society, but Thai women are given considerable authority, albeit informally, in the family, and far more freedom in society than are Chinese women—many Thai women run small businesses outside the home, they may own property in their own right, they enter the universities in large numbers, and some women have risen to high places in business and government. Finally, while the Chinese strongly oppose any dissolution of the family, divorce and separation among rural Thai and the lower classes in the cities is of common occurrence and excites no social disapproval (HRAF 1956: 196, 207).

The control which Chinese parents exercise over the marriage of their children must also be regarded as a factor hindering intermarriage with the Thai. Young persons are almost entirely dependent upon their parents for the arrangement of their marriages—while youths and girls have not infrequent opportunities to meet, dating and courtship practices prevalent in the West are simply not tolerated in Thailand. Chinese attitudes in these matters are not challenged, as they would be in the United States, for example, by the existence in the indigenous culture of contrary values and practices. Rather, among the Thai as among the Chinese, custom dictates that the sexes be separated before marriage and that marriage be planned by parents acting in what they regard as the best interests of their children. Very little room normally exists for the development of romantic love, as it is known in the West, which might help in the amalgamation of the two groups.

The fact that invariably young men and women wait patiently for their parents to find spouses for them, rarely question their authority, and almost never elope (as a Thai couple might) indicates the vitality of family control in this matter. Moreover, the tradition that the eldest son be married first, before any of his brothers, is so strictly followed among the Chinese in Thailand that it might as well be a law. Even when it imposes a hardship on other sons, they wait until their brothers are married before they themselves consider marriage.

Economic factors also act as barriers to intermarriage by forcing young men to remain dependent upon their parents and to respect their parents' wishes in matters of marriage. Marriage requires a considerable expenditure, for the numerous gifts, the dowry, and the entertainment custom demands. It is not unusual for the bridegeroom's family, which pays most of the bills, to spend from 15,000 to 20,000 baht (US$700 to $1,000), although of course the sum varies with the economic circumstances of the families concerned. These expenses are far beyond the ability of a young man just getting established in a career. Yet they are necessary expenses for the Chinese—weddings constitute a major event in the life of any Chinese family, and to trim down the display, or to eliminate it entirely by holding only a simple ceremony, would reflect unmercifully on the individuals concerned and their families. After marriage a young man is still dependent for years on his parents' help. To rent a dwelling of even the poorest sort in Bangkok calls for the payment by the prospective tenant of a large sum as 'tea money' (sometimes called 'key money', i.e. the sum given the owner as a bonus or gift for the privilege of renting a house or apartment). This sum may range from 3,000 to 10,000 baht. Additional expenses must be met—for furnishings, food, fuel, etc.—which would require a monthly income of at least 1,000 baht. Few young men starting out in business or the government expect to earn more than 600 baht per month. Thus, whatever the individual's desires, it is economically mandatory for the newly married couple to depend upon the bridegroom's parents for housing and other necessities. In view of this, the parents' consent to any marriage is a prerequisite which no one can easily disregard.

### ETHNIC PREJUDICE

Finally, ethnic stereotypes and prejudices must be regarded as a barrier to the amalgamation of the two groups. Neither the Chinese nor the Thai have any racial prejudice toward the other group which might hinder intermarriage. Both are Asians and both admire certain physical qualities of the other. Chinese readily admit the beauty of Thai girls—snapshots of Miss Thailand, the girl selected each year as the most beautiful girl in the Kingdom (comparable to the Miss America contest), are quickly bought by admiring Chinese. The Thai, for their part, regard a light skin colour as very desirable, and they have no hesitancy in saying that Chinese girls—who are usually somewhat lighter than Thai girls—have the decided edge in beauty.

The prejudices that exist are social and cultural, and of these there is no lack in either group. The Thai consider the Chinese uncouth because they are often loud and raucous in public, because they are noisy eaters, and have other food habits which the Thai deem very undesirable. They regard the Chinese as a dirty people who don't bathe often, who neglect their personal appearance and befoul the areas in which they reside. To them, the Chinese are grasping, excessively materialistic, interested only in making money. Undoubtedly these prejudices, minor as they might ordinarily be, have been fanned into larger issues by the frankly anti-Chinese utterances of Thai leaders and the running fire of unfavourable publicity given the Chinese by all newspapers.

Since the end of World War II, the amount and temper of this semi-official hostility toward the Chinese aliens in the Kingdom has been on the increase. At times it has taken spectacular turns. In November 1947, immediately following a *coup d'état*, in which the Phibun Songgram government regained power from the followers of Pridi Phanomyong, the Phibun group published a 'White Paper' which disclosed a Chinese plot to incorporate Thailand in a 'South China Republic'. The White Paper charged that 'two Chinese, born in Siam in the town of Ayuthia, are leading a large-scale Chinese invasion of Siam', and it went on to attribute the killing of the former King, the signing of a treaty with China, and a plot to overcome the army as part of this Chinese-directed scheme. Alexander MacDonald, American editor of the *Bangkok Post* at the time and a close friend of Pridi, declares there was no truth in any of these charges (MacDonald 1949: 178), but that did not impede circulation of the story.

An incident such as this is not unusual, for in the postwar years a host of derogatory statements have come from high government officials. Only a few can be cited here. A police official publicly attributed to the Chinese the dirt and uncleanliness of the Thai capital. Premier Phibun Songgram lost few opportunities to charge the Chinese with driving the Thai out of trades and crafts which were once exclusively Thai. The wealth of the Chinese (always a sore spot in Sino-Thai relations) he compared with the dire poverty of the Thai people—in an address to the Thai Labour Union in 1951 the Premier declared that one always found aliens, i.e. Chinese, enjoying the benefits of electric lights and a good water supply, while the Thai people have to be content with primitive living conditions. All these statements were reported in Thailand's newspapers along with other unfriendly comments and stories. The Chinese are charged with corrupting government officials. The rising cost of living is blamed on Chinese merchants, and Chinese trade guilds were described by one Thai newspaper as giving 'opportunity to aliens to suck out Thai blood'.

No Thai newspaper can be characterized as being pro-Chinese in any sense; at times many appear to be almost irresponsibly anti-Chinese. The editor of one Thai-language daily declared his attitude in the following terms:

> This newspaper has the objective of promoting the good living conditions of the Thai people. It has the duty to relieve the Thai people from the economic yoke caused by foreigners. This newspaper considers the interests and safety of the Thai people and Thai nation above other things. My new staff and I from now on are ready to sacrifice ourselves for the above aim
> (*Siam Mai*, November 16, 1951)

Such chauvinistic utterances when coupled with the equally nationalistic pronouncements of high officials serve only to exacerbate differences between the Chinese and the Thai people. We can note in passing that the Chinese as such are seldom mentioned in Thai newspapers. Reference is always made to 'aliens' or 'foreigners'—just why this caution is taken is not clear—but from the context of the term it is clear that the reference is to the Chinese. Even English language newspapers published in Thailand, which usually maintain a high journalistic standard, contribute their bit to this unfavourable picture. The majority of news items about the Chinese minority are concerned with crime, disputes, and Communist activities; and from reading these papers alone one could easily get the impression that the Chinese are an unstable part of the population. Actually just the reverse is true. Police officials report that crimes of violence—murder, robberies, assaults and the like—are infrequent among the Chinese immigrant group, and far more likely, in fact, to occur among the Thai.

The Chinese hold equally strong prejudices about the Thai. With them, however, derogatory opinions are rarely expressed publicly, either in newspapers or by Chinese leaders. The typical Chinese meets any unpleasantness with a smile or a resigned shrug. Yet by associating with the Chinese one soon realizes the depth of their contempt and bitterness. The Thai are characterized as indolent if not outright lazy, untrustworthy, and slippery in business dealings. A Chinese merchant will rather employ an Indian as a watchman or chauffeur than hire a Thai. Almost universal is the belief among the Chinese immigrant group that Thai women are morally loose and therefore undesirable as wives. This is certainly an instance of a double standard for the signs of blatant promiscuity on the part of Chinese males are everywhere apparent. Scores of houses of prostitution are located in the Chinese districts of Bangkok, and virtually every Chinese hotel in the country doubles as a call house.

Whereas the Thai feel exploited by Chinese shopkeepers, the same shopkeepers claim that Thai landlords, corrupt officials, and even the local police are constantly exploiting them. The Thai, say the Chinese, are not ambitious enough for business, thus they enter the bureaucracy or the police and squeeze hardworking Chinese merchants. The Thai blame the Chinese for the high cost of living, while the Chinese declare that Thai landlords demand 'tea money' and raise rents of Chinese tenants, thus driving up their living costs.

Rightly or wrongly, the Chinese have a strong sense of injustice done them and regard the Thai government as deliberately hostile. Restrictions on economic activities and the reservation of occupations to Thai nationals, while they may not yet have affected their economic position, are recognized as potentially serious threats to Chinese security. Efforts to limit the teaching of Chinese in schools is bitterly resented as a deliberate effort to destroy the unique cultural heritage of the Chinese. They resent the arbitrary and uncompromising way restrictions are announced and enforced, with the Chinese affected given little chance to make plans for the future. The arrest and deportation of Chinese particularly enrages the Chinese community, mainly because the public believes that those arrested were innocent of any wrong, or if guilty, that their offences were so trivial—selling eggs for a few cents above the fixed official price—as not to warrant the harsh sentence of deportation.

Chinese newspapers must be careful about criticizing the government if they wish to avoid suspension or suppression. Thus the Chinese press is ordinarily not jingoistic or openly provocative. However, Chinese dailies help to keep viable whatever resentments are present by faithfully reporting the effects of restrictions and controls. Usually the most pitiful—and atypical—case is described in merciless detail: for example, the indigent Chinese who committed suicide, leaving behind a wife and five little children, because he could not pay his alien registration fee.

A kind of ethnic stereotype based on informal religious practices serves also to separate the two peoples. Religious differences—as we shall see—stemming from Buddhism do not hinder amalgamation. The Chinese and Thai regard themselves as religiously akin, although differing in practices. The greatest tolerance is shown by the Chinese toward other religions and very much the same can be said of the Thai. Of all the reasons given for unwillingness to sanction intermarriage, differences in religion are never mentioned. But one must go beyond this. The religion of the Thai is compounded of three elements: Buddhism, Brahmanism and animism. The latter, spirit worship or animism, is an exceedingly powerful influence in the life of Thai on all levels of society, and in many ways animism has become so intertwined with Buddhism that no distinction is made in the popular mind between the two. One aspect of Thai animism is the belief in charms, among them the use of love philters. Love charms have an aura of black magic about them, and consequently are not openly discussed. Many stories are current about their use and effects, however, and from these the following information has been obtained.

In general love charms are thought to be useful not only in causing a person to become infatuated but in achieving an even more bizarre result. There are substances, it is said, which when given to a person over a period of time so accustom his body to the drugs or poisons they contain that if these are no longer given, the person will decline in health and finally die. Or in another version, two substances are given, one a poison and the other its antidote. So long as both are taken, all is well, but if only the poison is taken, the person will die very shortly. Thai women are supposed to be skilled in the use of such love charms. They were developed, it is said, in the old days when a woman married to an alien—Chinese or European—ran the risk of being abandoned when her husband returned to his homeland. To prevent this, she secretly put a philter in his food, then warned him that if he left her, he would sicken and die. If the man scorned the warning and left his wife, he was unable to get the necessary antidote and, as the wife predicted, became sick. Unless he returned to her, he soon died. Such devices, the Chinese say, are still used today by many Thai women. Thus, a man can never give up his Thai wife or mistress, or even oppose her in any way, under penalty of death. The moral is clear: keep away from Thai women. They are dangerous and deceitful, possessed of almost supernatural powers over their husbands.

How much of this folk belief is fact, how much fiction cannot be ascertained. Stories about the use of love charms appear in several books Westerners have written about Thailand, and in at least one of these written by a medical doctor the efficacy of these love philters on Europeans is accepted as a fact. The Chinese tell similar stories about the dire consequences which followed when Chinese married Thai women, and they seem to regard the possible use of charms as further instance of the hazards met when a Chinese marries outside his own ethnic group.

Finally, another factor must be considered in the separation of the two peoples. The Chinese, who value highly a stable, well-ordered society, are continually repelled by what they regard as the extreme instability and even lawless character of the Thai people. This is in many ways an erroneous evaluation, but it can be traced in part to the nature of the Chinese and Thai presses, and the world view each contains. Thai dailies fill their pages with sensational news and pictures—murders, suicides, divorces, stories of marital unfaithfulness, quarrels, etc. While such yellow journalism does sell papers, the cumulative picture of Thai society gained by an outsider is hardly attractive. Chinese newspapers, on the other hand, usually avoid sensationalism and concentrate attention on foreign news and business information. Thus they give an impression of a stable, diligent society, free from the disruptive criminal and delinquent tendencies current among the Thai. The contrast is striking and undoubtedly contributes to the maintenance of ethnic stereotypes.

Despite these prejudices and latent discontents, face-to-face relationships between the Thai and the Chinese are outwardly good. The two people mingle easily and freely in all public aspects of life. On a more individual level relationships are often unusually good. The majority of Chinese shopkeepers are genuinely liked by their Thai neighbours. Occasionally, however, violence flares up—a fight may break out between Chinese youths and *samlor* (pedicab) men, or a group of Chinese will attack an impertinent Thai bus driver—and these incidents give warning of the potentially serious cleavage between the two groups. The worst incident of this kind, and admittedly a special case, occurred in Bangkok immediately following the end of World War II. Thailand, officially leagued with Japan, was a defeated nation. China was one of the victorious allies. The Chinese in Bangkok staged a jubilant demonstration, raised Chinese flags, and sang nationalist songs. The demonstration touched off riots and street fighting between the Chinese and the Thai. Both groups armed themselves and the principal Chinese section of the capital became a small battlefield before the situation was brought under control. Incidents such as this are remembered, and those memories serve to re-enforce views already held: that mutual trust is impossible and close and intimate contacts undesirable.

### SOURCE OF CHANGES

In the continuing adjustment of the Chinese to life in Thailand, several categories of persons stand out as moving away most rapidly from traditional Chinese patterns. These persons may be the pace-setters for a new social orientation which by being less distinctively Chinese may be more in harmony with the future structure of Thai society.

Among the immigrant generation, men are far more susceptible and more receptive to change than are women. Men are given by custom greater freedom of movement and expression than women, and the demands of trade and commerce stimulate a still wider range of experiences. Chinese business men travel throughout Thailand, and many take periodic trips to the cosmopolitan centres of Hong Kong and Singapore. They show the effects of these contacts. Invariably men speak Thai more fluently than women, they learn new Chinese dialects, some even speak English —practically unheard of among immigrant women. All but the most old-fashioned and isolated have long since adopted Western-style clothing as standard for business wear. Many are as much at ease with a knife and fork as with chopsticks, and equally sophisticated about the intricacies of international trade and finance.

Through the agency of such men, changes are introduced into all institutions of the Chinese community, from the family on up, a process facilitated by the fact that men hold controlling economic and social positions in the family and the community. It seems inevitable that through the intermediary of husbands, fathers, and sons, the life of the Chinese woman will be gradually broadened to include experiences and contacts which tradition now denies her; and she will herself eventually become a more active agent of change than she has thus far been.

The second category of persons deeply influenced by alien cultural contacts is represented by second-generation Chinese, the sons and daughters of immigrants. Because of having been brought up in Thailand, they are, as one would expect, much more acculturated than their parents, in fact to such an extent that many have no trouble at all in passing for Thai nationals whenever they wish. These persons have many more opportunities than the immigrant generation for intimate associations with Thai—at missionary schools, for example, their companions are often Thai, and later as clerks in Western firms many work side by side with Thai. Through participation in Western institutions such as these they acquire a more fundamental understanding of Western thought and behaviour. Many speak English, and all seem eager to learn more about the West. In general males are more acculturated than females, but even among girls we find changes occurring—hair is cut and waved in the latest mode, Western-style dresses and skirts have become common, fewer second-generation married women carry on remunerative work at home, as many immigrant women do, and although the percentage is still small, more work outside the home than among the immigrant generation.

The younger generation in the Chinese community has few extreme types. Attention has already been called to the *A-sia*, a Teochiu term given to the playboy sons of wealthy Chinese. The A-sia does little or no work but spends his time in the pursuit of pleasure, gambling, drinking, and driving fast cars. Whether the A-sia represents marginal behaviour only, and not a model for others, is not clear. In general, his loose life is not at all characteristic of the typical second-generation Chinese male who is serious, hard working, and ambitious to succeed in business.

The second generation has already begun to asume positions of leadership in the community, and, through the families they have established, to mould the values and attitudes of the following generation. The second generation is even now too modern and westernized to be at ease in the traditional cultural atmosphere of the villages from whence their parents came, and the third generation will find an even deeper and broader hiatus between themselves and the traditional Chinese way of life.

The wealthy Chinese merchant, and those aspiring to that status, constitute another category of persons moving away from traditional standards and closer to Thai society and to the Western world. Under the absolute monarchy it was customary for the King to confer titles of nobility on some influential Chinese merchants titles comparable to those bestowed on high officials. Such men tended to identify their interests with those of the government and to draw closer to Thai society, assuming Thai names, dress, often wives, and moving in the company of officials. Yet they maintained their standing in the Chinese community, and in fact seem to have been useful intermediaries between that community and the Thai government. Titles are no longer conferred on either Chinese or Thai, but one finds a continuing need for persons to assume positions as go-betweens. Today this task falls to wealthy and influential business men who are chosen to positions of leadership in various Chinese associations where they can best serve the interests of the community. When necessary they intercede directly with officials —many are or become personal friends of the highest government figures—or on occasion act as agents of government policies, interpreting these to the Chinese. Understandably only the acculturated Chinese can fill such positions; few in the immigrant generation rise to such heights. But the smallest shopkeeper is convinced of the need to cultivate friendly relationships with local officials and the police, to assure their co-operation in times of trouble, and one finds even the neighbourhood policeman invited to Chinese wedding parties and similar festivities. On higher levels of commerce, many Chinese have found Thai officials likewise indispensable for continuing success in business, and consequently leading officials have been made nominal directors of Chinese companies. Opportunistic and shallow as these relationships may be, they should not be underestimated in view of the high economic and social position held by wealthy business men in the Chinese community and the influence they exert on the community's standards.

Equally important is the fact that any Chinese in the process of acquiring wealth also acquires an admiration for Western culture.

Western clothes, plastic belts, Parker fountain pens, wrist watches, radios, television sets, refrigerators, automobiles—the possession of these articles spells out a man's achievements so that all may see. But the West has made even deeper inroads. Western business methods are studied and copied, sons sent to Western missionary schools in Bangkok where they learn English and useful commercial skills, and some few merchants are boldly reaching out for direct trade connections with Europe and the United States. In Bangkok, a number of wealthy Chinese business men have moved out of the congested Chinese districts to large, modern houses in the new suburbs where the majority of the Europeans and Americans live. Some business men, as yet a small number, have become member of the capital's exclusive Western clubs.

In contrast to the wealthy business man, the Chinese intellectual and professional man is not an important figure in the changing social situation. There are few intellectuals in the Chinese community, if we define that term arbitrarily as a college graduate. Almost no immigrant might be classed as such, and ordinarily second-generation Chinese get no more than a secondary school education before being rushed into a business career. Some Chinese youth in this latter group—still a small minority, however—are sent to local universities and to institutions in Australia, England, and the United States for college training; however, the Chinese community has as yet little need for such specialists, consequently on their return to Thailand they find positions with semi-official organizations or Western business groups where their technical abilities can be used; a mechanical engineer, for example, might work with a government-run organization like the Thai Cement Company. Such men seem to identify themselves entirely with the most westernized elements of Thai society. They have no intellectual effect on the Chinese community. They do not write for the press or lecture, nor do they ordinarily become leaders of any associations. In the Chinese community, wealth rather than scholarship is the spur.

The Sino-Thai form another category of persons who may play a vital role in the breakdown of traditional standards. The offspring of Chinese-Thai unions are only slightly distinguished from the general population. The term *luk-chin* (literally, Chinese child) is applied by the Thai to such persons, but in actual usage all persons who have some Thai blood might be termed *luk-chin*. Most Sino-Thai are derived from unions of Chinese men with

Thai women—marriages between Chinese women and Thai men seldom occur. The Sino-Thai do not form a distinct, separate part of the population, as do the comparable group of *peranakan* Chinese in Indonesia, or the Anglo-Indians of India. In fact, the group is so indistinct socially that no statistics are compiled on the number of Sino-Thai. By all indications they must form a considerable part of the population, not the results of intermarriage in recent years but a generation or two ago.

The Sino-Thai is in no sense a marginal man who can find a place in neither group. On the contrary, he is accepted by both the Thai and the Chinese without prejudice. Most Sino-Thai identify themselves with either the Chinese or Thai groups; some may acquire positions in both at the same time. For example, a prominent Sino-Thai is a senator in the National Assembly (appointed to that position by the government) and at the same time is a director of the largest Chinese benevolent association in Thailand. Again, the male members of an old Sino-Thai family in Bangkok are separated into two groups: those holding leadership positions in the Chinese community, and those holding high posts in the Thai government. Both groups are on the best terms and each year hold a family reunion. A Sino-Thai may move back and forth between the Chinese and Thai groups—a Sino-Thai friend of the author who had been a police officer for more than twenty years later joined the administrative staff of a large Chinese hospital in Bangkok. Like all Sino-Thai he was fluent in a number of Chinese dialects and spoke excellent Thai as well. Following a customary practice among this group, he had two names one Thai and the other Chinese which was used among his Chinese friends.

Many Sino-Thai work for the government—possibly a good proportion of Bangkok's police officers are Sino-Thai and most amphur (district) offices have a Sino-Thai clerk or minor official whose language abilities are employed in dealings with Chinese immigrants. For the same reasons a number of Sino-Thai earn all or part of their livelihood by performing necessary jobs for Chinese immigrants who speak too little Thai to deal directly with officials—for a fee they obtain such things as gambling permits, hawking licences, or renewal of alien registration certificates. The Sino-Thai also enter business where because of their knowledge of both Thai and Chinese they can compete successfully with the immigrant Chinese. Some persons attempt to hide their Chinese ancestry, but most Sino-Thai speak of it with some pride, intimating that the addition of Chinese 'blood' added a desirable sturdiness to their characters, making them more industrious and persevering than the average Thai. Relatively little is known about the Sino-Thai group—in some respects they seem to facilitate the integration of the two ethnic groups, in other ways they take positions as intermediaries and thus keep the groups separate and distinct. Further research will be needed before their role in the assimilation of the Chinese minority can be estimated.

CHAPTER V

# TEMPLES, SPIRITS, AND FESTIVALS

ALTHOUGH the religious beliefs and practices of the Chinese differ in many respects from those of the Thai, these differences are not ordinarily a cause for antagonism or animosity. The Thai government has consistently encouraged by its own examples religious tolerance toward all groups in the Kingdom, the Chinese as well as others. Moreover, observers are impressed not so much by differences as religious similarities between the Thai and the Chinese minority. Both people are Buddhists. The Thai are followers of the Hīnayāna school of Buddhism, which emphasizes meritorious deeds by the individual rather than prayers to any deity, while the Chinese have been strongly influenced by the Mahāyāna form of Buddhism and like Chinese everywhere have freely mixed into it Taoist and Confucian elements. Many of the fundamental values of these two Buddhist sects are sufficiently alike for the Chinese and the Thai to recognize themselves as religiously akin. Both Hīnayāna and Mahāyāna Buddhism counsel tolerance toward others, an ideal which is closely adhered to by all Buddhists where religion is concerned.

The Thai and the Chinese are alike, too, in having a belief in spirits through whom the individual may gain protection in times of danger and uncertainty. Often these animistic beliefs appear to be of greater importance in the daily lives of the people than Buddhism itself. While the details of these beliefs and practices vary, both people share a common appreciation and respect for this world of the spirits, and in fact the Chinese have readily adopted certain Thai animistic practices.

The very fact, however, that these two people differ in places of worship, in their customs with regard to worship, in deities who are the object of prayer and petition, and in their festival days, makes religious separation inevitable. There is a greater degree of integration of the Thai and the Chinese in religious matters than characterizes economic, political and social affairs, but it is by no means complete. Yet unlike the situation with respect to the Chinese in other countries of Southeast Asia, in Thailand religion does offer one base on which cultural compromise is being achieved.

The religious experience of the Chinese may for convenience in analysis be seen as composed of two parts. On the one hand are the activities centred in the public places of worship—principally Chinese temples—which have remained a significant part of community life. On the other hand there are the religious activities centred in the home and its immediate environs. The overseas Chinese regard both temple and home observances as essential although, of course, individuals differ in the attention given one or the other. Chinese festivals and celebrations, many of which are religious in nature, provide another means of religious experience, one that is both temple-centred and home-centred. These festivals appear to have changed from their counterparts in China, as have indeed many religious practices of this minority, and yet the changes are not so great as to make overseas religious observances incompatible with that practised in the homeland.

Participation in religious activities and associations is now of interest primarily to the immigrant generation and to women. It remains to be seen what further changes will occur in this sphere of overseas life as the immigrant representation of the Chinese group is decreased, and the status of women generally is altered.

## TEMPLES AND THEIR RELIGIOUS GROUPS

Bangkok is justly famous among travellers from every continent for the beautiful Hīnayāna Buddhist monastery/temples *(wat)* of the Thai people, but its Chinese temples, on the other hand, are little known and easily missed. Unlike the colourful and sparkling Thai *wat*, which rise gloriously from their surroundings, the temples of the Chinese are hidden away in side streets and back alleyways, tightly squeezed and half enveloped by the shops and houses around them. The easiest way to locate temples in the labyrinth of the Chinese districts of the capital is simply to follow Chinese immigrant women who, dressed in freshly starched white jackets and black trousers, with baskets of incense and offerings on their arms, in the early morning hours stream toward a nearby temple. These temples, when finally found, are not rewarding in appearance. Usually they have a nondescript look, sooty and faded, and more likely than not will seem incongruous to a Westerner's conception of a place of worship. Yet one has only to visit a temple on a Chinese festival day, when it is teeming with worshippers and piled high with a variety of offerings to the gods, to realize the importance of these places in the religious life of the Chinese.

The largest and most active temples are located in the capital where the concentration of Chinese is heaviest; they occur infrequently in other parts of the country. Bangkok has about a dozen large and small edifices scattered throughout the Chinese districts of the city. They are neither Buddhist, Taoist, Confucian, nor animistic, but a combination of all these. The temples themselves are built of brick and stucco in traditional Chinese architectural style, with tiled roofs and dragons along the eaves. Fierce guardian gods are painted on the main doors, sometimes almost indistinguishable beneath the grime. Temples usually face an open courtyard where on festival occasions Chinese plays are presented. One feature of this courtyard is a fireplace where paper-money and similar offerings to the gods are burned; and here also vendors with caged birds offer passersby the privilege, for a small fee, of releasing a bird and thus doing a good deed before entering the temple. Beyond the red entry doors are a number of dimly lighted and smoky rooms and small courts; at the rear are the rooms for resident monks. At the principal altar immediately inside the door, and at smaller altars placed throughout the temple one finds the familiar Taoist gods, Mahāyāna Buddha images and not infrequently Thai Buddhist statues. Scarlet banners and embroidered lanterns, blackened with smoke and thick with a decade's accumulation of dust, enclose the altars and hang from the dark celing.

Landon (1941: 101) describing the situation of Chinese religion in the 1930's wrote:

> Chinese temples are receiving less and less attention. The general feeling among both Chinese and non-Chinese is that the temples will decrease in usefulness and influence in the years to come. There is very little religious teaching by Chinese for Chinese. Grass grows high in temple yards. The priests live quietly in their quarters and are, in fact hardly more than robed caretakers of the property.

Chinese temples in the southern part of Thailand seem to fit this description today, but there is little evidence that the temples of Bangkok have lost any of their original importance. They are attended regularly on the first and fifteenth day of each lunar month, and during the frequent religious festivals they overflow with worshippers. Many come on other occasions as well, whenever they need heavenly guidance and assistance, and even on any ordinary day one finds a scattering of worshippers. Financial support does not appear to present a problem, and several temples have recently been renovated and redecorated, a good indication of continuing popular interest and use.

We can distinguish three types of persons who become part of the temple organization or participate in its activities: the worshippers, the monks, and lay religious groups. Chinese temples do not have congregations in the Western sense of the term. Anyone may worship at any temple at practically any time, although the majority of people visit temples only on the first and the fifteenth day of each lunar month. No one 'joins' a temple in the Western sense of joining a church—people simply go to any temple they wish, and when the gods at that temple prove ineffectual, they go to another. Most of the worshippers are women—men are either too busy with business affairs or too little concerned with the spiritual realm to take a direct and regular interest. Worship itself is most often an individual matter of praying, bowing, burning incense and candles, or offering food, drink and paper-money before the figure of a particular god. Occasionally a Chinese monk attached to the temple will be asked to assist in the petitioning of a god, but more often the monks remain in the background and take no part in the rites or ceremonies. To the outsider all is confusion and distraction, with different prayers and petitions being offered at the same time, perhaps a monk chanting and striking a bell, fortune sticks being shaken and thrown to the floor, people coming and going. Yet this is the normal scene in a Chinese temple.

Although these worshippers constitute an informal, shifting, very loosely structured group, to the Westerner more like the customers in a market than a congregation, still they provide the main basis for the financial support of the temple. Without them, grass does indeed grow in the temple courtyard.

A number of temples have been built by dialect associations on their own premises and are supported entirely by the association but if one can judge by appearances, week after week, such temples are of very slight importance. They are not served by monks and in general they are ignored by the community—perhaps their main function is to gain a tax exemption for the association on the claim that association's premises are used partially for religious purposes. The majority of Chinese temples must depend for support almost entirely on the general public. No collections are ever taken in Chinese temples—the very idea would be highly improper—but money is collected in more indirect ways which are no less effective. Incense, candles and votive papers are sold at small stands found inside most temples, and part of the money received in this way goes to the temple. The votaries draw slips of paper (printed in either Chinese or Thai) on which fortunes or answers to petitions are printed: these are extremely popular ways to divine the future and moreover provide the temple with a good source of revenue. In addition, each temple usually has a cashier's cage where business-like young men accept donations from worshippers. As each donation is made, the donor's name is brushed in Chinese characters on a slip of yellow paper. These slips are later displayed for all to see and admire, and are subsequently burned in honour of the patron god of the temple. Any wish made when the donation was given is thereby sent directly up to the deity. No one gives very much in this way—perhaps 10 baht (US$.50) at the most—but the accumulation from thousands of worshippers over the course of a year is considerable. To this sum must be added the special fees paid for the services of monks, and the gifts to temples made by individuals and groups, which may run into several thousand baht. A Chinese temple, for all its appearance of neglect and confusion, is a smoothly running mechanism, and, as many Chinese wryly declare, a very profitable business in itself. The same comment, of course, can be made of some Christian churches.

Living at many of these temples are small groups of Chinese Mahāyāna Buddhist monks. Chinese monks are distinctive in general ways from Thai Buddhist monks. Although both wear garments of the same saffron-yellow hue, the Chinese monk's dress consists of a loose-fitting, long-sleeved jacket with trousers, usually of silk or other fine material, quite different from the voluminous toga-like robes of coarse cotton worn by Thai monks. Both groups shave their heads and are bound to observe similar rules of austerity, avoiding worldly pleasures and comforts. But while the Thai may remain in their monastic order for only a brief period of several months if they so wish, and may marry before they enter or after they leave the order, Chinese monks take vows of celibacy and service for life. Thai monks perform services throughout an individual's life from birth to death, and they are called into the home for various festive occasions, such as weddings and birthday parties, as well as in the event of sickness and death. Chinese monks, on the other hand, have practically their sole importance in times of misfortune or death. A Chinese does not ordinarily ask for their intercession until he feels himself in a situation of danger and uncertainty, and they are only invited into the Chinese home to conduct funeral services. A further difference between the two orders lies in the way each is supported. Chinese monks receive their subsistence from the temples to which they are attached; Thai monks depend upon daily food offerings from the devout, gathered each morning at their very doorsteps. Each order has its own distinct administration and leaders, yet there is a total absence of competition, rivalry, or hostility of any sort between them. There is, at the same time, very little fraternization, and in going about their duties in Thailand the members of each group keep pretty much to themselves.

Virtually all Chinese monks, like Chinese teachers in Thailand, are recruited directly from China. Almost no overseas Chinese enter the Chinese monastic order. Compared with the Thai, there are relatively few Chinese monks or monasteries in Thailand, as the following statistics show, an indication of the comparative position which the monastic order holds in the lives of each people:

6. NUMBERS OF CHINESE AND THAI MONKS AND MONASTERIES

| Year | *Chinese* | | *Thai* | |
|---|---|---|---|---|
| | *Monks* | *Monasteries* | *Monks* | *Monasteries* |
| 1937-38 | 52 | 15 | 127,367 | 18,934 |
| 1938-39 | 52 | 15 | 127,035 | 19,551 |
| 1939-40 | 52 | 15 | 105,045 | 18,826 |
| 1940 | 52 | 15 | 113,644 | 19,769 |
| 1946 | 52 | 15 | 111,839 | 18,630 |
| 1947 | 53 | 16 | 128,457 | 18,652 |
| 1948 | 54 | 17 | 161,989 | 19,150 |
| 1949 | 54 | 17 | 175,179 | 19,592 |
| 1950 | 55 | 17 | 176,377 | 19,704 |

The monastery is ordinarily associated with a Chinese temple, thus virtually all are located in Bangkok. In 1950, out of 55 monks 51, and out of 17 monasteries 15 were in the Bangkok area. Here they are, of course, vastly outnumbered by Thai monks and monasteries. In 1950 there were more than 6,000 Thai monks and over 180 Thai monasteries located in Bangkok alone.

In addition to its monks, almost every large Chinese temple in Bangkok has a religious association of lay persons, some groups composed entirely of women, others entirely of men. Membership in these associations is open to all adults, without regard to age or dialect affiliation. One becomes a member by paying a small fee and promising to abide by certain rules, principally abstinence from meat. Ordinarily a group will number several hundred persons, all Chinese and predominantly first generation. In most cases the Teochiu dialect is used in such groups simply because most of the members are Teochiu.

Two typical associations in Bangkok are the Lien-hua Nien-fo She (蓮華念佛社), a man's organization, and the Chung-hua Fo-hsüeh She (中華佛學社), an association for women. These Buddhist associations perform religious services in the temples and in individual houses. On the first and the fifteenth day of each lunar month the association meets at its temple for special services, and on specially designated days more elaborate ceremonies are held. Some associations, when a member or the relative of a member dies, conduct religious services at the home of the deceased; such services supplement but do not replace the usual funeral services by Chinese and Thai monks.

The funeral services performed on such occasions are simple but impressive. A small altar covered with beautifully embroidered cloth is erected, with a porcelain back-screen of Bodhisattva images. Three or four members of the association, either men or women, dressed in flowing robes that reach from the chin to the ankles, perform the ceremonies. In the usual service lasting about half an hour there is chanting, the soft ringing of a bell, and the use of a small drum and gong. At its conclusion the robes are taken off, the altar dismantled, and all packed away in convenient boxes or baskets. Such services are usually conducted in the early morning because the members, business men and housewives, have no other free time.

Some associations of lay persons organized under the name of a temple are less formal and active. They prescribe no distinctive robes for their members, nor do they conduct any special services. They simply seek to encourage regular attendance at the temple and adherence to religious principles.

In addition to these various lay groups who engage in part-time religious activities only, groups of Chinese women, sometimes called 'nuns', live permanently at some of the larger temples in Bangkok. These women wear no distinctive dress and are loosely organized—there are no 'orders'; they are simply women who live at temples, doing whatever household tasks need to be done: cleaning, cooking, sewing, and at times taking part in religious services. The women who join such temple groups are well past middle age. Most have no families or close relatives in Thailand, and the temple becomes for them a kind of refuge or 'home'. They live entirely on the temple's charity. Probably no more than half a dozen groups of this kind exist, and most do not exceed a dozen women. A Chinese temple across the river from Bangkok in the suburb of Thonburi which is devoted entirely to women has an unusually large group of about one hundred 'nuns' living there permanently. There, as at other places, the women are under the authority of an older Chinese monk, or abbot. The author on a visit to this abbot at New Year's found his room so filled with tables holding bowls of oranges that it was difficult to find a place to sit. These oranges were gifts of the people in the neighbourhood—the orange for the Chinese is a symbol of good luck and happiness, and the hundreds of oranges presented to this monk were material representation of the esteem in which he was held. In the course of this visit a young Chinese girl accompanied by an older woman entered the room, both people from the neighbourhood who had come to present their good wishes. The older woman was Cantonese and could not speak the only dialect the abbot understood, Teochiu, and the young girl thus had to interpret for her. The deference which such Chinese women show to monks is in striking contrast to the indifference of many Chinese men in the community.

Beyond these formally organized and rather permanent associations one occasionally finds small groups of women banded together in an informal club for a specific religious purpose—to collect money for a temple or a benevolent association, or to save money themselves so that the group can make a pilgrimage to a nearby Buddhist shrine. Once this goal is achieved, the group is dissolved. Such groups are formed only by women.

Religious associations are exceedingly popular with women. Most immigrant women since the time of their coming to Thailand have belonged to one or another of the associations described above. These organizations are respected but they and their leaders rank low in the prestige hierarchy of the Chinese community. They are not stepping-stones to more socially prominent positions. Some of them (the monastic order and the temple 'nuns') facilitate a limited kind of withdrawal from the larger society, and all turn the attention of members away from the material life of the Chinese community to the spiritual realm. None leads to a significantly closer integration with Thai society, but rather all serve to perpetuate the separation of the two ethnic groups.

The ancestral halls which are so characteristic of the villages of South China are almost entirely absent in Thailand, although structures patterned after them are found in the Chinese community. One exquisitely beautiful building constructed by the Chao-Yang regional association, a subdivision of the Teochiu Dialect Association, has been referred to earlier. Built as a faithful replica of the traditional ancestral hall, it is such in design only. It is open not, as in China, to only one clan, but to anyone from the Chao-Yang region (near Swatow), regardless of surname. This hall, like the ancestral halls of China, contains memorial tablets for deceased persons, but here again one notes differences between overseas practices and those of China. Only persons who have died in Thailand are commemorated, and several names are put on one tablet. Although many Chinese not members of this association are inclined to dismiss this hall as a money-making scheme of the association's leaders, it does show a weakening of clan ties and their systematic replacement by regional ones among the overseas Chinese.

In China, memorial tablets of deceased family members up to the fifth generation are kept in the home where they form part of the family ancestor shrine; other tablets are put in the clan ancestral hall. Almost no overseas Chinese family in Thailand follows this custom any longer. Tablets for persons who have died in China are kept, presumably, by the branch of that family in China, and persons who have died in Thailand are honoured, if at all, by having tablets placed in Chinese temples there. All the large temples in the capital have one room set aside for this purpose. There can be found row upon row of wooden tablets similar in size and shape to the traditional ancestor tablets, but not similar in their use. The tablets kept in Bangkok commemorate men, women and children indiscriminately. Moreover, the names of several unrelated persons may be placed on one tablet—this is cheaper than having but one tablet for each person. A few temples, in addition to keeping these tablets, have initiated the practice of storing in individual boxes the ashes of the deceased for whom the tablets are erected. Memorial services which in China might be conducted in the home are shifted in Bangkok to these temples. Chinese women in particular like the new arrangement inasmuch as it relieves them of some chores connected with maintaining home ancestor shrines, especially the necessity to prepare daily food and drink offerings to the deceased.

## HOUSE SPIRITS AND ACTIVITIES

The typical Chinese immigrant home in Thailand is often a drab and dismal affair, with the only spots of colour provided by household 'shrines' (called *shen-k'an* 神龕 in Mandarin) where various spirits are worshipped. Ordinarily these deities include a God of the Earth, God of the House, God of the Kitchen, and a God of the Sky; but in addition to these principal spirits many houses periodically make offerings to lesser gods in and about the home. Small pieces of red paper representing these gods are pasted to walls and doors, or woodcuts of Chinese Buddha figures may likewise be used. Many shops also have various cabalistic pictures and devices fixed over the front entrance to ward off evil influences—one of the most popular in Bangkok is a small opened fan. Near such devices one finds a small tin can fastened to the wall where incense sticks can be placed for burning. Finally, in addition to all these gods, there is often an ancestor shelf, but not ancestor tablets, prominently located in the home or shop.

A brief description and explanation of the principal gods will provide an understanding of the smaller ones as well. The God of the Earth consists of a piece of red paper, about eight by three inches, on which has been written in black or gold ink the Chinese characters for this god. The shape of the paper and the characters used are shown in the accompanying sketch. This piece of paper is pasted close to the threshold on the outside of the street door or on the outer street wall of the house.

The God of the House is also a piece of red paper, about 10 by 12 inches containing characters reading 'God of the House' or some optimistic or honorific phrase such as, 'Gather together treasure hall' or 'Silver-tree has bloomed'. This paper is pasted close to the floor on an inside wall near or facing the street door. Sometimes a wooden frame is fitted around the paper so that a boxed effect is created. Or, the paper may be fastened to a wall directly beneath a small table so that the table seems to enclose or frame the paper. Offerings to this spirit—incense, wine, food—are placed on the floor or on the bottom shelf of the box, when the latter is built, and the top of the box or the table is used to store the cups, dishes, and bottles needed for the daily offerings.

The God of the Kitchen is also a rectangular piece of red paper with characters in black paint reading 'Sure Luck Kitchen Master'. This paper is stuck on the wall of the kitchen area above the stove.

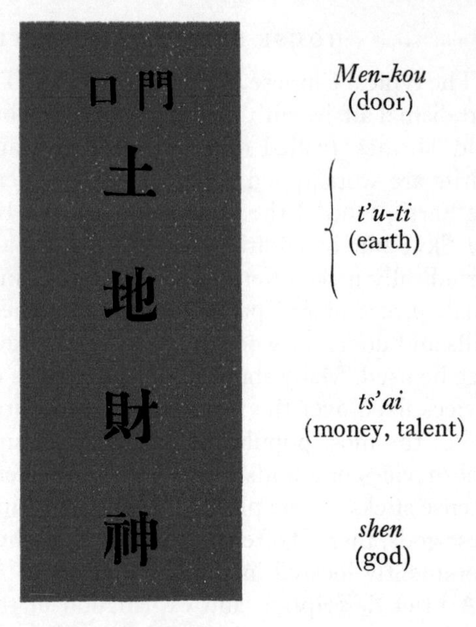


*God of the Earth*
*Of Chinese in Bangkok*

Traditionally this god is believed to return to heaven before the New Year to report on the family, and to assure a good report honey or jam is smeared on the god's mouth. Actually, this god is not commonly seen in overseas Chinese homes in Thailand and many people seem unaware of the practice described above.

The God of the Sky is also made of a rectangular piece of red paper about 10 inches by 12 inches on which is written the characters signifying this god. It is fastened to a wall under the open sky, that is, on the rear outer walls of the house or on one wall of a roofless court if placed within the house proper.

In some houses a kind of general god takes the place of all the individual ones described above. This consists of a piece of red paper, about 10 by 12 inches, on which has been brushed in large, bold strokes the Chinese characters for 'god', plus some laudatory phrases in smaller characters. This paper is fastened to the inside wall of the house, often facing the street door, slightly higher than a person's head, and offerings similar to those for the other spirits are made periodically. Not infrequently a Chinese shop or home will display a large picture of the heavenly triad, Kuan Kung (關公), Chou Ts'ang (周倉), and Kuan P'ing (關平) painted by a local Chinese artist, which like the general god, is designed to protect the place from evil influences.

The 'Ancestor Shelf' normally seen in Chinese homes in Thailand is simply a piece of red paper about 10 by 12 inches with characters in black or gold paint. The paper is fastened to a wall inside the house, over a doorway or to one side of it, about eight feet above the floor in the room which opens directly on the street. The paper gives the surname of the family, often the number of generations it has existed, and lists the names of those close relatives such as parents, grandparents, wife, or husband, who have died in Thailand. A small shelf is built beneath the paper, where incense and food offerings can be placed. Often an elaborately decorated frame encloses the paper, sometimes with small coloured electric lights similar to those used in the United States for Christmas-tree decorations. Not every house by any means has an ancestor shelf, and ancestor tablets as such are rarely found in the average overseas Chinese home.

The number and variety of spirits worshipped within the home depends on the inclination of the individual family. There seems to be a variation according to dialect group, but virtually every overseas Chinese home contains some of the gods described above. The attention given to these shrines varies from family to family and in any case becomes the responsibility of the wife. In general, incense is burned morning and evening, and one of the commonplace sights in the Chinese districts of Bangkok are Chinese women kneeling on the sidewalk at the corner of their houses, burning sticks of incense to some spirit. On the first and the fifteenth day of each lunar month, as well as on the occasion of all the principal Chinese festivals, food and drink offerings are made to the spirits before the family eats its first meal. More attention is given to the ancestor shelf. In addition to the offerings on the occasions listed above, incense and candles are burned and special food and drink offerings are prepared and presented to the ancestral spirit on the birth and death days of the deceased who are commemorated by the shrine, and on the occasion of such festivals as New Year, Ch'ing-ming, and Chung-yüan.

All the god papers are renewed once each year on the occasion of the New Year, and as this holiday approaches Chinese vendors begin to appear selling bright, new papers already freshly printed with the appropriate characters.

## RELIGIOUS SYNCRETISM

Religion is one sphere at least where a considerable degree of integration occurs between the Chinese and the Thai. Hīnayāna and Mahāyāna Buddhists are sufficiently alike for the Chinese to accept certain Thai practices without difficulty or contradiction in values. Moreover, Thai Buddhism is an *inclusive* religion which does not demand absolute allegiance—a person accepts what he likes, participates where he cares to, while retaining, if he wishes, his old beliefs and practices. Consequently the Chinese find it easy to accept selectively certain Thai practices without the necessity of changing in any fundamental way their essentially Chinese religious habits. Some specific examples of this may be cited.

The Chinese, although they are free to do so, do not ordinarily attend services at Thai *wat* on *wan-phra* (holy days), as do the Thai. When there is sickness in the family, however, or some similar misfortune, then it is likely that the Chinese wife will seek the intercession of the gods, often at both a Chinese and a Thai temple. Some *wat* are favoured over others by the Chinese, because of extraordinary powers attributed to figures of the Buddha there, or because a Thai monk there has a popular reputation as a healer.

One *wat* located across the river from Bangkok in Thonburi contains a huge statue of The Buddha, called 'Sam Kuo Khoon' by the Chinese, which they worship as the guardian god of Thailand. The Chinese crowd into this temple during the three days when Chinese New Year is celebrated, seeking the support of the god during the coming year. Also, thousands of Chinese each year visit a Thai shrine at Phrabat (about 80 miles from Bangkok) which contains a 'footprint' of The Buddha, the pilgrimage to Phrabat being one of the most popular excursions that the Chinese make. They worship also at several animistic Thai shrines in Bangkok. One called by the Thai 'Lak Muang', or Stone of the City, where the city deity resides, attracts almost as many Chinese each day as Thai. They are also frequently visitors to other shrines in the capital revered by the Thai as the loci of powerful spirits.

All these holy places are open to the public without restriction, and anyone—Chinese, Thai, Indian, or European—is welcome to participate in any of their activities. Chinese religious values undergo no change by such action. They simply worship the Thai statues in the same way they worship images in their own temples. In China these immigrants sought to honour or appease any powerful god or spirit or to appeal for assistance in times of need. In Thailand they merely extend the range of these sacerdotal activities so as to include powerful spirits and gods peculiar to this new environment.

This constancy of religious values is clearly shown by considering the aspects of Thai Buddhism the Chinese do not accept. The monastic order is a basic institution in Thai Buddhism and almost all Thai men sometime in their lives enter the order as novices or monks. Yet one almost never sees a Chinese, immigrant or succeeding generation, becoming a novice or monk. Questioned as to why they do not, the Chinese simply reply, 'We Chinese have different customs from the Thai people'. One second-generation Chinese youth was more explicit: 'Where would my father get a bookkeeper while I am being a monk? My wife would not like the idea either. She thinks I run around too much already and she would not believe I went into the monastery to become a better person'. As has been pointed out above, rarely does a Chinese enter a Chinese monastery either.

Practically all Thai householders offer food to Thai monks in the early morning as an accepted and every essential part of their religious life. Presenting this food has a definite value as a means of making merit and thereby assuring one's future salvation. The Chinese householder only rarely does this, and Thai monks ordinarily by-pass Chinese settlements on their daily rounds.

Yet the Chinese show respect to Thai monks, sometimes more than to Chinese monks. It is not unusual to hear overseas Chinese declare that Chinese monks are interested only in making money but that Thai monks are sincerely concerned with their religion. The Chinese use Thai monks for the same purposes they would Chinese, to perform funeral services for instance. Monks are never seen at Chinese weddings, however, nor are they asked to perform services in the home, as they commonly do among the Thai people. Here again fundamental values differ. For the Thai, the monk or novice has a positive function: he enables the layman to make merit, and the more his services are used, the greater the merit accumulated. The Chinese regard the monks as intermediaries between the individual and powerful gods and spirits. When the gods are favourable, there is no need for the services of monks. They are sought only in times of misfortune—in the event of sickness, ill luck, death—when the gods must be appeased and again made favourable. The less one has to do with monks at other times the better.

## FESTIVALS AND HOLIDAYS

Chinese holidays, which occur at periodic intervals throughout the year, provide a popular means for relaxation from the daily routine of business and work. Most of the festivals have a basically religious significance, but this is often overshadowed by the purely social and entertainment aspects of the celebrations. Certain festivals are celebrated by the community as a whole, with parades, displays and public dinners. In other instances the day is observed within the home, with only the immediate family in attendance. All festivals, without exception have undergone changes from China, usually because of a conflict between traditional standards and practices and the new demands of business life in Thailand, but change seems to characterize the public observances far more than the private, intimate family celebrations.

The Chinese in Thailand observe some eight major festivals or occasions during the year: Chinese New Year; Lantern Day; Ch'ing-ming; Fifth Month Festival; Star Day; Chung-yüan; Mid-Autumn Festival; and the so-called Winter Festival. These occasions are by no means of equal importance, and some are more characteristic of one dialect group than another. Many festivals that are observed with great fanfare in the capital are but quietly celebrated in the rural areas where the Chinese are less numerous—in these latter cases the public display would be reduced and the essential celebration limited to the family group. The descriptions offered here are based on observations and participation in festivals held in Bangkok which as the centre of Chinese community life can be regarded as forming a model for celebrations elsewhere in Thailand.

1. *The New Year celebration.* The New Year festival, by far the most important of the entire year, begins on the first lunar month and lasts from three to five days, depending on the inclination of the individual concerned. Preparations for the New Year begin a week or more in advance. After consulting a handbook of auspicious days (books based on the lunar calendar giving such information are kept by every family), the Chinese housewife visits a nearby temple to thank the gods for assistance during the past year and to ask for their continuous help in the future. Temples are crowded at this time, and the offerings are much more elaborate than at other times. It is not unusual to see entire roast pigs being carried to the temples, placed before favourite gods, and when the petition

has been made, carried home again. Small boys have their hair braided into topknots decorated with red string in anticipation of the holiday. All during New Year's Eve the housewife is busy preparing food for the occasion—according to custom, nothing may be killed on the first day of the New Year—and making up scores of red paper packets, each containing a small sum of money, for distribution as gifts to children. All god papers in the home are renewed at this time, the areas thoroughly cleaned, and special offerings make to the spirits. By New Year's Eve business has come to a virtual standstill. In the afternoon of this day Chinese business houses give dinners for all their employees, and in the home such meals are given to servants. Some merchants spread out on the floors and adjacent sidewalks of their shops an elaborate offering of food, drink, incense, and candles to the spirits of the old year. By late afternoon many shops have already boarded up their entrances and the streets are practically deserted as each family prepares to greet the New Year from the privacy of its own home. Unlike China, no fire-crackers are heard as the new year arrives—Thai law forbids their use—but occasionally one or two may be exploded surreptitiously within the confines of the home.

On New Year's day children rise early to pay their formal respects to their parents, and later visit other relatives and friends to wish them a happy new year. The red paper packets containing money are given at this time to the children. The streets of the Chinese districts are thronged with people in their best and newest clothes, and the entire community has a festive air. Everyone lets himself go in having a good time—eating, some drinking of Chinese wine and whisky; going to movies, which run extra shows throughout this period; strolling about the streets, visiting relatives and friends. Increasing numbers of second-generation Chinese take this opportunity to go on short vacations to seaside resorts. In the afternoon some dialect associations stage 'dragon dances'—a long dragon made from cloth and *papier maché* and manned by several young men cavorts to the beat of drums and cymbals—and hold formal dinners later on in the evening of New Year's Day. Virtually all Chinese business is closed down, and so well is this custom followed that shortages of food quickly develop, driving up the prices of foodstuffs, such as pork and poultry, as much as 100 per cent. For the majority of small shopkeepers, the New Year period is the only time during the entire year, including Saturdays and Sundays, that they stop work entirely. Although

Chinese New Year is not recognized by the Thai government as an official holiday, it is both a commercial and bank holiday for all Asian and Western businesses, a clear indication of the importance of the Chinese in the business life of the capital.

Yet even during this most important celebration some immigrant shopkeepers have begun to temporize with tradition in order to profit from the crowds that throng the streets. Many coffee shops remain open for business, the less conspicuous side door rather than the front being used for entry. Shops selling fruit and canned goods—both items are used as gifts by the Chinese—remain open throughout the New Year period. Street vendors of food, drinks, clothing and trinkets do a land-office business. Beggars are very much in evidence because their pleas are sure to be rewarded. Gold shops which sell ornaments and jewelry likewise do a brisk business. Moreover, while almost all Chinese shops are closed on the first day of the New Year period, many more are open on the second day, and by the end of the third day, business is practically back at its usual level. Some retail stores in Bangkok are in fact giving their employees a short vacation before the New Year so that they can remain open for business for at least part of this holiday.

2. *Lantern Day*. Compared to the carefree celebration of the New Year, this is a quiet and principally religious celebration, but one which children look forward to because of the special confection prepared for this occasion. Lantern Day falls on the fifteenth day of the first lunar month, and in the villages of South China marked the formal end of the New Year celebration and the resumption of work. There, according to Chinese immigrant reports, it was celebrated by a procession with a Buddha image through the village, the hanging out of lanterns at each home, and in the evening the holding of a special dinner for the immediate family. In Bangkok, however, no procession is held and few lanterns are hung out, but offerings are made to temples and small dinner parties are held at home. For this occasion Chinese confectionery shops make models of pagodas and stylized lions of hard white sugar. These are purchased by individuals and then along with fruit, cakes and noodles are presented to Chinese temples.

The overseas Chinese go to the temples on Lantern Day to see whether the gods are favourably disposed toward them during the coming year. They find out by throwing to the floor two small pieces of wood *(bei)*, each of which has both a flat and a round side: if the round side of one and the flat of the other turn up, then the gods are favourable, and in return for their help so quickly given, the individual buys some of the fruit, cakes and confections at the temple, promising to repay double the next year. If the initial try with the pieces of wood is not favourable, then the individual tries again and again, each time raising the number of times he promises to repay the next year. This continues until a favourable answer from the gods is received, and with each try the interest on his debt, as it were, increases. The confections are taken home to be eaten by the children in the family as a special treat. Chinese temples are crowded on the evening of this day with both men and women making offerings of sweets as well as oranges, noodles, incense, and candles, and having their names inscribed on lists of donors.

3. *Ch'ing-ming* which falls on the 29th day of the second lunar month, is still faithfully observed by the overseas Chinese in Thailand but in a quite different manner from in China. In China it was usually the occasion for a day-long holiday in which the entire family took a leisurely trip through the country side to the tombs of the ancestors. After the offerings were made to the spirits, and the grave site cleaned and set in order, a picnic would then be held nearby. In Bangkok rather than individual tombs located in the countryside, there are only Western-type cemeteries on the immediate outskirts of the city. Beginning before sunrise of this day, individuals and families hurry to the nearby cemeteries carrying baskets filled with food, drink, incense and paper-money. Usually they come by auto and bus, and by six o'clock the roads leading to the Chinese cemeteries are jammed with pedestrians and cars. In these cemeteries it is customary to place the partially cremated remains in small tin boxes, the latter being stored in large warehouses. In preparation for Ch'ing-ming cemetery officials have set out the thousands of such boxes with a clerk in charge of each section. A person obtains the box holding the remains of a relative, and taking it a little distance apart from the crowd, opens the box and makes the traditional offerings by burning paper, incense, and paper-money and presenting the dishes of good and drink which he has brought with him. Chinese musicians who circulate among the throng may be hired to play briefly. Occasionally fire-crackers

are shot off. The rites are over in a few minutes. The box is returned to the attendant and the individual hurries home again to open his shop in time for the usual morning trade. For those whose relatives are actually buried in graves at the cemetery, the traditional ritual of cleaning the grave site is performed, although Chinese coolies or small Thai boys are hired on the spot to do much of this work. For those persons who have no relatives buried in Thailand, Ch'ing-ming has lost much of its old significance. Some go to the cemeteries along with friends, but many simply remain at home with no special observances to mark the day.

4. *Fifth Month Festival.* Falling on the fifth day of the fifth lunar month, this festival is sometimes called the 'Dragon-Boat Festival' because in China it was the occasion for races between boats shaped like dragons. In Thailand much of the holiday flavour of this day has been lost, although its observance in the home makes up to a certain extent for this. There are no boat races. Instead the Chinese worship at their temples and make offerings to the temple gods, at various animistic shrines, and to the household spirits. This task usually falls to the women. At home in preparation for this festival the Chinese housewife makes small cakes of glutinous rice and nuts, and these after being offered ritually to the gods, are served to the family as a special treat. Usually enough cakes are made to last for several days, much to the delight of the children. Some special dishes will be added to the evening meal on this day, and in the evening it is customary for adults to visit friends, play mahjong with a small group at a restaurant, or go to the movies. A brief festival, it serves mainly to break the monotony of everyday life and give those who have worked hard for several months an excuse for relaxation and enjoyment.

5. *Star Day* which falls on the seventh day of the seventh lunar month, is a minor Chinese festival with a social rather than a religious significance. It originated with the legend of the Cowherd, *Niu-lang* and the Spinning Girl, *Chih-nü*, in Aquila and Vega, who live on the opposite banks of the 'Heavenly River', or Milky Way, but once a year on this day are reunited on a bridge of magpies (the Leda constellation?). Tradition, according to overseas Chinese accounts, requires that Chinese girls wait for the convergence of the stars and at the precise moment when it occurs try to thread a needle—should a girl succeed, this indicates that she will be happily married during the coming year. In Bangkok the observance

has changed somewhat. In anticipation of this day, small groups of young unmarried teen-age girls form clubs, pay dues throughout the year, and use the accumulated fund to buy cakes for a small informal party the evening of Star Day. The girls don their finest clothes and in the early part of the evening, before darkness falls, they can be seen sitting in front of their parents' shops, chatting with each other, or strolling from place to place to visit other girls. Chinese youths like to wander about on this evening, usually in groups of two and three, to admire the girls, and if possessed of enough courage, to chat idly with them under the chaperoning eyes of the girls' parents. This is one of the rare occasions when the unusually strict supervision of unmarried girls is relaxed to some extent. Star Day is especially observed by the Cantonese dialect group, but virtually ignored by the numerically dominant Teochiu group.

6. *Chung-yüan* falls on the 15th day of the seventh lunar month. In China it is not so much a festival as a memorial occasion when offerings are made to the ancestral spirits and the family graves are swept and put in order. In Bangkok the observance and significance of this day varies with the different dialect groups. The Cantonese, for example, go to the local cemeteries for simple memorial services, but the number of such visitors on this day is much less than on Ch'ing-ming. The Teochiu dialect group on the other hand is more inclined to observe the day at home. According to local Teochiu belief, the spirits of the dead are released to roam the world on this day. They are mischievous and even dangerous, and must be appeased. Thus merchants set out tables in front of their shops on which are placed various foods and drink—chicken, rice, sweet cakes, unopened bottles of whiskey, soda-water, and Coca-Cola. Candles, joss-sticks, oil lamps, or electric lights are burned around this table. A pail of water with a metal dipper is kept close by, for the spirits to wash after eating. Paper-money is burned at the curb (and if these fires threaten to get out of control, the pails of water are handy extinguishers). From time to time handfuls of dry rice, containing small coins are thrown around the shop entrance to tempt the spirits to take it and leave the family in peace. Small boys wait about and scramble for these coins. By evening the food and drink is taken inside and forms the basis for an especially elaborate evening meal.

On this day the streets of the Chinese districts are comparatively quiet, with most of the shops closed, or, if open, desultory about doing business. The usually crowded alleyways are easy to walk through. Some children are playing about, a few musicians may be seen going from door to door offering their services for a small fee, but the majority of people remain at home. Occasionally Chung-yüan coincides with the beginning of the annual Thai school holiday, and the entire city therefore has a quiet holiday air.

7. *The Mid-Autumn Festival*, which falls on the fifteenth day of the eighth lunar month, is a joyous festival both in China and in Bangkok. In the latter place it rivals the New Year celebration for popular enthusiasm and community-wide activity. On the evening of this day, every Chinese shop that can do so sets up a richly decorated table close to the sidewalk, and often extending into the sidewalk, on which is placed an elaborate display of special cakes, bottled drinks, cups of tea, several kinds of fruit, and various merchandise—canned milk, cologne water, face powder, silk trousers, etc.—in fact anything sold by the shop making the display. Each table contains also an amount of ceremonial gold and silver paper, some fashioned into gold bricks, which will be burned at the curb when the celebration is over. Around the table are placed incense sticks—some as large as baseball bats—candles and brightly coloured Chinese lanterns in the shape of fish, airplanes, and pagodas. Some displays feature traditional Chinese paintings of mountain scenes as backdrops, with the entire shop front being covered. So much time is required to set up a finely decorated table that not infrequently several families will band together to make one especially large display. Over each a Coleman gas lamp is usually hung, giving off intense heat but making the entire area almost as bright as day.

The displays are set up beginning about seven o'clock in the evening, and from then until midnight dense crowds stroll through the streets, completely blocking all traffic and in fact making it impossible to use a car at all. People are happy and carefree but there is no rowdyism. In the open vegetable market areas stages are erected where professional actors present Chinese plays, and around these the crush is so great that movement is virtually impossible. Younger children with all kinds of lanterns run about until midnight, and groups of teen-age girls in their best dresses stroll gaily by.

Women are particularly in evidence, and this festival is popularly regarded as of interest principally to women. The Mid-Autumn Festival is also known as the 'Moon Festival' because of the popular belief that the Moon Goddess comes out on this occasion to hear petitions and to offer help to women. The displays of food and goods mentioned above are in honour, therefore, of this Goddess. On this day also offerings are made in the various Chinese temples and to all the household gods as well. Chinese stores for several days before begin to advertise the sale of 'moon cakes'—large and small sweet cakes made with coconut and dates, both round and crescent-shaped—which according to tradition are to be eaten at midnight by the assembled family while seated beneath the full moon. The local Chinese explain that this custom is to commemorate a Chinese rebellion against the Mongols centuries ago when slips of paper announcing the rebellion were hidden in small cakes and distributed to the Chinese population. Many overseas Chinese thus regard the Mid-Autumn Festival as a time for remembrance of their homeland and they make it an occasion to strengthen among the younger generation emotional ties with China. As with the other Chinese celebrations, the Thai take no part in this one nor do they show any interest. Festivities end at midnight, and by the next morning the Chinese community has returned to its usual business-like tempo.

8. *The Winter Festival*, on the twenty-fifth day of the eleventh lunar month, is a quiet affair which has as its principal function the integration of the immediate family. The overseas Chinese believe that on this day the household gods return to heaven to report on the activities of the family for the past twelve months. To assure a good report, the Chinese housewife has prepared sweetened balls of flour, about the size of marbles, which after being offered to the gods to 'sweeten' their report are eaten by the family as a special confection. According to local belief, a person becomes one year older after eating these flour balls, and by eating them he is also assured of good fortune in the coming year. The evening meal on this day is more elaborate than that usually served, and it is the occasion for the entire family, including married children, to return to the home of their parents. No special events take place in the community as a whole, and business or work is not interrupted.

In addition to these eight major occasions, there are a few purely religious festivals observed by sections of the Chinese community.

Portions of the Chinese minority in Thailand also observe the national day of the Chinese Nationalist Government, which falls on October 10 and is popularly called the 'Double Ten' celebration, or the national day of the Chinese Communist Government, which falls on October 1. However, while 'Double Ten' brings forth some kind of public display, October 1 is usually passed by quietly without any overt celebration for fear of offending the Thai authorities who look with disfavour on any pro-Communist celebration.

Neither Thai nor Western holidays, such as Christmas or New Year's are ordinarily observed by the overseas Chinese, although these occasions may coincide with the major Chinese holidays and festivals. Those who regularly observe Thai holidays can be separated into two categories: (i) persons employed by large businesses—insurance companies, banks, export-import houses—which observe official Thai holidays, and, in the case of European and American firms, Western holidays as well; and (ii) small shopkeepers living in predominantly Thai districts who likewise find it expedient to conform at least in part to the practices of their Thai neighbours. The vast majority who do not observe Thai holidays are motivated often by economic considerations. Because Thai government workers throughout the Kingdom are released from work on these days, retail business is excellent, and it would be folly for any merchant to close his shop when sales are likely to be at their peak. But there are other reasons. Practically all Thai official holidays during the year are either in observance of religious events connected with Hīnayāna Buddhism or are in celebration of recent political events, such as the establishment of the Constitution. The Chinese participate selectively in Thai Buddhism but do not take it over in *toto*. Thus for them Thai religious festivals have little significance. Since the Chinese do not take part to any extent in politics, they have little reason to observe Thai political holidays.

In general the Chinese retain the habits of industry and hard work for which they were noted in their homeland. If they change at all, they tend to change in the direction of their compatriots in Thailand, and the Chinese communities there place a premium on industry and perseverance. Ordinarily the longer a person works the more he makes; the relationship is as direct as that. Thus while Thai government employees receive a total of about 20 official holidays during the year, in addition to a one or two-week vacation and sick leave, the average Chinese shopkeeper and itinerant peddler works Saturdays and Sundays; he will absent himself from work for at most only three days during the entire year, exclusive of a day now and then, perhaps to attend such ceremonies as weddings and funerals.

This intense devotion to industry, greater in many cases than in China, is caused chiefly by the urban business environment. In the Chinese community competition is too keen, the struggle for profits too intense for any shopkeeper to take whole days from his work. Even the funerals of parents, which in China would take unqualified precedence over all other interests, in Bangkok are so arranged as to make a minimum of interference with the family's business—the period of mourning is shortened, and if possible funeral and memorial services are held at a nearby temple or Thai *wat*, rather than in the home where they would interfere with routine business activities.

Despite such changes as these, religion continues to play an essential role in the life of the overseas Chinese. Religion provides a measure of psychic security and comfort for the individual in times of crisis and misfortune, and it also, through public activities, serves to unify the overseas Chinese community and to strengthen in-group sentiments. Many religious activities reaffirm the values of co-operation and mutual aid which is the keystone of the Chinese community itself. Religion helps to reinforce emotional ties with China and it is one means for inculcating the younger generation with the finer details of Chinese cultural patterns which will facilitate their integration into Chinese commercial and social institutions. Religious activities and values will in the future be reinterpreted by the overseas Chinese, as they have been in the past, and some practices will disappear, but Chinese religion serves too many socially desirable ends for the individual and for the community to be quickly discarded or replaced by something else. This is a favourable augury in so far as relations between the Chinese and Thai are concerned, for of all the activities the Chinese minority engage in, those relating to their formal religion are most readily appreciated by the Thai, and the reverse is true also. Here, then, is a community of interests which may be utilized to overcome difficulties in other spheres.

CHAPTER VI

# ECONOMIC ORGANIZATION AND INTERESTS

FEW descriptions of Thailand today, or of Siam as it was called formerly, or of Ayuthia as the Kingdom was known in the 16th and 17th centuries, are without some mention of the Chinese and their mercantile way of life. The Chinese trader has even found his way into Thai folktales, he is a familiar comical character in the popular theatre, and he figures in Thai jokes almost as much as the mother-in-law does in American humour. No town of any size is without its cluster of Chinese shops, restaurants, hotel and rice-mill, and the economic life of the largest city and capital is dominated by Chinese enterprise. The smaller rural villages may lack Chinese shops as such, but by bicycle or by boat, traders come almost daily, selling everything that anyone can be expected to buy. This overwhelming concern of the Chinese for commercial activities, and their consequent occupational separation from the Thai people, is one of the striking features of Thailand's social structure, and in recent historical times a major source of friction between the two peoples. Initially a convenient and culturally acceptable division of labour, this occupational separation has given the Chinese minority immense economic power, but at the same time has excited fear, resentment and a growing measure of intolerance on the part of many leading Thai. Their present economic position, related as it is to so many fundamental institutions and values, is the major obstacle to the further integration of the Chinese minority.

In the sections which follow we shall examine more closely the economic and occupational separation that exists today and which existed formerly, calling attention to the historical and cultural influences which have promoted the present divisions. Following this, we shall review the government's efforts to limit Chinese economic power and assess the effect of these measures on Chinese business and on Chinese assimilation.

## OCCUPATIONAL PATTERNS

Below the uppermost stratum of hereditary royalty, there were until recent times two main levels in Thai society: the peasantry at the bottom and at the top a highly respected and privileged body of government officials. Between these two main levels the Chinese immigrants of the 19th century entered as traders, middlemen, and skilled craftsmen, in small numbers initially but in growing strength after Thailand was opened to Western commerce about the middle of the 19th century. Already ensconced in domestic and foreign trade long before the advent of the first Europeans, the Chinese during the 19th and 20th centuries extended their mercantile activities, becoming in fact a necessary adjunct to Western commercial expansion. In the West's exploitation of this Asian market, the Chinese functioned as essential middlemen, funneling manufactures from European import houses in Bangkok to the population throughout the Kingdom. Having virtually no competition from the indigenous peoples, whose concern with trade was largely limited to dealings in agricultural produce, the Chinese during the course of the last century won a virtual monopoly of all retail trade in the Kingdom and control as well of rice processing and marketing. In gaining this position they have leaned heavily on western import-export houses, banks, and shipping companies, and the symbiotic relationship thus developed has been mutually profitable.

During this period also the Chinese won a firm foothold in the construction trades and related occupations. Bangkok was established as the national capital only at the end of the 18th century, after the complete destruction of Ayuthia, the ancient capital, by Burmese armies. From a small river town, Bangkok has grown during the last century into one of the largest cities of the Far East, with over a million residents today. For this expansion of the city, the construction of public and private buildings, streets, canals and port facilities, the Chinese furnished the bulk of the skilled and semi-skilled labour, and the steady demand for their services during the past 75 years particularly has been a major attraction for immigrant Chinese. They were indispensable too in the extension of a canal network through the rich central plain and the building of railroads and roads to link the capital with the provinces. The Chinese immigrants' ready adoption of these craftsmen occupations is not surprising. In China a farmer was by necessity a jack of several trades, and such skills as carpentering, bricklaying and housebuilding brought additional income during the slack agricultural season. In Thailand these skills were quickly utilized, and what was lacking in knowledge was made up for by the ambition and perseverance of the immigrants.

Thus as both entrepreneurs and workmen, Chinese immigrants extended their hold over virtually every processing and marketing occupation in the country. Generally speaking, the Thai were concentrated in the two main occupational groups mentioned earlier. They formed the vast peasantry, growing rice on which the country's economy depended. They also filled the steadily expanding ranks of the government bureaucracy and related service organizations. Trade and commercial pursuits were by and large left to the Chinese and other alien peoples.

While these occupational distinctions between the two peoples still hold true, the lines during the past few decades have become much less rigid and sharp. Today one must speak not of absolute occupational separation but of proportions; during the past two decades in particular an increasing number of each group have crossed over into occupational fields formerly monopolized by the other. Some Chinese aliens have managed to obtain and hold jobs with such semi-government organizations as the railways, and a small number of second-generation Chinese have successfully sought careers as government officials. Likewise, there are numerous Thai business men and artisans (although they form as yet a minority when compared to the numbers of Chinese in these occupations). Thai women have a secure place as market vendors, street hawkers of foodstuffs, and proprietors of small shops. Moreover, an increasing number of Thai young women with clerical skills are finding their way into Chinese businesses and offices.

A 1952 survey (Skinner 1957: 301–304) of the working population of the Bangkok area pinpoints the present extent of occupational concentration. The Chinese (including both persons who were Chinese nationals and those who were ethnically Chinese) formed the majority of the workers in the following occupational categories:

7. OCCUPATIONAL CATEGORIES

| *Occupational Category* | *Total Number of Workers* | *Percentage* | |
|---|---|---|---|
| | | *Chinese* | *Thai* |
| 1. Weavers and dyers | 8,770 | 97 | 3 |
| 2. Shoemakers | 1,960 | 96 | 4 |
| 3. Metal workers (base and precious) | 7,540 | 87 | 13 |
| 4. Building trades | 1,420 | 82 | 18 |
| 5. Hotel and restaurant employees | 4,110 | 88 | 12 |
| 6. Carpenters and furniture makers | 8,480 | 86 | 14 |
| 7. Market sellers and hawkers | 7,940 | 86 | 14 |
| 8. Barbers | 1,350 | 75·5 | 24·5 |
| 9. Miscellaneous technicians and craftsmen | 11,370 | 71·5 | 28·5 |
| 10. Business owners and managers | 124,140 | 71 | 29 |
| 11. Business clerks | 8,210 | 65·5 | 34·5 |
| 12. Tailors and dressmakers | 6,600 | 60 | 40 |

NOTE: Data in source have been reworked. The distribution of seamen and actors has been omitted because so far as these occupations are concerned the distribution in the capital is not representative of the country as a whole.

This survey showed the Chinese and Thai about equally represented in the preparation and processing of foodstuffs and as market gardeners. The Thai, on the other hand, formed in the Bangkok area a clear majority in such high-status occupations as government officials and clerks, professional and semi-professionals, industrial and administrative specialists, and in such lower status jobs as hairdressers, automobile, bus and truck drivers, and domestic and service workers. For the country as a whole, of course, the Thai form the vast majority still of the farmers and fishermen; rice farming is almost entirely in Thai hands.

To round out the picture, mention must be made of the two major extractive industries: tin mining and rubber, both centred in the southern provinces of Thailand. In both the Chinese form the dominant group. Formerly virtually all tin mining was done by Chinese—tin mining in fact drew Chinese to Thailand and Malaya centuries ago—but during the past thirty years Australian companies using modern dredging methods, and a minimum of labour, have produced an increasingly large proportion of Thailand's tin. Nevertheless, as independent miners and labourers, the Chinese still outnumber any other ethnic group. Chinese control of the rubber industry is unchallenged; the smallholders who make up Thailand's rubber producers are predominantly Chinese, as are the tappers, processors, and exporters.

What of the future occupational and economic position of the Chinese minority? Two trends are now apparent. The great role of the Chinese in filling Thailand's pressing need for unskilled and skilled labour seems to be passing. The need still exists, perhaps more acute than formerly, but increasingly it will be Thai rather than Chinese who will satisfy it, for several reasons. The number of immigrants in the ranks of Thailand's Chinese is falling, and historically immigrants have filled the need for low-paid labour. At the same time the population of the Kingdom is growing at a good rate, and in a steadily swelling flow Thai peasants are migrating to the cities and towns where they find employment as unskilled and semi-skilled labourers. Efforts by the government to train Thai for various trades and crafts has already helped to break down the once rigid vocational separation. Occupationally, therefore, we can expect Thai workers eventually to take over and replace Chinese unskilled and skilled labourers, and fill any need for this kind of worker created by the expanding economy. One sees evidence of this trend on every hand in Thailand today. The driving of passenger tricycles (*samlor*), a low-paid occupation that is the modern equivalent of ricksha pulling, is monopolized by Thai young men who come by the thousands to the capital, particularly from the rural northeast provinces. When a cotton-spinning factory was established near Bangkok about 1950, the Chinese management first employed Chinese, but has since turned to Thai women who would readily accept the low wages and without demanding working conditions. Road workers, garbage collectors, street cleaners, excavation coolies, stevedores, bus, taxi, truck and trolley drivers —all such low-paid and manual occupations are filled by Thai workers today, in some cases to the exclusion of Chinese.

As Thai have moved to the lower rungs of the vocational ladder, the Chinese have shown a steady drift into the ownership and management of what might be termed 'big business', meaning by that term complex commercial organizations such as banks, insurance companies, export and import houses, transport firms and travel agencies, construction companies, and light manufacturing industries. Just what this change means for the future of the Chinese minority is difficult now to say. Certainly, it gives the big business man more money with which to buy influence and protection, but at the same time it demands an acceptance of Thai and Western modes of conduct, less dependence on the family as the base for a business organization, and by necessity a partisan relationship with powerful military and political figures in the Kingdom. More will be said of this in the sections which follow.

## THE CHINESE IN BUSINESS

All observers of the overseas Chinese are agreed that their *forte* is commerce, and those not actually engaged in trade of some sort look forward to the day when they can pursue a commercial career. Precise statistics are lacking, but we can reasonably suppose that today at least 70 per cent of Thailand's Chinese, immigrants and their immediate descendants, are engaged in some form of commerce and industry. What are the factors which tend to bar outsiders, i.e. non-Chinese, and thus help to perpetuate their control of domestic commerce?

One of the most powerful factors favouring the Chinese is the nature of their businesses as family enterprises, employing family members exclusively, and being passed on eventually to a son to be operated again as a family enterprise. We have elsewhere called attention to the physical and social propinquity of the typical business and Chinese home. The usual dwelling in the Chinese community is a two or three-storey compartment building; the shop or business occupies the ground floor, facing directly on the street, and the back rooms and upper floors are used as living quarters by the proprietor and family. So pervasive is this pattern that even when a person has only an office in a large building, usually there are rooms immediately behind the office area where he and his family may live. This makes it relatively easy for a merchant to draw upon his wife and children as shop assistants. Ordinarily both husband and wife wait on customers, and the wife assumes full charge when the husband is absent. As the children grow up, jobs are found for them. Initially they merely help their parents and run errands, later taking over the task of serving customers and keeping the books, and eventually, in the case of sons, succeeding their fathers as owners. In this situation the family is the primary economic and occupational unit. To become part of the business, one must first become part of the family, a very difficult matter for a non-Chinese. The family functions simultaneously as a vocational training institution, and from the earliest years the children of the proprietor are being schooled in the details of business. Trade and commerce become almost second nature; little wonder then that the Thai without this practical tutelage find it so difficult to compete successfully with the Chinese.

For the smaller shop the immediate family provides enough personnel. The larger merchants must look elsewhere. In hiring, first priority is given to close relatives, second priority to more distant relatives, and after these to Chinese of the same dialect group as the proprietor. Except when it cannot be avoided, Thai are not hired by Chinese companies. Some prejudice is involved here. The typical Chinese business man regards Thai employees as indolent, lacking in business acumen or interest, and apt to be dishonest. But these attitudes may simply reflect practical considerations. Thai employees lack the necessary fluency in Chinese, both the local dialects and written Chinese; this is a tremendous handicap inasmuch as Chinese is often necessary with customers, with other merchants and with wholesalers; moreover, the firm's books are kept in Chinese as well as Thai, and letters and notices are usually in Chinese. If employed at all, Thai are kept at the periphery of the business, as minor clerks, and seldom admitted to the more responsible posts.

The customary informal method by which employment is obtained in the Chinese commercial community also works to exclude non-Chinese. Thailand has no employment offices, and newspapers carry want-ads only rarely. Jobs are secured through friends and relatives who can recommend prospective employees to business men they know. A recommendation carries with it some responsibility for the employee's conduct and character, and is not lightly given. The system tends to favour relatives over non-relatives, members of one's own dialect group against outsiders, and, without question, Chinese over Thai.

The Chinese community is rife with stories concerning the hazards of employing non-Chinese. The following one was cited to the author by a Chinese business man who was the compradore for a western bank in Bangkok. As compradore he was paid a commission by the bank on all Chinese business he brought to it, but like many Chinese business men he never had paid income tax on this money, as required by law. A clerk went through the bank's books and secured evidence on the sums paid the compradore during the several preceding years. He then went to an official in the government's income tax office and suggested that the compradore be blackmailed, offering to split any money received. The official agreed, and the compradore was duly called in and informed that he owed several hundred thousand baht in delinquent taxes. He was given the choice of paying for silence or facing prosecution. The compradore was helpless; he paid up. The clerk was Thai—had he been Chinese, the compradore declared, he would have been more loyal; or if he had tried blackmail, the compradore would have gone directly to his father and stopped the racket. However, the compradore was determined thereafter to insist that the bank employ only clerks approved first by him. These would, of course, be Chinese.

On the entrepreneurial level, the obstacles faced by non-Chinese are formidable. In a commercial situation in which written agreements are rare and a person's word must be his bond, where everyone is either a creditor or debtor and speculation with the narrowest of margins is common practice, to be sure of your colleagues' intentions is all important; mutual trust is impossible without mutuality of values. The average Chinese business man is sure of other Chinese business men; he is not quite so sure of Thai. A Chinese merchant summed up his feelings in this way:

> Chinese who go bankrupt seldom if ever are taken to court by their creditors. Instead, all the creditors hold a meeting, with the bankrupt owner absent, and they go over his business accounts to see how much is left for them. They often settle on 20 or 30 per cent of their investments. And no hard feelings will result, since it is felt that the bankrupt owner tried honestly to make a go of his business. In fact, the creditors will usually leave him a sum of money to start up his business or another business anew. Of course this procedure can be used only so long as all creditors agree—and Chinese creditors always do. A business man can depend on good treatment from other Chinese. He knows he will not be dragged into court by a creditor refusing to take a small percentage of the money owed him. A Thai creditor might do this.

The Thai entrepreneur trying to break into the commercial community must contend with other problems. Imported goods brought into the country mainly by Western import-export concerns are channeled out to retailers through Chinese compradores, and the larger non-western wholesalers are Chinese. No one refuses to do business with non-Chinese, of course, but terms are not so liberal, prices may differ from those offered Chinese merchants, credit is tighter, and when difficulties arise, as they are bound to in the up-and-down course of domestic commerce, the entrepreneur is pretty much on his own. An added problem is the mercurial nature of trade, sometimes good, sometimes poor, which makes a knowledge of the local market indispensable. As one Chinese importer explained:

> A person has to study and work in the business of Bangkok for years before he is able to understand all the ins and outs of it. There are strange depressions when no one buys, and other times when buying is good. A person has to be close to the Chinese to know just why this is so, and what is coming next, or else he stands to lose by shipping in products when no one will buy, or not having goods when people want them. For example, during the month of December there is little buying because people are getting ready for Chinese New Year, accounts are being settled, and there is not much money for buying new things. But after the New Year, business spurts because of the many bonuses given to employees which increase purchasing power. Or again, for the last few months there was no buying by Chinese merchants—they were calling in their money, not putting it out. Reason: word had gone around that the Thai Government would make the owners of various businesses—pawnshops, opium dens, rice mills, etc.—pay a higher tax and greater squeeze. The merchants wanted to have the money on hand to meet this demand by the officials. So, they did not buy goods. A foreigner or a Thai who tried to get into the swing of business here would be helpless unless he were close enough to the Chinese community to understand trends like this.

Not least significant among the factors favouring Chinese control of commerce and industry are the views taken of commercial pursuits by Thai and Chinese youth. Put simply, the Chinese take to business as ducks to water: there is no other medium for them. Upwardly mobile Thai youth look elsewhere.

Not only are opportunities continuously open in Chinese business establishments, but these are eagerly sought by the younger generation in the Chinese community, to the exclusion of other occupations and professions. Few second-generation youths attend the local universities where they might qualify as doctors, lawyers, engineers and teachers. Few indeed see any attraction in government work, but turn to trade and commerce as a far more lucrative calling. In the last ten or fifteen years, when this second generation has come of age, government salaries have suffered from the inflation of Thai currency. In many instances they are totally inadequate for the necessities of life. At the same time the chances to make money in business have increased tremendously. A successful Chinese businessman in Bangkok summed up the advantages of business over government employment:

> In the first place, there is discrimination against children of Chinese parents in getting government jobs; those with Thai parents are preferred. Second, clerical jobs in business pay more than such jobs in the government. As for example, a clerk in a government office will get about 400 baht a month, and a clerk in a Chinese firm will also start at about 400 baht a month. But the Chinese firm will give the clerk all his meals in addition to his salary; he works longer hours but gets his breakfast, lunch and dinner at the expense of the firm. Also, he will get a bonus at Chinese New Year which is never less than three times his monthly salary, which, in this case would amount to

> about 1,500 baht. Chinese firms regularly figure a bonus for their employees from the total profits and are very fair about it. At times this bonus amounts to a large sum. One clerk for a Chinese company dealing in rubber exports whose salary was 1,500 baht per month got a bonus last New Year's of 100,000 baht. This was an exception of course and was due solely to the greatly increased price of rubber in that year. But still there are these opportunities when a young man works for a Chinese firm, all legal too, which government work does not begin to equal.

A second generation Chinese drew the following contrast between careers in business and those in government:

> Within a period of ten years a clerk in the government can rise to be chief of a section or office. As such his pay would be about 1,500 baht a month, but in addition he would have the chance to make money by taking bribes or gifts. This would be illegal and he would have to be careful all the time he was doing it. His promotion would depend on how well he pleased his superiors, not on how hard he worked.
>
> A clerk working in a Chinese business house has the chance in about ten years to become the manager of the business—that is, he runs the store or office while the owner goes around drumming up business. Such a manager will get a salary of about 1,500 to 2,000 baht each month. But in addition he will get a yearly bonus of from 50,000 to 80,000 baht which is not reported to the government and on which he does not have to pay income tax. Sometimes he will get a car for business use and occasionally a house will be given him by the owner for his own use. After he has been a manager for a while, he can form his own company and then he has unlimited chances for making money. Anyone who works hard can be a rich merchant eventually.

Obviously, not all Chinese-run shops offer this kind of opportunity for advancement. Many family enterprises lead only to a mediocre economic and social position at the very best. Yet enough young men do rise to the upper reaches of business to inspire the majority in the community to follow their lead.

Thai youth have other goals. One of the striking features of the Thai ethos is the prestige accorded government officials as a group and government service as a career.[1] This is no new phenomenon. For centuries the way upward from the peasantry has been by way of official rank, and during the period of modernization extending over the last hundred years government posts have been especially valued because of the social and economic rewards they offered.

Under the absolute monarchy—that is, until 1932—government service provided virtually the only means by which a commoner could enter the select society of nobles and royalty. It was then the practice of the King to confer non-hereditary titles on officials as they advanced in the civil service, and Landon (1939: 207) declares that these titles 'formed one of the chief magnets that drew the talented youth of the country into government service'. The Revolution put an end to the conferring of titles, yet otherwise left untouched the prestige of the service as a white-collar occupation and a ladder to a higher position in society.

The civil service has five ordinary grades plus two special categories for the highest career officials. Upon reaching the higher ranks an official becomes entitled to certain perquisites of office: a car with chauffeur may be assigned to him; he may live in government housing, and so on. Advancement within the service depends largely on seniority and the approval of one's superior; consequently the official in charge of even a small office commands a degree of respect and deference unusual in western bureaucratic systems.

Civil service employees benefit from a liberal system of leave which is integrated with Buddhist activities. There are about 20 holidays during the year, or an average of almost two each month, when all government offices are closed, and several of these are for Buddhist festivals and celebrations. In addition an employee is permitted up to 30 days paid vacation leave each year, as well as sick leave. Moreover, the government grants a three-month leave with pay at least once during an official's career in order that he may enter the Buddhist Monastic Order, as required by local tradition. Considering the religious and social values attached to serving in the Monastic Order, this special monastic leave is undoubtedly one of the major advantages of government employment.

Before the disastrous inflation of the currency following World War II, when the value of the baht slid from about US$·40 to $·05, the civil service paid very well and provided a comfortable and secure livelihood, and some observers suggest that the postwar corruption has more than made up for any losses through inflation, at least for some. Except for gross misconduct or malpractice, a civil servant is seldom discharged. He may retire after 25 years service with a pension and bonus. He and his family are entitled to free medical care in government hospitals, and his children may be educated in private schools at half the tuition rates charged others. At least part of public housing projects has been reserved for officials.

Many educated Thai enter the professions, yet even this often means working for the government, as teachers in government schools or doctors in government hopitals. Some Thai are found in business pursuits, and the government has long tried to stimulate this trend. Yet the average Thai would rather work for his government than for any other organization, and it has continued to be the major employer of Thai middle school graduates. The director of the largest government commercial school in Bangkok—established to train Thai boys for business careers—admitted to the author that almost all his graduates, by preference as much as necessity, have gone to work for the government. Those pursuing higher education as well think primarily in terms of future goverment employment.

According to Thompson (1941: 244) up to 1925 the government had readily absorbed all male graduates of the middle schools. In 1934, even after government lists had been drastically reduced, some 78,000 persons, 1·19% of the male population of the Kingdom, worked for the government. The census report for 1947 shows over 210,000 persons directly employed by the government—about 15% of the total non-farming working population of the country—and the percentage would be even higher were we to count the employees of semi-government organizations like the railroads and the communications services.

The bureaucracy has swelled steadily as new services are added to the government, yet increases in population, and the numbers seeking employment at all levels, in particular the growing number of middle school graduates, have made it progressively more difficult for government offices to absorb all who expect employment. The pressure was felt more than thirty years ago, and the first step was taken in 1925 to relieve the situation when King Prajadhipok introduced the Civil Service and Pensions Act, one provision of which required that all applicants for government employment be of Thai nationality. More recently the government has urged the Thai to look elsewhere for employment, principally to the only other major labour market, commerce and industry. To clear the way, and at the same time to win back some measure of control over the country's economy, the government has instituted a number of limitations on alien economic activities.

## GOVERNMENT RESTRICTIONS ON THE CHINESE

The dominant influence of the Chinese over the Thai economy went virtually unquestioned until the early years of this century when a sense of uneasiness about this minority's power began to pervade the leadership group in the government. The nascent anti-Chinese attitudes of this period may possibly be traced to the influential Western advisors to the Thai government, particularly the British in this group. Few felt friendly toward the Chinese, for reasons which we can only surmise. For one thing, they carried to Thailand a prejudice against trade as a way of life and of merchants who used their money to gain social position to which their family background and education did not entitle them. Moreover, they quickly saw parallels between the Jewish concern with commerce in Europe and the interests of Chinese merchants in Southeast Asia; what was a prejudice against Jews in London became in Bangkok a prejudice against Chinese. It is worth noting that the most venomous expression of anti-Chinese feelings published at this time was written in 1914 by King Vajiravudh (Rama VI), who because of an English education and long residence abroad was more English in his interests than he was Thai. In his articles, published under a pseudonym, the King referred to the overseas Chinese as the 'Jews of the Orient' and excoriated them for their calculated exploitation of Thailand's bountiful hospitality (Landon 1941: 22–43). It was not until the Revolution of 1932, however, that this latent anti-Sinicism came to the fore and found ready expression in restrictive legislation aimed at the Chinese.

The first constitutional government after the Revolution came into office at a very inauspicious moment when the entire world was feeling the effects of the Western economic depression. Poor world markets for her rice, rubber, tin and teak meant a smaller national income for Thailand and decreasing revenues for the government. Rather than an expansion of the bureaucracy, nationalist leaders like Pridi Phanomyong advocated a reduction in size and at the same time measures to stimulate an interest in commerce among the Thai people as an alternative to government employment. To this end a Thai Chamber of Commerce, distinct from the Chinese Chamber of Commerce, was established in 1934 to promote purely Thai business ventures. These early efforts failed —most educated Thai continued to petition the government for jobs. As the national leadership shifted from civilian to military men in the latter 1930s, and ultra nationalists like Phibun Songgram came to the fore, a more aggressive and comprehensive anti-Chinese policy was instituted.

This policy had two immediate objectives. One was to gain administrative control over Chinese businesses which heretofore had successfully evaded government efforts at supervision and regulation. To this end all businesses were required to register with the authorities, sign-boards in foreign languages had to include Thai translations, and firms were ordered to keep their accounts in Thai so that they might be more easily inspected. Within a short time an income tax and business tax were instituted which, it was anticipated, would bear most heavily on Chinese merchants. A second objective of the government was to force Chinese (and other foreigners) from certain commercial fields, thereby creating employment for Thai nationals and, perhaps of more importance, permitting the immediate nationalization of revenue-producing industries.

The dearth of Thai with vocational and commercial skills soon became apparent, and the government subsequently established vocational and commercial schools to train Thai youth in such skills as carpentry, cabinet making, barbering, typing, shorthand, accounting, etc. This, however, was a later development of the government's policy. Direct restrictions on Chinese economic activities, regarded as a popular shortcut solution to the Chinese problem, initially won the attention of the country's new leaders.

Landon (1941: 219–259) provides the best summary discussion of measures directed against the Chinese, as well as other foreigners, before World War II. Beginning in December 1938, when Luang Phibun Songgram assumed the premiership, and running through the following year, the blows against foreign interests fell almost capriciously on large and small alike. The measues taken included the following:

1. *The formation of the government-controlled Thai Rice Company with the avowed purpose of ending Chinese control of the rice industry*. The Thai Rice Company was to buy, mill, and export rice in direct competition with Chinese companies. It was an ambitious but premature plan, and from the very beginning the Company found itself dependent upon Chinese know-how and labour. Chinese millers sold their factories to the government at handsome profits and then assumed managerial posts in the Thai Rice Company. Despite concessions from the government, the Thai Rice Company apparently failed to cut deeply into the Chinese rice industry. It was, however, an ominous presage of the strongly nationalist temper of the new government.

2. *A law reserving the bird's-nest concession to the government or its agents*. The nest of the swift (there are eight species of swiftlets of the genus *collocalia* which make edible nests) forms the main ingredient of the famous 'bird's-nest soup' prized by Chinese everywhere as a gourmet's delicacy. The concession to collect

these nests from islands off the coast of Thailand had formerly been given to Chinese firms who exported them at a handsome profit throughout Asia.

3. *The 'Salt and Tobacco Act' passed in March 1939 which put the salt and tobacco industries under government control.* The majority of salt producers and the leading salt exporting companies were Chinese, and these were soon forced out of business. As with the bird's-nest concession restriction, the number of persons involved was not large, but the suddenness of the restriction came as a shock to the entire Chinese community. Nationalization of the tobacco industry was not, strictly speaking, an entirely anti-Chinese measure. Both Chinese and European firms produced cigarettes in Thailand, and both were eventually forced to sell out to the government. However, in the Thai Tobacco Monopoly which was eventually established no immediate attempt was made to eliminate Chinese managers or workers, a sensible policy inasmuch as the prerequisite skills were lacking among the Thai.

4. *A regulation of the Ministry of Education forbidding alien food hawkers to sell their wares in the environs of the Ministry and on the grounds of government schools in Bangkok.* Later the same year other ministries likewise forbade alien vendors to sell their wares on government premises, and the restriction spread from Bangkok to the provinces. The Thai are noted for their enjoyment of snacks throughout the day, and food vendors do a thriving business near government offices and schools, especially so since these places lack their own cafeterias. Chinese vendors have long had an important stake in this business, and these restrictions, when rigorously enforced, could have threatened the livelihood of a considerable number of low-income families.

5. *A law governing the slaughtering industry*, the intent of which was to put this industry and the retailing of meat in the hands of Thai nationals. This act is understandable only as an ultra-nationalist measure, for there was less demand by Thai for jobs as butchers than probably any other occupation. The Thai then as now abhor the deliberate killing of animals as a gross violation of a fundamental Buddhist teaching that all life, human and animal, is sacred; the good Thai Buddhist will not even kill insects, so strongly is this teaching held. Undoubtedly, this law encouraged some Thai to enter the slaughtering industry but the net result must have been minimal. This industry, as well as the retailing of meat, is today

firmly in Chinese hands, a good indication that this law did not seriously affect many Chinese.

6. *A law restricting the driving of vehicles for hire to Thai nationals.* Henceforth aliens were no longer issued licences to drive taxis, buses and trucks. Judging by the situation at the present time, this law was strictly enforced, and the opportunities to become drivers and chauffeurs quickly seized by the Thai. In 1939 there were probably not a great many persons, aliens or Thai nationals, engaged as hired drivers, and not many aliens to be forced out of these occupations. Thus this was scarcely a catastrophic blow to the livelihood of many Chinese. Coming in the wake of other restrictions, however, it served to unsettle further any Chinese confidence in the future, and thereby weakened the economic position of the entire Chinese community.

7. *The 'Siamese Vessels Act of 1939'.* This restricted ownership of ships trading within Thai waters to Thai nationals or companies in which the partners or stockholders were predominantly Thai. The law also provided that not less than 75 per cent of a crew manning a Thai vessel in Thai waters must be Thai.

8. *The 'Fishing Act of 1939'* reserved the right to fish in Thailand's territorial waters to Thai nationals.

9. *The 'Liquid Fuels Act'* sought to give the government control over the processing and marketing of gasoline and oil throughout the Kingdom. Following this measure, the two foreign companies, Shell and Standard Oil, withdrew completely from Thailand. Immediately after the war, however, this law was repealed and the oil industry again turned over to private companies.

In addition, the government proclaimed its intention during that turbulent year of 1939 to establish a number of Thai co-operative societies in rural areas to compete directly with Chinese rice-millers and middlemen, and to operate government tin mines and thus eliminate dependence on Chinese and British mines in southern Thailand. The government also declared its intention to control the rubber industry which was then as now principally a Chinese enterprise in southern Thailand.

By the end of 1939, the nationalist upsurge responsible for these various anti-foreign measures seems to have run its course, and no further economic limitations on aliens were written into law until the full flood of the war years. From late 1941 until the end of the war in 1945 Thailand was a Japanese military base; she officially counted herself an ally of Japan and the declared enemy of such allied nations as the United States and Britain. These circumstances encouraged a revival of extreme nationalism and further restrictions affecting the Chinese in particular. A Royal Decree of June 2, 1942 specified twenty-seven different occupations and professions that were henceforth to be 'reserved only to the Thai in all the localities throughout the Kingdom' [2]—and this time the list struck directly at many Chinese entrepreneurs and retailers. In 1949 this Royal Decree was superseded by another, which reduced the number of restricted occupations to seven but retained the principle of reserving certain occupations for the Thai people.[3] In 1952, two more occupations—female hair dressing and dressmaking—were added to the list of those reserved for Thai only. Strictly speaking, these prohibitions applied to aliens only, i.e. non-Thai nationals. Offspring of Chinese, if they were born in Thailand and would thus claim Thai citizenship, were not affected. There is evidence that the laws were in fact interpreted to make this distinction between aliens and offspring of aliens.

There has been no further *legislative* curtailment of Chinese economic activities since the 1952 decree. However, the Government has extended the restrictions on aliens through the issuance of ministerial regulations and directives, in which form they attract much less publicity but lose nothing in effectiveness. Moreover, anti-Chinese practices are often carried out as the personal policy of an official in the course of administering his department, with the tacit approval, if not the encouragement, of the government.

Understandably government offices maintain a discreet silence on this subject, but the local Chinese newspapers quickly pass along to their readers any suggestion of discriminatory practices. It must be emphasized that newspapers in Thailand are frequently inaccurate or dishonest in their reporting; consequently one cannot judge accurately the extent and the nature of the restrictions directed at the Chinese. There is little doubt, however, that the anti-Chinese measures mentioned in these newspaper reports would be immediately approved by Thai inside and outside government circles. Moreover, whether these restrictions are fact or only rumour, they are believed by Chinese reading local newspapers and thus shape Chinese attitudes as much as laws actually on the books. There follows a sample of what newspaper readers were told in 1951–1952 of limitations on the Chinese.

According to reports in Bangkok newspapers: (i) Chinese are no longer chosen as retail agents of tobacco, wine, sugar or canned goods produced by government factories; (ii) butchers' permits are not being issued to Chinese; (iii) the Ministry of the Interior has forbidden alien vendors of drinks or foodstuffs to sell or bring their goods into Ministry offices, and has instructed municipalities throughout the country to forbid aliens to monopolize stalls in food markets; (iv) aliens will be barred from selling cloth for use by Buddhist monks or as religious offerings; (v) aliens will not be allowed to own coffee shops; (vi) they will not be permitted to drive tricycles for the private use of others; (vii) aliens will be forbidden to sell pork at retail; (viii) aliens have been forbidden to serve as porters or hawkers in railway stations; these occupations are being reserved for Thai nationals; (ix) a survey is being made of the construction industry and various skilled trades to determine which to close to aliens; (x) the Civil Service will order the discharge from government offices and organizations not only aliens (a small number are employed as specialists and in menial occupations) but all persons of alien parentage, i.e. locally-born offspring of Chinese aliens; (xi) the railways, a government organization, will no longer do business with alien-owned transport companies, such as trucking concerns, which might sabotage the transport system in the event of war; (xii) alien-held leases of silos near railway stations will not be renewed when they expire; (xiii) alien's dock licenses will not be extended beyond their expiration dates; (xiv) the government intends to give its own Thai Rice Company a monopoly over all rice exports (which have long been the province of Chinese firms); (xv) the government will nationalize all trade and commerce in order to terminate alien control of business which has been responsible for the rising cost of living.

Such rumours and reports, endemic in the postwar period, point to the conclusion that the government is actively considering increasing the number of occupations and professions reserved for Thai nationals only, despite official disclaimers and some opposition from liberal political groups. Proponents of this legislation were strengthened by Marshal Sarit's seizure of power in 1957. According to reports from the Interior Ministry in late 1958, an additional thirteen occupations would soon be labelled 'For Thai Nationals Only'. The list is strongly reminiscent of the 1942 law, cited earlier, and would include umbrella-making; hand-weaving; brick-making; fruit gardening; the manufacture of mattresses and pillows; of bamboo and rattan articles; and the production of coconuts, sugar and charcoal. In addition Chinese might be barred from operating boats along the country's rivers and canals. The reason given for such legislation: 'to protect the people from the industrious Chinese community in Thailand'. It was admitted, however, that previous restrictive laws had not been effective, mainly because many second and third generation Chinese could validly claim to be Thai nationals and thus not subject to the restrictions.

The possibility of requiring all businesses to employ a certain proportion of Thai nationals, and thus a smaller proportion of aliens, has been considered for many years. Landon (1941: 242) mentions that in late 1939 all factories, both government-owned or private, were ordered to employ at least 75 per cent Thai labour; but there is no evidence that such a regulation, if indeed issued, was ever enforced. Early in 1950 Premier Phibun was quoted as saying that the government planned legislation requiring every foreign firm, including small Chinese shops, to employ a 'certain percentage' of Thai. By 1952 a bill was introduced into the National Assembly which would have required every business to hire at least two Thai nationals, but again nothing came of it. In 1956, however, the long-sought legislation was finally enacted, but in a much milder form than observers had anticipated. Under the 'Vocational Assistance to Thai Act, B.E.2499', industries, trades and businesses with ten or more employees will be required to have a certain percentage of their employees of Thai nationality, the percentage to be determined later but not to exceed 50 per cent. Immediately a survey of all businesses in the Bangkok area was begun as a preliminary to the setting of definite percentages and enforcement of the law. In January 1959 the first list of ten small industries required to employ a minimum of 50 per cent Thai nationals (if more than ten workers were employed) was announced: welding; metal plating; shoe-making; furniture manufacturing; weaving; automobile construction and repair; motor cycle construction and repair; construction, assemblying, and repair of radios; building construction; and match factories.

What will this latest measure mean for the Chinese community? Virtually all the industries listed are indeed in Chinese hands, but this does not mean that a significant turnover in labour will occur. Firstly, all the industries listed are small and even in total their employees would not account for much in the entire labour force.

Secondly, alien workers already employed in these industries will be allowed to retain their jobs; only newly-employed workers must be Thai nationals until the required ratio is attained. Any firms, of course, may employ Thailand-born Chinese, offspring of Chinese immigrant parents born in Thailand, who have legitimate claims to Thai citizenship. Those of this group who have up to this time not claimed Thai nationality, in order to avoid onerous military service, may now find compelling economic reasons to do so. Thailand-born Chinese as well as aliens may thus be stimulated to apply for naturalization. In short, this decree is not likely to do what its sponsors apparently hope, that is, increase employment opportunities for 'pure' Thai, but it will force a section of the Chinese community to decide whether it wishes to remain Chinese in nationality, and pay the price, or accept the responsibilities of Thai citizenship.

A clue to the possible effect of this measure on Chinese enterprise is provided by what has already happened to certain Western firms in Thailand. The government has for years impressed upon these firms that it does not favour their employing Chinese alien labour, and most have stopped hiring Chinese whenever possible. An informal survey of the three largest European firms in Bangkok in 1951 showed this to be the case. The 600 employees of Firm A, a saw-mill, included no Chinese aliens; the 300 employees of Firm B, export-import house, included but two Chinese; and the 200 employees of Firm C, also an export-import house, included four Chinese aliens. These firms are free to hire the Thailand-born children of Chinese aliens, if these have retained their Thai nationality, and there are sufficient numbers of these so that the firms have not suffered in the least from a shortage of qualified labour.

### EFFECT OF RESTRICTIONS

In considering the effect of the numerous restrictions, actual and proposed, we need repeat here as elsewhere, that the Chinese are not singled out for discrimination in the strict legal sense. No law has ever been enacted specifically denying to the Chinese in Thailand rights which are granted to other alien groups. On the contrary, the very laws which partisans of the Chinese regard as tantamount to persecution are applicable to *all* aliens without exception. Almost all the measures cited above are directed at the genus 'aliens'. The Thai government is careful to have restrictive laws and regulations apply to all aliens in the execution of measures which affect its Chinese minority. By following this course Thailand has successfully countered charges, brought by both the Chinese Nationalist and Chinese Communist Governments, that it has singled out the Chinese minority for discrimination and persecution.

The fact is, however, that the Chinese constitute far and away the largest alien group in the Kingdom. The 1947 census reported the presence in Thailand of some 527,000 aliens of whom 476,582 were Chinese nationals. In other words, almost nine out of every ten aliens at that time were Chinese. Consequently this community is most affected by measures directed toward aliens in general, a fact which official statements concerning impartiality cannot hide. Moreover, since restrictions placed on aliens have always been concerned with activities in which Chinese are prominent, if not predominant, it is obvious that the Chinese, rather than aliens in general, are the prime target. The government measures mentioned above are basically anti-Chinese and are regarded as such by the Chinese in Thailand.

Yet the simple cataloguing of these restrictions may create an erroneous impression of their total effect. Thus far, this minority as a group has not been greatly disturbed economically, although individuals certainly have suffered. The group's freedom of action has been somewhat circumscribed perhaps, but it would be a gross exaggeration to conclude that the Chinese in Thailand are an oppressed minority. Some reasons for the ineffectiveness of these economic measures may be advanced. First, the occupational restrictions actually enforced have rarely touched the callings which are the main economic foundations of the Chinese community, particularly retail shopkeeping, peddling, rice-milling and vending and saw-milling. Second, by acquiring Thai nationality (through naturalization), using Thai names for business purposes, taking on Thai citizens as dummy business partners, registering a business in the name of a wife or child who is a Thai citizen, or simply by buying licenses and bribing officials, Chinese aliens have circumvented the restrictions which apply directly to their occupations. It is commonly said that the Chinese can buy their way around almost any restriction, despite the government's warning that any alien found trying to bribe Thai nationals in order to obtain rights denied to aliens would be deported and his property confiscated, and his Thai confederate sentenced to ten years' imprisonment or subject to a fine of 20,000 baht.

A further reason for the ineffectiveness of restrictions is that restrictive legislation is often not well enforced. Barbering, for example, has been restricted to Thai nationals since 1941, yet a survey made by the Bangkok Municipality in 1949 showed that fully 62 per cent of Bangkok's barbers were Chinese aliens, and that more than half the barber shops were owned by Chinese. (*Bangkok Post*, March 3, 1949). It appears that only when Thai individuals are able and willing to engage in the occupations reserved for them is the exclusion of aliens enforced. This explains the frequent reiteration of restrictions in the matter of hawking food and drink on government premises, and the butchering and retailing of meat. The restrictions remain on the books, however, and can be enforced whenever circumstances seem to warrant; thus they are a handy threat for purposes of coercion.

The working assumption underlying many of these restrictive measures and plans is that the Thai people are excluded from commercial occupations because the Chinese have monopolized all trade opportunities. Trade and industry in the Kingdom are dominated by Chinese, and Chinese immigrants and their descendants do comprise the majority of the labour force in commercial occupations. Yet this is only part of the picture. The Chinese younger generation by reason of practical training, often in family enterprises, have the essential skills and know-how for business careers, far more than the average Thai, and it is natural that the former would be preferred by both Chinese and Western business concerns, even if no other considerations entered into their employment. Moreover, man for man, the Chinese are more diligent, more careful workers than the Thai. Even the Thai when they want a job done and done well—building a house, for example—will hire Chinese rather than Thai workers.

Finally, as we have pointed out earlier, an important part of the explanation for continued Chinese domination of the trades and of commerce is that many Thai do not regard these occupations as the most desirable. The ambitious Thai young man only too often prefers to work for the government, and this basic value has not been greatly affected by the various measures instituted to break the trade monopoly of the Chinese. This statement should not obscure the fact that traditional values are weakening, and that in the future we can expect many more Thai to seek their livelihood in the crafts and in commerce. As the statistics on occupations cited earlier indicate, many Thai have already entered these fields, undoubtedly encouraged by the government measures to protect their interests. Many more will do so as vocational and technical schools turn out an increasing number of Thai with skills useful to commerce and industry.

While the Chinese minority has not yet been seriously affected economically, these varied restrictive measures, and even broader range of threatened limitations, have had two general consequences of a curiously opposite nature. It has been impossible to disguise the basically anti-Chinese motivation behind the restrictions, actual and proposed, and this patent fact has drawn the rank and file Chinese closer together in their various protective associations: the trade guilds, dialect associations, and the Chinese Chamber of Commerce. The second-generation no less than the first-generation Chinese value the buffer services of these ethnic organizations. The first consequence, therefore, is a strengthening of cohesion within the Chinese community.

The second consequence is a development of closer ties with the élite members of Thai society. The larger Chinese business men, in order to protect their extensive interests from economic controls and eventually nationalization, have formed financial alliances with leading Thai politicians and military men, who are simply made directors of Chinese companies at a handsome remuneration. A person with substantial financial interests in a business is not likely to destroy it. By the end of 1952, it is estimated that 'hundreds of government officials and other members of the Thai élite were either fully "cut in" on Chinese businesses or serving on the boards of Chinese firms in a "protective" capacity [and] a majority of the most influential Chinese leaders had formal business connections with government officials and other members of the new Thai élite' (Skinner 1958: 187). There is little evidence that these Thai were more than paper directors, and individuals kept their positions only so long as they remained politically powerful and thus useful to their Chinese friends, but on the higher levels both groups found good reasons to work together. This development stands in rather marked contrast to the apparent conflict of economic interests one finds at the lower economic levels.

### LAND OWNERSHIP AND RESIDENCE RESTRICTIONS

In considering the economic limitations on the Chinese minority, mention should be made of one further restriction, that concerning land ownership, and one additional chauvinistic threat, to force all aliens to live in special reservations. The latter in particular provides a good example of the kind of thing which does nothing to solve any problem but which helps to hold the entire Chinese community together, thus impeding the attainment of the very goal sought by the government, to curtail the minority's in-group solidarity and influence.

In 1943, with the passage of a law entitled 'Land Pertaining to Aliens Act, B.E. 2486' Thailand's free-and-easy attitude toward alien land acquisition abruptly changed. All aliens were henceforth denied the right to purchase or otherwise acquire land for any purpose. The only exception recognized were aliens whose homelands had concluded treaties with Thailand specifically permitting the ownership of immovable property. Inasmuch as China has no such treaty with Thailand, the Chinese have felt the full weight of this restriction. To the Chinese, who see only the effect upon them, the law seems directed at them specifically, and they regard it as further evidence of the anti-Chinese attitude of the government. The fact is that the law is not overtly directed against the Chinese—Chinese as such are not mentioned in this legislation—and so far as interpretation by Thai officials is concerned, it has been made to apply with equal force to all aliens, Westerners as well as Chinese. Yet as the largest alien group, the Chinese cannot but be affected more frequently than other foreigners.

Apart from the fact that it was a war-time measure, enacted at a time when ultra-nationalists were in the saddle, it is difficult to understand the rationale for this measure. Despite the absence of any such restriction prior to 1943, there is little evidence that the Chinese or other aliens were acquiring extensive holdings of land. Thailand has a surplus of good farmland, much of it still uncultivated. Unlike the Indian minority in neighbouring Burma, the Chinese through their moneylending practices in the rice growing areas were not dispossessing Thai farmers and becoming absentee landholders. Farm tenancy prevails in Thailand but the landowners are Thai, not foreigners.

As with other restrictive measures, Chinese and other aliens have found ways to evade the intent of the law. Land is purchased in the name of wives or children who have Thai nationality, or through Thai friends. In the latter case, the Thai buys the land and registers it in his name, but signs a note or a mortgage for the full value to his Chinese friend. Yet even these loopholes are being gradually closed, for the Chinese at least. Thus a Bangkok newspaper reported early in 1952 that 'the Ministry of the Interior has requested the Lands Department to study carefully all transactions for sale or mortgaging of land in order to prevent land being indirectly owned by aliens'. The government was said to be taking steps 'to prevent aliens from buying land under the names of Thai citizens', and the Ministry of the Interior emphasized 'that wives or children have no right to purchase land for their husband or father'. According to reports, provincial governors have received an official circular warning against land sales to Chinese through the intermediary of Thai nationals. The circular declared that land so purchased would be promptly expropriated.

For the rank and file Chinese in the cities and towns, the most common means of adjusting to this situation is to rent the land desired but to own buildings on this land. Ordinarily a plot of land is leased for a ten-year period, without buildings, and at a low figure. Buildings are erected by the lessee for his own use or to be sub-leased. At the expiration of the land lease, all buildings become the property of the landlord. In cities like Bangkok this practice leads to cheap construction, concentration of the Chinese in a few over-crowded areas, high rentals, and little security for the lessee or tenants. It cannot be regarded as a desirable substitute for the ownership of land as a means of encouraging immigrants to put down roots in the new country.

Yet even renting land or buildings to Chinese has been discouraged. In certain provinces Thai have been cautioned not to rent their lands to aliens for business purposes because this would 'make it impossible for Thai people to earn an independent living of their own in the future'. The Royal Estates Department has reportedly been instructed not to renew alien-held leases, but to reclaim land for use by Thai nationals when leases expired.

A case can be made for restrictions on the activities of aliens in order to protect the interests of citizens. It is more difficult, however, to justify discrimination against Thai citizens of Chinese extraction. Yet one finds such discrimination in several spheres as the previous discussion of restrictive measures has indicated. The government's land policy provides further illustration of this. It is reliably reported, for example, that in some localities officials now require prospective land buyers to prove Thai ancestry for three generations, failing which the application is rejected. Bangkok newspapers reported that the Public Welfare Department, in announcing the completion of a low-cost housing project in Bangkok in 1951, informed applicants that not only must they be Thai citizens but their grandfather must have been born in Thailand. A cabinet decision of August 1952 limited the leasing of Crown land to 'pure' Thai or ex-servicemen only, and subsequently an order was issued that Thai nationals born of alien fathers and still using alien surnames were to be prevented from acquiring rights to any land. All these measures point to the fact that in the eyes of some officials there are two classes of citizens, only one of which, the 'pure' Thai, is accorded full citizenship rights.

Before the War, the Chinese were not restricted in the areas in which they might live or engage in business, although during the War they, along with other aliens, were forced out of certain designated military areas. Chinese were not segregated or interned as were other aliens whose governments were at war with Japan. They were too important in the national economy and too numerous, of course, to be interned.

Since the end of the War, however, sporadic demands have arisen from various official quarters for residential restrictions on the Chinese, and indeed plans to do this, ostensibly to improve internal security, are already being carried out. These measures, while directed at aliens in general, affect the Chinese more than other foreigners and are prompted essentially by fears of a Chinese fifth column in the event of Communist disturbances.

A bill giving the government extraordinary powers, including the authority to remove aliens from strategic areas, in the event of a national emergency, was passed by the National Assembly in February 1952. Officials were instructed to purchase land if necessary from alien owners (acquired legally before 1943) in these areas and under no circumstances to renew leases of government land to aliens. Farther than this the Government declared it had no intention of going until the Kingdom was actually in a state of national emergency. However, a spate of disturbing rumours and accounts of restrictions on the Chinese began to appear in the Chinese press. It was reported that aliens, i.e. Chinese, would soon be forbidden to live within ten kilometres of rivers, railways, bridges, and dams, or adjacent to police stations—enforcement of such a restriction would force virtually every Chinese in Thailand to move! At Chainat, the site in central Thailand of a large dam, the entire Chinese community was said to fear forced removal. One newspaper declared that some provincial authorities had already begun to act:

> The order to move out aliens from certain places was already carried out in Prachinburi. According to a person from the province: Chinese doing business around the provincial train station have been notified to get ready to move out. Although the time was not stated, this has been a shock to the Chinese. According to the Interior Ministry's order, this task should be fulfilled within this year. (*Chung-yüan wan-pao*, February 12, 1952)

Chinese living in certain provincial areas likely to be declared restricted areas in the event of a national emergency began to move elsewhere, greatly 'annoyed and frightened', as one paper reported.

Undoubtedly the newspapers were guilty of deliberate exaggeration for few Chinese appear to have been removed. But, on the other hand, there is no evidence the government, or the officials responsible for the alleged near-panic in certain communities, took effective steps to scotch the rumours or reassure the Chinese of its intentions. The Chinese Communist government, always eager to champion the rights of the overseas Chinese for its own ends, quickly made the most of the situation, and by radio and press itself assured the Chinese in Thailand that it was giving serious consideration to their plight.

An obvious manifestation of this latent anti-foreign sentiment occurred late in 1951, when a bill designed to oust all aliens from the Province of Bangkok and twenty-seven other provinces was introduced into the National Assembly. Under this bill aliens would have been 'deported' from the restricted areas within sixty days after its passage, with the Chinese obviously most seriously affected. This bill was lost in the confusion following the November *coup d'état*, in which the military leaders simply dismissed the National Assembly. Yet the idea of segregation was not forgotten, and three months later the Director General of Police, General Phao Sriyanon, one of the most influential politicians in Thailand at the time, stated publicly that the government intended to set aside a part of each province in which aliens would be forced to live. This procedure, he declared, was modelled on American policy with regard to minorities! The Emergency Administration Bill approved by the new National Assembly in 1952 did not quite confirm General Phao's opinion. The measure provided only that in the event an Emergency is declared, the government may forthwith forbid aliens to enter into any place required to safeguard the stability or safety of the Kingdom. This could apply, of course, to any place where Chinese presently reside or do business.

Nevertheless, the idea of restricted areas for aliens has continued to appeal to certain Thai leaders as a short-cut solution to the problem of the Chinese minority, as the following recent quotations from the Bangkok press indicate:

> After attending a Cabinet meeting, Premier Thanom [head of the government which replaced that of Phibun Songgram following the 1957 *coup d'état*] said yesterday that in his opinion the proposal for setting up overseas Chinese residential areas would be convenient for official control. He pointed out the fact that there are 'Chinese Towns' in the Philippines and the United States. (*Shih-chieh* and *Hsin-pao*, May 27, 1958)
>
> Prince Wan, the Thai Foreign Minister, was asked by reporters for his opinion about limiting aliens to certain residential areas. He replied that he knows nothing about this matter because it only concerns the Ministry of Interior. He added, however, that the government has the right to restrict aliens to certain areas, but that a committee must be established to make rules for such an action. (*Siam Radh*, May 28, 1958)
>
> Nai Suraphong Trirat, Mayor of Bangkok, told reporters that it had been found that all the recent fires in Bangkok and Thonburi had been caused by Chinese. He added that these fires had not only caused damage to the Chinese but also to Thais who were living nearby. He went on to say that he was of the opinion that as fires broke out frequently in the municipal areas and these had all been lighted by Chinese, the latter ought to be placed in restricted areas in order to control them more easily and prevent cases of arson.
> (*Siam Radh*, *Siam Nikorn*, *Chao Thai*, November 12, 1958)

Other leaders, and ones with more authority for carrying out such a measure, have rejected the idea as both impractical and unjust, and thus far their opinions have been a sufficient deterrent.

Such schemes as this, and other restrictions on the Chinese in Thailand, are based on the assumption that what hurts the Chinese will help Thailand. A more serious error could scarcely be conceived. The Chinese are the most energetic and capable element, from the viewpoint of commercial know-how, in Thailand's population. Their talents and interests and capital are essential to the further development and improvement of the country's economy. The problem, as other Southeast Asian governments have learned by experience, is not how legally to throttle Chinese enterprise and initiative but rather how best to encourage its further development for the good of the entire country.

CHAPTER VII

# CHINESE SCHOOLS AND EDUCATION

THE Chinese in Thailand, like their compatriots in the other nations of Southeast Asia, have organized Chinese schools for both boys and girls, making it possible, until recently, for their children to obtain both primary and secondary education within the cultural boundaries of the Chinese community.[1] The growth of Chinese schools has coincided roughly with the modern development of a Thai system of popular education. Formal education for the Thai traditionally was entrusted to Buddhist monks in monastery schools, but for the last several decades, under the impetus of westernization, education has become increasingly a matter of secular interest. Direct government concern for education dates from 1891 when the Ministry of Education was first organized and given jurisdiction over all schools throughout the Kingdom. A Primary School Law passed in 1921 made education compulsory. There is now an extensive government-supported educational system, from primary schools to national universities which compares favourably with the educational program of any other Southeast Asian country.

The lines between these two educational systems were initially sharply defined. Thai schools, using the Thai language as the sole medium of instruction, prepared students for life in a Thai cultural milieu; the other was unmistakably and almost aggressively Chinese, and its medium and content of instruction not greatly different from that of schools in China itself. Conflicts between the government and the Chinese community over the latter's schools arose and grew in intensity, fired by the development of nationalism in China and in Thailand. The Chinese quite rightly recognized their schools as the most effective institutions beyond the family itself for imparting their own cultural values and patterns to the younger generation; the cohesion of their community depended on the maintenance of these values and patterns. Significantly, the first serious restrictions on Chinese activities in Thailand were in the field of education, an indication that the government had also correctly assessed the strategic role of Chinese schools as barriers to the integration of this minority.

Restrictions on Chinese schools have sometimes been half-hearted, often opportunistic, and, by Chinese community standards, arbitrary and unjust. No other Southeast Asian government has gone so far in limiting the scope of Chinese education. As a result of these controls, and of pressures arising within the Chinese community for changes in educational procedures, the lines between Thai and Chinese schools have been blurred; Chinese schools have increasingly become Thai schools where special, but minor, attention is given to Chinese instruction. In the field of education, therefore, a long stride has been taken toward the acculturation of the Chinese minority. Other Southeast Asian governments are already copying the education policies of the Thai government regarding the Chinese.

## RISE AND DECLINE OF CHINESE EDUCATION

Schools in Thailand can be separated into two general categories: government schools, or those operated by the central government and municipalities; and private schools, or those established by non-official organizations and individuals, and deriving most of their support from tuition fees. Private schools in turn include Thai schools in which Thai is the principal medium of instruction, western missionary schools which offer instruction in both Thai and English, and Chinese schools—the latter are simply private schools in which Chinese is one medium of instruction and whose curriculum includes Chinese subject matter, history, literature, geography, and so on. The Thai government, until recently, called these institutions 'Chinese Language Schools'—although strictly speaking even today they are more than that—but Ministry of Education officials are now inclined to regard them as Thai private schools which differ from other schools in that they are allowed to use Chinese for certain courses. Otherwise these schools must conform to the same curriculum requirements as other Thai schools and the Ministry of Education exercises direct control over them through its Private School Section.

Whether established by private persons or community organizations, Chinese schools have three sources of revenue. All schools charge tuition fees and in the cases of those run by individuals, these fees account for all income; contributions from community-minded merchants and organizations provide continuing assistance for schools operated by associations; and in recent years the Thai government itself has granted Chinese schools a small subsidy—this is more of a reward for performance than a major source of support, however.

The economic aspect of education should not be minimized when seeking reasons for the rise and persistence of Chinese schools. By almost any standard, school construction costs in tropical Thailand are low, and usually only classrooms with simple wooden benches need be provided. Unburdened by large capital expenses and assured moreover of a steady demand for education, schools have often become quite profitable businesses in themselves. Historically, however, other considerations have been of greater importance to the development of Chinese schools.

An interest in education was shown by the earliest Chinese settlers in the nineteenth century—the American Presbyterian Mission in 1852 established a school 'for the sons of Chinese'—but not until the 1911 revolutionary ferment reached the overseas Chinese did the minority in Thailand make a concerted effort to establish their own schools. The Hua-yi school founded in 1909 by followers of Dr Sun Yat-sen marked the beginning of overseas Chinese education in Thailand. This school, looked upon by many Chinese as a revolutionary institution, used Teochiu, or the Swatow dialect, as the language of instruction, although its financial support came from all dialect groups. A Hakka school was established in 1913, a Cantonese in 1914, a Fukinese in 1915, and a Hainanese school in 1921. The first Chinese girls school was founded in 1917. By 1920 there were about thirty Chinese primary schools in Thailand. In 1925 two Teochiu-sponsored institutions, the Chung-hua School and the Hing-min School, were amalgamated and renamed the Pei-ming Middle School, the first Chinese secondary school to be opened in Thailand. By 1932, on the eve of the Thai revolution, there were some 200 Chinese schools in Thailand, of which six were middle and normal schools.

These schools, writes Graham (1924: 256–257) 'were at first looked upon by the Siamese with suspicion, as it was thought that they inculcated revolutionary principles and checked that free mixing of Chinese and Siamese blood which had been so much to the advantage of Siam'. By 1924 Graham (256–257) reported 'large numbers of boys and girls, children of immigrant Chinese merchants and shopkeepers' attending Chinese schools. Landon (1941: 267) connects the rise of these schools during this period with the increased immigration of Chinese women, and the consequent establishment of the all-Chinese home 'by which Chinese social and cultural life was strengthened'. Skinner (1956: 169) sees the increase in Chinese schools as a response to the demands of the growing Chinese business community: 'The usefulness of efficient bookkeeping and filing in large firms, the introduction of banking, the greater reliance on correspondence with Chinese firms in Singapore and Hongkong'—all these drove home to the Chinese in very practical terms the need for greater literacy in Chinese. Many things were involved—pride in one's cultural heritage, Chinese nationalism, economic opportunism, shortage of adequate alternative educational institutions, and, not to be overlooked, the sudden availability of teachers as intellectuals fled the chaotic conditions and economic depression in China in the decade after 1920.

Whatever the reasons, Chinese schools mushroomed throughout Thailand. Statistics on Chinese education, like data on virtually every phase of life in Thailand, are apt to be confused. According to official records, 1933–34 saw the greatest number of Chinese schools: 271 in the whole of Thailand. (*Statistical Year-Book* 1933–34, 1934–35: 418). Landon (1941: 264), however, cites 1936–37 with almost 260 schools as the peak year. If not simply schools but number of pupils are taken as the crucial index, then the year 1937–38, with a total of 16,711 pupils in Chinese primary, middle, and normal schools, is the prewar high-water mark in Chinese education. It is generally agreed that only after 1939 did the number of Chinese schools, and the number of pupils in those schools, decrease drastically, as the following table indicates:

8. CHINESE SCHOOLS IN THAILAND AND IN BANGKOK PROVINCE

| *Year* | *Primary* | *Secondary* | *Special* | *Total Schools* |
|---|---|---|---|---|
| 1937-38 | 197 (99)* | 20 (9) | 13 (11) | 230 (119) |
| 1938-39 | 187 (104) | 25 (14) | 6 (6) | 218 (124) |
| 1939-40 | 38 (10) | 9 (6) | 14 (3) | 61 (19) |
| 1940 | 6 (6) | 2 (2) | 8 (6) | 16 (14) |
| 1941 | 2 (2) | — (–) | 1 (–) | 3 (2) |
| 1942 | 2 (2) | — (–) | 3 (2) | 5 (4) |
| 1943 | 2 (2) | — (–) | 2 (1) | 4 (3) |
| 1944 | — (–) | — (–) | 2 (1) | 2 (1) |

NOTE: Figures in parentheses show the number of schools in Bangkok Province (*Statistical Year-Book of Thailand*, 1939-44: 127).[2]

Reasons for the decline are to be found not in the Chinese community but in the steadily growing opposition from the Thai government after the 1932 Revolution. While the absolute monarchy had initiated controls on Chinese schools, the demands were minimal and either easily met or as easily ignored. The Private Schools Act of 1918, for example, extending government control over all private schools, required schools to register with the Ministry of Education and fulfil other demands: principals had to be literate in Thai and the Thai language had to be taught at least three hours per week. We can doubt that this law was ever strictly enforced, however. The essentially benevolent attitude of the government toward Chinese education is exemplified by a speech King Prajadhipok delivered to Chinese schools in Bangkok during a tour of inspection in 1927. In this speech he accepted the principle of Chinese education and simply urged Chinese pupils to be good Thai as well as good Chinese:

> I thank you all most sincerely for the excellent arrangements you have made to receive me on this occasion; for they reflect your friendly feelings towards me. My object in paying visits to your schools is to show my friendship to the Chinese who are resident in this country, and also as a token of my goodwill towards the schools themselves.
>
> The Chinese merchants have established these schools for the education of their children in their own tongue, to fit them for future commercial and other careers. Apart from their education in Chinese, you also give them facilities to learn Siamese and acquire other forms of knowledge of this country. The schools therefore are very useful; for, in addition to providing children with knowledge which will enable them the better to take up their future professions they also make it possible for the Chinese to know more of the country they live in; and an ability to read and write in the vernacular will certainly place them on a more intimate footing with the Siamese.
>
> The Chinese race may be said to be akin to the Siamese race. In this country Siamese blood and Chinese blood have mixed in such a manner that in many cases it is impossible to separate them. A large number of high officials, both active and retired, have Chinese blood in them. I myself have some Chinese blood in me. Again, many Chinese have lived in this country so long that they have become Siamese. For these reasons the Siamese and Chinese have lived amicably together for generations. I do not wish for anything better than that they should continue to live thus harmoniously for all time. I trust that you have the same feeling as I do in this respect and that you will teach your children to entertain such sentiment. In your schools, you teach your students to love their motherland, that is, China; that is natural and quite right. But apart from teaching them to love China, I trust that you will also teach them to love Siam; for you who live in this country have received good treatment from the Government, and are given rights equal to the Siamese themselves. You are happy and prosperous in this country, and the firm standing of Siam must be your desire. If Siam is faced with dangers and suffer therefrom, unhappiness equal to that of the Siamese will be your lot. I trust therefore that your feeling towards enemies of the Siamese Government, internal or external, is that of detestation, and that if occasion should arise, you would be possessed of a desire to assist in their destruction. Should Siam at any time come face to face with danger, it is my hope that assistance will be forthcoming from the Chinese.
>
> If you will try to inspire in Chinese children such a feeling as I have mentioned, the Siamese and the Chinese will certainly live amicably

> together. Such reciprocal friendly feeling will be a source of happiness to both, who are racially akin, and enable them to exist in perpetual harmony.
>
> In conclusion, I wish the Chinese merchants and householders, the teachers and pupils of the schools, who are assembled here, complete happiness, absence of ailments, strength in body and mind, and success in their enterprises.

The Thai Revolution of 1932 which overthrew the absolute monarchy provided the justification for a more intransigent policy. The revolutionary 'coup group' consciously sought to consolidate its position by replacing the old popular loyalty to the King with a new loyalty to the Nation. Accordingly, Thai nationalism was deliberately encouraged as a means of unifying all the people. Chinese schools which served to perpetuate minority differences and to extol an alien way of life were a divisive force, splitting part of the nation from its new leaders. Furthermore, the revolutionary government was pledged to the promotion of education so as to create a population that was 50 per cent literate in the Thai language within a ten-year period; when that standard of literacy had been attained, the reins of government, held temporarily by the 'coup group', would be given over to the people. Chinese schools with their emphasis on the learning of an alien language rather than Thai subverted this basic objective of the Revolution.

The offensive against Chinese schools was soon opened. One of the first targets was instruction in Chinese. In 1933 regulations were drawn up limiting the time which might be devoted to studies in a foreign language, such as Chinese, to no more than six of the 28 hours in the school week (Landon 1941: 271). A later law (Private School Act of 1936: Section 20) stipulated that no subject might be taught in a foreign language without the specific approval of the Minister of Education. By 1939 this law was being interpreted so as to restrict the teaching of Chinese to only two hours each week in Chinese primary schools, although secondary schools were permitted to teach and to use Chinese as a language of instruction for 18 hours each week (Landon 1941: 277).

In addition to the language restrictions, two other controls were instituted. The first concerned qualifications of teachers. Educational authorities began strictly to enforce a regulation requiring alien teachers to pass the fourth *pratome* (primary grade) examination in the Thai language before being licensed to teach. Hitherto teachers had been permitted to defer this examination almost indefinitely. This order together with the limitation of instruction in Chinese, stopped the large-scale importation of Chinese teachers, and thus had a fundamental effect on Chinese schools: from now on their staffs contained an increasing proportion of local-born teachers who by interest and ability were much less effective mediums for the inculcation of Chinese cultural values.

The second control concerned the content of instruction. Chinese schools, together with all other private schools, were made to conform to the more rigorous regulations of the Ministry of Education regarding syllabi, schedules and textbooks. The government banned books used in Chinese schools which were 'so patriotically Chinese so as to stand in the way of the pupils' assimilation of the new Thai national spirit', or which were anti-foreign or which dealt with political theories, such as Communism, objectionable to the government. In 1934 a list of some fifty banned books was published; in 1938 an additional 43 books were proscribed.

Schools which violated any regulations did so under threat of immediate closure. Initially goals outstripped means—without trained personnel supervision of all Chinese schools was impossible. Gradually regulations were more efficiently enforced, and as a consequence the number of Chinese schools, and pupils in schools, began to decrease. By 1941 there were no longer any Chinese secondary schools operating in the whole of Thailand, and by 1944 all Chinese primary schools as well had been closed. Chinese schools remained closed throughout World War II, partly in response to the demands of the Japanese military which dominated the Kingdom from late 1941 until the end of the War in 1945.

For a brief period after the end of World War II, when the government found itself unable to cope effectively with its many postwar problems, the number of Chinese schools, both licensed and unlicensed, shot up to over 450 (Skinner 1950: 8) with anywhere from 100,000 to 175,000 students, according to various estimates. But by 1947 order was restored; the government began to crack down, with a strict enforcement of controls. Many fly-by-night schools simply folded up; others had their licences revoked for violations of regulations. At this time the government introduced a new limitation on Chinese education: the banning without exception of all Chinese secondary schools. By the end of 1951 a total of 244 Chinese primary schools remained in the whole of Thailand, 40 of these located in Bangkok and in the neighbouring community of Thonburi. The Ministry of Education had earlier publicized its intention to license but 154 Chinese schools of all categories for the entire Kingdom. There has been no wholesale closing of schools, but the 154 goal is being gradually and quietly approached as Chinese schools are closed for one reason or another and the government follows a policy of granting few licences for new schools. By 1958, according to the Ministry of Education, only 185 Chinese schools remained in the entire Kingdom. The drop in school enrolment was even more spectacular: from well over 100,000 in 1948 to about 63,000 in 1958.

With the situation well in hand, the government has relaxed some prewar controls on Chinese schools. Primary schools now devote up to ten hours each week to instruction in Chinese, but schools which give only six hours to this language are rewarded by special government subsidy. On the other hand, the number of subjects which may be taught in Chinese has been cut to four: Chinese reading, Chinese writing, Manners and Behaviour, and Common Knowledge (an omnibus course which combines history and geography). Alien teachers are now given two years in which to pass the required examination in the Thai language, meanwhile teaching on a temporary licence. But examinations for teachers are now more thorough, re-examinations are more frequent, and no extension of the time limit can be expected. Scores of Chinese teachers have had their licences withdrawn because of failure to pass the language examinations.

The ban imposed on Chinese middle and normal schools remains, despite periodic requests from the Chinese community and the Embassy that it be removed. This means that Chinese education in Thailand is legally limited to the four years of primary school, plus one preparatory kindergarten year. In 1959 there were two Thai-language secondary schools in Bangkok, operated with financial backing from Chinese individuals and organizations, which had been given permission to teach Chinese as a foreign language in for a total of six hours weekly. But even this is regarded simply as an experiment, and its extension to other secondary schools is doubtful.

The postwar Communist scare has given the government additional justification for curtailing Chinese schools. Communist publications are banned from all schools (yet, paradoxically, schools are authorized to use pro-Communist Chinese textbooks). To eliminate the danger of a more subtle Communist influence, even Chinese songs must be specifically approved by the Ministry of Education before being sung in any school. The police have not hesitated to raid schools suspected of mixing Chinese and Communism, seizing teaching materials and taking principals and teachers into custody. Since 1950 a score or more Chinese schools in Bangkok and up-country have thus been closed down on charges of political activities. Police have begun to screen all private school teachers and to order teachers charged with Communist sympathies blacklisted. For a period beginning in 1954 special inspectors, usually retired police officers, were posted in all Chinese schools to make certain that all regulations were being followed.

While the objective of this determined campaign is to root out Communism in Chinese schools—and there is no reason to doubt the sincerity of this goal—the net effect, of course, is to eliminate not only Communism but Chinese schools as well, and on the whole to reduce further the influence of Chinese education in Thailand. Few Thai officials would regard this latter consequence as undesirable. The danger in this campaign, and in others in which the Chinese are involved, is that anti-Communism can become an excuse for essentially anti-Chinese measures.

One good rule of thumb in assessing the situation of the Chinese in Thailand is that no restriction should be taken completely at its face value. The Chinese have a well-deserved reputation for exploiting every possible loophole to avoid compliance with official controls. In general two legal loopholes in the educational regulations are used to teach Chinese. If a family has money, it can hire a private tutor. If not, night schools may be used. According to law a school is defined as having at least eight students; thus a Chinese tutor may enrol seven students, teach them for one hour only, and pass on to another group of seven students. In this way he can teach scores of students each day without having to register as a school or to obtain a teaching certificate. Moreover, night-schools, i.e. schools opening after 4 o'clock and running until 9 p.m., are not subject to the limitations on other private schools, and provide an easy way to give, legally, advanced instruction in Chinese. Kindergartens are not counted as part of the primary school programme, thus young children may be enrolled in Chinese kindergartens and given all beginning courses in Chinese, without breaking any educational regulation. The Chinese community will continue to use stratagems such as these, and the government will probably continue to ignore them, as being less dangerous. Its means for supervision and control, particularly in terms of qualified personnel in the Ministry of Education, have become increasingly efficient and effective. Unless there is a drastic change in the government's policy, Chinese schools will never again reach the peak they held in the immediate postwar years, but neither is it likely they will disappear entirely. What we can expect is the continuation of certain trends, to be discussed below, which have greatly altered Chinese education over the past two decades.

## CHANGES IN CHINESE SCHOOLS

Reasons for the government's recent tolerance may be found in the fact that Chinese schools have been largely divested of their once alien character. Judging by the composition of their teaching staffs, these schools are in fact more Thai than Chinese. Originally Chinese schools were taught by an all Chinese staff with the exception of a lone Thai language teacher. Now the reverse is typical: the staff of many a school is virtually all Thai, with only a few Chinese language instructors. Figures supplied by the Ministry of Education for registered Chinese schools in Bangkok illustrate this, for in each of these years cited Chinese schools employed more than twice as many Thai as Chinese teachers:

9. TEACHERS IN REGISTERED CHINESE SCHOOLS
THAI *vs.* CHINESE

| *Year* | *Thai Teachers* | *Chinese Teachers* |
|---|---|---|
| 1945 | 25 | 11 |
| 1946 | 89 | 37 |
| 1947 | 146 | 72 |
| 1948 | 255 | 98 |
| 1949 | 561 | 261 |
| 1950 | 558 | 254 |

In the postwar period Chinese teachers have become increasingly difficult to find, and more expensive when finally located. The Ministry of Education will accept only graduates of certain approved middle and normal schools in China—college graduates are not particularly welcomed—and all diplomas must be certified as genuine by the Chinese Embassy in Thailand. The candidate must, moreover, have a valid identity card and residence permit before applying to the Ministry of Education. There he must ordinarily use personal influence and strategically placed gifts to obtain approval in the form of a teaching certificate (qualifying him for a certain level of teaching at a specific school), and a licence. The permit is valid for two years only, after which he must take a Thai primary school diploma examination testing his knowledge of the Thai language. If he fails, he may get his licence extended for an additional two years, and take another test. If he fails again, he can never teach in Thailand.

This procedure, with known pitfalls and unexpected obstacles as well, has helped to reduce the number of qualified persons. Chinese teachers have become increasingly expensive, a good indication they are in short supply. Schools must pay Chinese language teachers twice as much as Thai teachers. Illustrative in this connection is the sitution at the Kwang-chiao School in Bangkok, the largest Chinese primary school, with over 1,700 students. The Kwang-chiao School employs 63 teachers, 23 (or about one-third) are Chinese language teachers. A Thai teacher at the school in 1959 received a salary of 400 baht monthly, while the average Chinese teacher received 800 baht monthly. Yet, even with this added incentive, it is almost impossible to secure new Chinese language teachers. Recruitment among the local-born Chinese has not been practicable. Men in this group prefer business careers to any of the professions, and women, who in other countries might be expected to fill the need for teachers, are still closely tied to the home. As the figures above show, it is Thai and Sino-Thai men and women, graduates of government teachers training colleges, who have stepped in to keep the Chinese schools in Thailand operating, and this indirect government help stands in rather startling contrast to the history of official opposition to Chinese schools.

The change we have noted above, in the composition of teaching staffs, has also served indirectly to reduce the number of Chinese schools. As teaching salaries have risen, schools operating on narrow profit margins have had to close down. Moreover, as Chinese schools generally have become more Thai in their faculties and content of instruction, and therefore less Chinese, individuals and groups in the Chinese community, who might ordinarily be counted upon to back Chinese cultural activities, have been less willing to extend financial support. One observer writes that 'probably more schools closed voluntarily for financial reasons between 1950 and 1954 than were ordered closed by the government for political activities or failure to conform to other regulations'. (Skinner 1957: 370)

We have already called attention to the restrictions on the use of Chinese in all schools; this now amounts to only two hours daily maximum, and for many schools only one hour a day is devoted to Chinese. But even in these remaining Chinese-language courses the content of instruction has been 'nationalized' in recent years because of textbook changes, and this has further reduced the schools' 'Chinese' character. Before the War, textbooks used in Chinese schools in Southeast Asia were published mainly by two large printing concerns in China (the Commercial Press and the Chung-hwa Book Company, both in Shanghai) and were identical with textbooks used in China itself. Thus, pupils attending Chinese schools in Thailand were given as strong an indoctrination of Chinese nationalism as students in China proper; China was accorded paramount attention, invariably referred to as 'our country', and little attempt was made to foster an appreciation of local Southeast Asian traditions and history.

Such texts, however, were patently out of place in the new post-war world of Southeast Asia; local government demanded less emphasis on China, and more on their own country. About 1950 a group of publishers in Singapore established the Shanghai Book Company there, presumably with Chinese Communist funds, to bring out Chinese school texts especially suitable for Malaya and other countries of Southeast Asia. In these books expressions of extreme Chinese nationalism were carefully avoided, while at the same time attention was given to political and social developments in Southeast Asia. In 1951 the Shanghai Book Company texts were approved by the Thai government for use in all Chinese primary schools, replacing thereby the old prewar books.

To combat the pro-Communist influence of the Shanghai Book Company texts, the Chi-sheng Book Company was organized in Hong Kong, with the backing of Nationalist China, to publish Chinese texts to meet local needs in Southeast Asia. These likewise made an honest effort to reduce to a minimum Chinese nationalism, without, however, eliminating an appreciation of China; for example, these books reproduced both the Thai and Chinese Nationalist flags, side by side, with the text under the Chinese flag reading, 'Respect your national flag', and that under the Thai flag, 'Love your country's flag'. In 1957 a series of the Chi-sheng Company texts were published for Chinese schools in Thailand and subsequently approved by the Thai Ministry of Education; these were to be used as alternatives to those of the Shanghai Book Company by any school so wishing.

Whether the books used are Communist or Nationalist inspired, pupils in Chinese schools in Thailand today are devoting more attention and time to Thailand, and less to China, as compared to prewar days, and are urged to think of Thailand as their 'own country' rather than identifying exclusively with China. Undoubtedly these changes have helped to weaken the divisive and separatist nature of Chinese schools and to encourage the government to take a more tolerant view of these institutions. Yet with the present drastic reduction in hours devoted to Chinese instruction and a further watering of Chinese courses, a student gets now only a very attenuated knowledge of Chinese history, literature and geography, and a limited ability to read Chinese. Chinese schools in Thailand have long been noted for their poor quality when compared to those elsewhere in Southeast Asia; these latest changes serve to weaken them further as mediums of Chinese knowledge. The effect of this will be discussed later.

Probably one of the most important forces changing the character of Chinese education is the realization on the part of parents that a very practical value accrues from knowing the Thai language. The success which second-generation Chinese have had in business, even surpassing their fathers in many instances, is popularly attributed in no small measure to their fluency in Thai and their facility in a Thai cultural *milieu*. Before the War, the normal reaction of Chinese parents impatient with restrictions on Chinese schools in Thailand was to send their children overseas for a Chinese education. In the 1930's thousands of children were despatched to China and to Chinese schools in Malaya. It is now clearly evident that such children were done a gross disservice, for they returned to Thailand as cultural misfits, unable to speak or read Thai with the fluency required for business, burdened with alien values and knowledge and, in short, greatly handicapped in efforts to make a living in Thailand. It is paradoxical that many of these people who spent years acquiring a completely Chinese education in China, now spend years of study at private night-schools in Bangkok learning the Thai language which they were sent to China initially to avoid learning.

Chinese parents have had to be shown by experience that education cannot be entirely Chinese if it is to be economically useful. In 1933 the government's attempts to reduce the Chinese instruction and correspondingly increase that of Thai provoked an outburst of popular indignation—sponsored by nine prominent members of the Chinese community a petition of protest signed by over six thousand parents and three hundred business firms was presented to the government (Landon 1941: 271). But in 1951 the revocation of the teaching licences of several score Chinese teachers, because of their failure to qualify in Thai, raised only a flicker of interest. One very effective lever to gain voluntary compliance with the Ministry of Education's standards is the requirement that graduates of all primary schools, whether Chinese or Thai, pass the same Thai language qualifying examination; failure to pass this examination means the student does not get a primary school certificate and cannot continue his education in any middle school in Thailand. His education ends after four short years, which is a severe penalty for people who put an exceedingly high value on education.

Both Thai and English are recognized now as essential commercial languages, and the Chinese Chamber of Commerce periodically requests permission to open a combined commercial secondary school which would teach Thai and English rather than Chinese. Today Chinese parents eagerly enroll their children in Western-type secondary schools in Bangkok run by Christian missionaries, Catholic and Protestant, rather than send them to Chinese schools abroad. These schools teach no Chinese and emphasize Thai and English instruction. Changes have certainly occurred in Chinese thinking about their schools, but it is reasonable to conclude that the social and economic factors mentioned above—the scarcity of Chinese teachers and the practical value of knowing the Thai language and Thai customs—have been at least as instrumental in bringing about the present attitude as arbitrary government controls and restriction on Chinese education.

### PERSISTENCE OF CHINESE SCHOOLS

Although the alien character of Chinese schools has been considerably modified during the past twenty years, we have no evidence that the Chinese community has given up its desire for separate schools. Public schools can be a great assimilative force both for immigrants and their children, but the maintenance of separate schools by any group serves to perpetuate differences and thus retard social integration. Why do Chinese schools persist? Both the Chinese minority and the Thai Government furnish the answer to this question.

Chinese schools, even in their present form, help to perpetuate Chinese culture and nationalism. This has been the basis for the government's opposition to these schools from the beginning, but it is also one reason for the Chinese community's desire to maintain them. Chinese schools provide virtually the only means by which spoken and written Chinese of the Mandarin dialect, the *kuo-yü* or national language of China now, can be learned. Moreover, because of the high level of illiteracy among the immigrant Chinese, it is only in these schools, or by private instruction, that a child can learn written Chinese in any dialect. The 1937 census showed a total of some 576,000 aliens in Thailand aged ten years and over. Of these, 357,100 (about sixty per cent) were reported to be illiterate. Since eight out of ten persons listed as 'aliens' were Chinese, these figures can be interpreted as referring particularly to the literacy level of the Chinese. As immigrants are supposed to have passed a literacy test as a requirement for entry into Thailand (a test frequently avoided through connivance with inspectors), possibly many illiterate Chinese claimed to be literate in the census tabulations. A more accurate measure of literacy, and of ability to use written Chinese, is provided by data on educational level of aliens. The 1937 census reports that of the 576,000 aliens counted, less than 20,000 (about five per cent) had completed primary school. Even for native speakers, written Chinese presents formidable difficulties; usually several years of schooling are required for even a minimal fluency in Chinese characters. It can be assumed, therefore, that the great majority of Chinese aliens in Thailand who had not completed primary school were for all practical purposes illiterate. Exceedingly few of these immigrants speak Mandarin, nor do they pick up a knowledge of this national Chinese language after arriving in Thailand. Ordinarily immigrants speak only their local dialect, Cantonese, Hakka, Teochiu, Hainanese, or Fukienese, and acquire some fluency in Teochiu (if not native speakers) because this latter dialect is useful in business transactions.

Thus the low-income Chinese immigrant home differs from those of immigrant groups in Western countries in its inability to pass on to the second generation the national language of the homeland. Yet there is a compelling demand throughout the community for this kind of cultural connection with the homeland, and it is thus only through the Chinese school that this demand can be satisfied. Chinese parents are not interested in producing scholars in the classical sense, but they do insist that their children be able to read and write Chinese. Participation in the normal day-to-day life of the community requires that one know written Chinese, and conversely, a person's inability to read and write Chinese severely limits the range of his activities. Many shop signs are in Chinese characters only. Even to clerk in a Chinese store a boy must know written Chinese since most bills and notices from other companies are in Chinese. Bulletin board notices and all publications of Chinese associations are in Chinese. The home shrines, the ancestor tablets found in Chinese temples, the genealogies displayed sometimes at the surname clubs are all in Chinese, as are wedding and birthday party invitations and funeral notices. Given these social, religious, and economic values associated with the written language, it is little wonder that efforts to eliminate Chinese schools altogether, or to restrict drastically the teaching of Chinese, have met with such emotional resistance from the entire Chinese community. Very few schools, even with the incentive of the special grant from the government, have reduced their Chinese language instruction to six hours per week. The ten hours weekly that may now be devoted to Chinese language work gives students only a fair fluency in written and spoken Chinese. Newspapers and modern novels may be read without undue difficulty, but the Chinese classics, with their special vocabulary, are beyond students' ability.

Ordinary Thai schools do not teach Chinese with the recent exception noted earlier. In the 1930's some government schools offered Chinese, but instruction in this language was gradually reduced until by 1939, according to Landon (1941: 277) only one government school in Bangkok taught Chinese and only two students were studying this language. Understandably the government has been unwilling to promote Chinese in its schools while curtailing the use of this language in Chinese institutions. In 1951 inquiries revealed that no Thai schools in Bangkok were using Chinese as a language of instruction, but two government schools were offering Mandarin Chinese as a foreign language. One of these, a secondary school, found the response so poor that officials planned to drop this elective from the curriculum. The Bangkok Commercial School, a secondary vocational school, has taught spoken and written Chinese for about 20 years as a required subject for all students, according to the headmaster, but very few Chinese students attend this school. The fact that the Chinese have neither used the facilities of the few Thai schools where Chinese is taught, nor petitioned the Educational Ministry for increased Chinese language instruction in Thai primary schools, suggests that Chinese schools satisfy other needs, apart from formal language instruction, which Thai schools by their very nature cannot fulfil.

Chinese parents declare that Thai schools fail to impart proper 'moral training' and perhaps in this somewhat vague objection can be found the basic reason for the persistence of Chinese education. These schools, the most important institution outside the home for the growing child, are a means by which children can be insulated to a certain degree from Thai society and its alien influences, and herein lies probably their strongest appeal to parents eager to preserve their cultural identity in a foreign land. The child who attends a Chinese school not only is taught about China and impressed with her cultural achievements—more so than in any Thai school—but of immediate importance he makes playmates and companions of other Chinese children, and associations with these over the years serve to reinforce his attachment to Chinese rather than exclusively Thai standards. The acquisition of 'bad habits' which Chinese parents attribute to mixing with Thai companions is therefore avoided. Conditions which might lead to intermarriage between the two ethnic groups are also avoided, while those favouring marriages within the Chinese community are encouraged. This latter consideration is significant in view of the fact that Chinese parents are permitting their children a greater freedom in the choice of a marriage partner—yet despite this trend, ethnic endogamy continues to prevail within the Chinese community.

The foregoing does not imply that children of Chinese descent seldom form friendships with Thai children. Ethnic lines are by no means that exclusive; indeed, it is the rare Chinese who does not have one or more Thai friends whom he has known well for years. But the child who attends a Chinese school has fewer opportunities and reason for forming close friendships. What he may do outside of school is another matter, but at least such friendships lack the common identification of a shared educational experience, and are so much the weaker. Nor has the abolition of Chinese secondary schools helped to break down ethnic divisions. Observers note that many Thai secondary schools established by Chinese associations or individuals attract not a mixed group of students from Thai and Chinese homes but almost entirely those from

Chinese homes. Thus, these schools constitute a divisive force within Thai society.

The schools serve another function which is hardly realized by the Chinese themselves. Although all Chinese schools teach Mandarin, but no other Chinese dialects, they provide invaluable opportunities for children to learn the local dialects, especially the commercially useful Teochiu, through contacts with schoolmates, friends, and acquaintances who are native speakers of these dialects. Second-generation non-Teochiu Chinese questioned on this matter report learning Teochiu by associating with Teochiu companions. Chinese schools provide one of the best means for the learning of this dialect for children from other dialect groups.

Despite the fact that the Thai government is ostensibly hostile to the principle of Chinese schools, much of the responsibility for the persistence of these schools can be placed with the government itself for two reasons. First, the Thai educational system has directly encouraged the development of private schools, of which Chinese schools are an important part, as an essential adjunct to government schools. In fact the government has assisted Chinese schools to meet their operating costs. Secondly, although the government has at times curtailed the number of Chinese schools in Thailand, it has been slow to provide adequate substitute public education which might attract the children of Chinese immigrants.

The Ministry of Education defines academic standards and qualifications for a first-class private school. Private schools are encouraged to fulfil these qualifications, i.e. improve their plant, facilities, and instruction, so as to receive official recognition. Only schools so recognized, as first class institutions, are eligible for government assistance. The government will lend money for the construction and enlarging of private institutions, and government subsidies are given to private schools with good records. The 1948 budget carried an item of eight million baht (equivalent to US $400,000) for private schools aid (United Nations: 1950:14) and as education costs have risen since that time, the government's measure of help to private schools has also gone up. For example, in 1952, when the salaries of teachers in government schools were increased, the Minister of Education asked that the government's subsidies to private schools be increased to enable these schools to raise salaries also; the request was subsequently approved and an item of two million baht was added to the sum to be allocated to private schools. The following figures obtained from the Ministry of Education, shows the total education budget and the amount ear-marked for private schools:

10. THAILAND'S BUDGET FOR EDUCATION AND AID TO PRIVATE SCHOOL
*(in Baht)*

| *Year* | *Total Budget* | *Private School Aid* |
|---|---|---|
| 1949 | 95,989,761 | 9,875,000 |
| 1950 | 128,796,786 | 13,895,624 |
| 1951 | 158,392,280 | 24,055,000 |
| 1952 | 215,545,022 | 29,745,559 |
| 1953 | 273,139,779 | 37,530,000 |
| 1954 | 300,987,713 | 39,991,000 |
| 1955 | 250,979,271 | 44,320,500 |
| 1956 | 268,719,768 | 45,562,500 |
| 1957 | 277,681,590 | 60,660,500 |

Chinese schools are always included in this program of aid. When their records are satisfactory, and all regulations have been observed, they too are given subsidies by the government to enable them to meet operating expenses. A typical Chinese school in Bangkok in 1951, according to its principal, received the following support from the government: for each student enrolled, the school was paid four baht a year (one baht worth about U.S. $·05). With 1,500 students, this school received a yearly sum of 6,000 baht. For each teacher, Thai and Chinese, the government allotted the school (which in turn gave the teacher) 200 baht; teachers holding the highest teaching certificate were paid 400 baht, in addition to the regular salary received from the school. Such payments are equivalent normally to about half a month's salary for each teacher. A brief survey in 1959 showed a somewhat different system of subsidy for Chinese schools. For those teaching but six hours of Chinese weekly the government allotted 12 baht per student yearly and for each teacher with a permanent licence, 100 baht yearly. The total amount received by one large Chinese primary school was well over 25,000 baht yearly from the Thai government. While these subsidies account for only a small part of the total expenses, they are a factor in enabling these schools to meet their responsibilities and thus keep their doors open.

From the very beginning of compulsory education, some thirty years ago, Thailand has met the growing demand for schools only with the help of private institutions, which include Chinese schools. The Primary School Law of 1921 required every child between the ages of seven and fourteen to attend school regularly. This law was not enforced evenly throughout the entire Kingdom, yet in the first decade the number of pupils grew from 241,508 to 788,846, and swamped the government's facilities. For a time storerooms and pavilions in *wat* (Buddhist temples) were turned into schools, and Buddhist monks, resuming their traditional role in education, took charge of government schools. Gradually school buildings were erected and more lay teachers trained, yet through the 1930's crowding was severe and standards remained low. One observer writing of this period declared that 'to obtain salutary results is a superhuman task. Only the most primary of primary education can be expected.' (Landon 1939: 125). This was, incidentally, the very period when Chinese schools had their phenomenal growth, and it may well be that the obvious inadequacies of government schools provided the Chinese community with further justification for establishing a separate, and more effective, school system. An indication of the inadequacy of Thai educational facilities is shown by the fact that by 1934 only one-third of those eligible had attained a primary education. Kindergarten and pre-nursery education was virtually neglected, and only private schools were concerned with these levels of schooling.

The demands on the educational system have increased since the end of World War II, throwing a still greater burden on the already overcrowded government schools. In 1951 a shortage of 10,000 primary school teachers was reported, and according to estimates government school facilities were then available to only two out of every 500 pupils seeking enrolment. Still the plight of government schools would be even worse if there were not hundreds of private schools to take some of the burden from government institutions.[3] In short, the government has 'solved' its education problem by encouraging the development of private schools. It has thus avoided the large expenditure necessary to expand its own school system. This policy has undoubtedly saved money, but it has scarcely touched what we must regard as the number one internal problem of the Thai government: the integration of the Chinese minority. Assimilation very often begins in a public school classroom, and until Thailand has a top-notch school system which will draw in all children, much of the separatism which characterizes the Chinese minority will be perpetuated.

Whether Thailand can afford a modern public school system is another question. Educational expenditures, expressed as a percentage of the national budget, increased only from 13·3% in 1937–38 to 14·3% in 1948.[4] During this period and continuing to the present, expansion of the military and police establishments took an increasingly larger share of government revenues, making it that much more difficult to allocate funds for education. Paradoxically, the Chinese provide an excuse for much of this military expansion in recent years. To counter the threat of aggression from Red China, Thailand has greatly expanded and modernized her armed forces, and to meet the danger to internal security posed, in part, by the large Chinese minority, the police organization has been similarly enlarged and equipped. The military danger has seemed the more pressing, thus government funds have been more easily diverted to military expenditures than to education, and the educational aspect of the minority problem put off for another time.

## FUTURE PROSPECTS

Judging by the decline in numbers of schools—from 271 in 1933–34 to 195 in 1956—Chinese education has suffered a marked setback during the past 25 years. If, however, the number of children attending Chinese schools are compared—17,000 during 1937–38 and 63,000 today—then we can only conclude that Chinese education is in a stronger position today than two decades ago, even taking into consideration increases in the Chinese minority population during that period. Until we have further data it would be premature to speak, therefore, of a decline in Chinese education.

There can be no doubt, however, that the Chinese character of the education offered by these schools has indeed declined during the past three decades. Today there are fewer Chinese teachers, fewer hours devoted to Chinese, fewer subjects taught in Chinese, and a much thinner coverage of China and her culture in the textbooks used by all schools.

These changes in turn have made it exceptionally difficult for students from Thailand to continue their education in Chinese colleges and universities of both Mainland China and Taiwan. Taiwan's experience with such overseas Chinese students is that they require several years of preparatory work in special schools before reaching the language level required by a Chinese university or technical school, and without a doubt the Communist government has had comparable disappointments with its overseas students. This adds years to one's education, frustrates ambitions, and in the long run dims perceptably the appeal of education in a Chinese institution of higher learning. Understandably, therefore, more and more locally born Chinese in Thailand are enrolling in Thai universities and technical schools. A poll taken of the students at Bangkok's universities in 1957 showed that fully twenty-five per cent of the students had at least one parent who was Chinese, and ten per cent of the students could either read or speak Chinese, suggesting that these local institutions are attracting a considerable number of close descendants of Chinese immigrants.

One exception to the general trend toward Thai and away from Chinese education must be noted, however. South Thailand seems to have become a special centre of Chinese culture in education at least, more so than Bangkok itself. Reports indicate that it is customary for Chinese families to send their children to Chinese primary and secondary schools in Penang and other centres in Malaya, with which South Thailand has closer economic and cultural ties than with Bangkok. These students presumably would be more interested in continuing their Chinese education at university level in Mainland China and Taiwan, and better prepared educationally to do so.

Chinese schools have shown themselves to be adaptive institutions responsive to both the needs of the Chinese community and the demands of the government. Like schools everywhere, they face the perennial task of fitting their programmes to the needs of the society in which their students will live and work. The Chinese are far too practical to support a school system which is patently out of touch with reality, and inasmuch as Chinese schools are almost entirely dependent upon voluntary support, they must satisfy local demands. We can expect, then, that Chinese schools, if they are to survive at all, will adjust to certain trends whose influence is unmistakable.

The first of these is Thai nationalism, which demands political loyalty and, negatively, opposes all influences which might weaken national unity. Communism and foreign nationalism are alike anathema. If indeed Chinese schools become vehicles for either, then their doom is sealed. Even if Thailand came under the control of a group far more leftist than now runs the country, there is good reason to doubt that *Chinese* Communism would be tolerated. In its subtle flavour, Chinese education in Thailand may well continue to be pro-Communist, pro-Kuomintang, and pro-China, but it must be obviously and unmistakably pro-Thailand first of all. If the postwar battle of the textbooks is an indication, all but the extremists in the Chinese community know and accept this, as have indeed both the Communist and Nationalist Chinese governments. Rather than a source of separatist sentiment, Chinese schools will increasingly become the means by which the Chinese minority identifies with the larger Thai society, although this process of mutual adjustment would be more rapid if there were but one school system unifying the entire nation.

Another major influence is the accelerated Westernization of Thailand, along with other countries of Asia. If Chinese are to hold their present preeminent position in Southeast Asian economies which are fast coming under direct and indirect Western influence, they must acquire the skills increasingly demanded of business leaders and institutions: fluency in Western languages, particularly English, and the ability to apply Western techniques of accounting, business management, advertising, and sales promotion. The younger generation must also be trained to enter such rapidly expanding professional fields as medicine, dentistry, nursing, teaching, law and engineering. Chinese schools have lagged behind both Thai and missionary schools in the amount and quality of English instruction.

Up to the present no attention has been given to commercial training as such in any Chinese schools, a curious fact indeed considering the pre-eminent commercial interests of this minority; and until very recently they simply ignored English-language instruction. A good example of what Chinese schools might do in this connection is provided by some western missionary schools in Bangkok, both Protestant and Catholic. These offer a curriculum weighted with English-language work and practical commercial subjects. The outstanding example is Assumption Commercial College, a Catholic-run secondary school for boys, which has become so popular among the Chinese that its student body is now almost completely Chinese. Local institutions wanting to emulate it are handicapped by a shortage of both qualified instructors and teaching materials; however by 1959 two Thai secondary schools (Shih-dai and Mei-kwai), established in Bangkok with Chinese community backing (and catering principally to Chinese youth), were giving special emphasis to English-language instruction, using in fact the Assumption College text books. In a single year the Shih-dai School had doubled its enrolment, a good indication of the popular demand for this kind of instruction.

Two pressing and immediate problems will speed the Chinese community toward acceptance of modifications in its thinking about education. One, not new, has never been more serious. It is the unmasked impatience of the present government, and a large part of the Thai people, with a militant, demanding, troublesome minority; not only are concessions of any kind unpopular but to demand them, or to offer any organized opposition, would encourage repressive measures by the government against the Chinese. Other governments are setting similar examples of intolerance in this regard: the Philippines' efforts to exclude the Chinese from retail trade and the Indonesian government's removal of all aliens retailers from the rural areas. For the overseas Chinese, this is the time to compromise, to remove the sources of friction, and so far as education is concerned, to accept integration rather than seek separation.

The second problem concerns young Chinese who normally would enter Chinese middle schools were these allowed to open. Observers estimate that only ten per cent of the graduates of Chinese primary schools now go on to Thai secondary schools, and that less than one per cent leave Thailand to continue their education elsewhere. There is reason to believe that until recently the graduates of Chinese primary schools were too deficient in Thai-language work to enter Thai secondary schools; the graduates of Chinese secondary schools, when these were open, certainly did not qualify for Thai higher education. The majority of Chinese youth today simply end their education at the halfway point, after four years of primary schooling, with serious consequences to their immediate adjustment and subsequent advancement financially and socially. Concern about these foot-loose young people will force the Chinese community to accept the Thai educational system as preferable to nothing. The best the community can hope for is government permission to establish private secondary schools in which Thai will be the medium of instruction with Chinese or English offered as a foreign language, along the lines of the Shih-dai School. This is likely to be the next most significant development in Chinese education, making of the schools a broad avenue leading to Thai and Western institutions of higher learning.

Chinese education in Thailand is entering a new phase in which the schools can do far more for assimilation and acculturation than they have previously. As changes occur in these pivotal institutions, it can be expected that organizations as well as individuals in the Chinese community will accept as normal a degree of integration with the dominant Thai society, something considered impossible only a decade ago. More essential than ever is there need for Thai leaders to encourage this development by accepting the Chinese as participating members of the larger community and to grant them the full rights of citizenship.

CHAPTER VIII

# CITIZENSHIP AND POLITICAL INTERESTS

THE average Chinese in Thailand is well aware of economic, occupational, and educational limitations imposed by the Thai government—probably one or another of these has pinched him personally. But few seem to know or indeed to care about the restrictions on citizenship, nationality rights, and political activities in general, nor are these restrictions given much publicity in the Chinese press. This merely points up the fact, recognized by all observers, that the overseas Chinese are primarily concerned with making a living, or amassing a fortune, and thus take only a passive interest in the formal political life of the country in which they live. In this disinterest in politics they differ not at all from the great majority of the Thai people, who since the establishment of a purportedly representative government twenty-five years ago have themselves been content to stand aside while a small group of intellectuals and military men run the country.

The government for its part has been loathe to welcome the Chinese immigrant and his immediate descendants into the Thai nation or to encourage an active interest in Thai political affairs. It must be recalled that the Chinese took no positive part in the 1932 Revolution when the absolute monarchy was replaced by the present constitutional government, and consequently gained nothing from that event. The new parliament had no members chosen by or representing as such the Kingdom's largest minority, nor was there any official specifically charged with presenting its views to the government. Indeed for the Chinese the 1932 Revolution marked the beginning of a harsher regime. To the new leaders, the absolute monarchy had been far too permissive with the Chinese, permitting them to gain an unusually privileged position economically and educationally. Rather than furthering privileges for this minority, Thai administrations since the Revolution have sought to erect barriers against Chinese influence and power, first in the fields of education and economics, and most recently in political activities. These latter have resulted specifically in limitations on citizenship, naturalization, and the rights of citizenship, the details of which will be discussed in the sections that follow.

However, the government's policy for the Chinese, or descendants of Chinese aliens, in this field follows a curiously vacillating course. Whereas in education and economic activities one can plot a steady line of limitations without any backsliding on the government's part, in the case of citizenship and nationality, the government has several times reversed itself, starting out with a liberal conception of rights, then drastically limiting these so far as aliens or their immediate descendants were concerned, and later rescinding these restrictions and returning to a more benevolent policy. All this points to divided opinion within the ranks of government leadership, and a flexibility in policy that is lacking in other spheres where the Chinese minority is concerned. It indicates, too, if we are to judge from the latest enlightened swing of opinion, a realization that members of the Chinese minority must be accepted into the Thai national society as citizens, whatever other limitations may be imposed on them.

## CITIZENSHIP BY BIRTH

The policy shifts that have occurred are well illustrated by laws which specify those categories of persons who are regarded as natural-born citizens. Thailand, like other nations of the world, traditionally took the position that any person born on her territory, regardless of the nationality of his parents, was a Thai citizen by birth. This *jus soli* principle of nationality was specifically recognized in the Kingdom's first nationality law, usually referred to now as the 'Law of R.S. 130', which became effective in 1913; the relevant part of this statute was the following:

SECTION 3. The following persons are Thai:

*i.* Every person born to a Thai father on Thai territory or abroad;
*ii.* Every person whose mother is a Thai and whose father is unknown;
*iii.* *Every person born on Thai Territory;*
*iv.* Every woman of foreign nationality who is married to a Thai;
*v.* Every alien who has acquired Thai nationality by naturalization.

The Nationality Act of B.E. 2495 (1952) reaffirmed this principle in SECTION 7 which declared the following persons to be Thai subjects by birth:

*i.* Any person, whether born within or outside the Kingdom, whose father is a Thai subject;
*ii.* Any person, whether born within or outside the Kingdom, whose mother is a Thai subject but who has no lawful father, or whose father is a person without any nationality;
*iii.* *Any person born within the Kingdom.*

These laws had the effect, therefore, of conferring Thai nationality on *all* local-born children of Chinese alien parents. The actual citizenship rights of such children, as will be shown subsequently, were often inferior to rights granted native-born citizens of Thai parents, but at least until 1952 they were considered a part of the Thai nation by reason of birth in Thailand.

Within a year of the 1952 law, however, the government had had second thoughts about its Chinese minority and abruptly rescinded its former liberal policy. Under the Nationality Act B.E. 2496 (1953) Section 7 of the 1952 Act, quoted above, was repealed and replaced by this provision:

SECTION 7. The following individuals shall receive Thai nationality at birth:

*i.* *Any person born of a Thai father either inside or outside the Kingdom;*

*ii.* Any person born of a Thai mother outside the Kingdom and an illegitimate father or a father having no nationality;

*iii.* *Any person born of a Thai mother inside the Kingdom.*

In brief, by 1953 only those persons having at least one Thai parent were granted citizenship by reason of birth in Thailand. Children of Chinese alien parents, although born in Thailand, were considered to be aliens, no different under the law from their parents born in China. If they wished later to obtain Thai nationality, they had to follow the same naturalization procedures prescribed for all aliens.

This was not so severe a blow as it might seem, however. Indeed, this 1953 law, which was tantamount to declaring local-born Chinese to be aliens henceforth, excited no comment whatsoever from the Chinese community. Reasons for this are not difficult to find. Up to very recent times Chinese immigrants have not been particularly eager for their children to become citizens of Thailand. Parents have deliberately ignored any rights their children might have had to Thai citizenship, whenever possible registering them as Chinese nationals. The compelling reason in the case of sons was military service. All Thai men when reaching the age of 18 are liable to compulsory military service in the armed forces. The Chinese in Thailand abhor the thought of their sons performing such service. It is not that the status of the soldier as such is considered degrading, but rather that they fear the effect of military life on their sons' characters. In the army, they insist, a boy associates with bad companions; divorced from the supervision of his parents, he becomes lazy and learns immoral ways. His character ruined, he becomes a burden to his family after leaving the service.

This reasoning sheds a revealing light on the Chinese view of Thai society. Inasmuch as a boy's companions in the armed services are mainly Thai and the values he learns are Thai, this is perhaps but another way of saying that to the Chinese the Thai way of life is undesirable. Aliens are not conscripted, thus one sure way to avoid military service is to claim alien status.

Thai nationality might be avoided in a number of ways. Some years ago, before vital statistical procedures were systematized, parents could delay registering births until a child was several years old, and then claim that he had only recently arrived from China. Or, if a child were sent to China for schooling, on his return to Thailand he entered the country as a Chinese alien, concealing the fact of his birth in Thailand. Later on, however, once such a person were safely past the age for military service, a shift to Thai nationality might be attempted, and he would claim now to be a Thai citizen to avoid payment of alien registration fees or to obtain other privileges of Thai citizenship. Ordinarily a second-generation Chinese would speak the Thai language fluently enough to pass easily as Thai; if the authorities investigated thoroughly, of course, he ran the risk of being exposed and punished with imprisonment or deportation.

In the light of these facts it would be easy to excuse the principle of the 1953 Nationality Act which denied citizenship to local-born children of alien parents. In the long run, however, this act had an unfortunate effect. It can be argued that the Chinese problem will be lessened to the extent that the Chinese minority is integrated into the Thai national life, as, in other words, the 'pro-Chinese community' group is decreased and the 'pro-Thai society' group is enlarged. This nationality act, however, did just the opposite. Many second-generation Chinese—all those whose parents were aliens—were denied any right to Thai nationality, treated under the law as aliens, and forced therefore to identify with the Chinese community. This is not the best way to facilitate the assimilation of any minority.

It was perhaps considerations such as these that led to a reversal of government policy and a restoration of the citizenship rights through the Nationality Act of B.E. 2499 (1956). This latest law states:

SECTION 3. The provisions of the Nationality Act of B.E. 2495 amended by the Nationality Act of B.E. 2496 are repealed and replaced by the following:

SECTION 7. The following are Thai by birth:

*i.* Any person whether born within or without the Kingdom whose father is Thai;

*ii.* Any person born outside the Kingdom of a Thai mother but having no lawful father or whose father is stateless;

*iii.* Any person born within the Kingdom.

SECTION 4. Any person born in the Thai Kingdom whose mother was not Thai while the Nationality Act of B.E. 2496 was in force shall have Thai Nationality.

The 1953 law is thus swept away and any local-born person denied citizenship under its provisions is through the 1956 law granted citizenship automatically. This more liberal policy is restored at an auspicious time, for the Chinese are more willing today to accept Thai nationality status, presumably because of the economic advantages that go with such status. There remains the disadvantage of military service, which all male citizens may be called upon to perform. But methods short of deliberate denaturalization have been evolved by the Chinese minority to avoid such service. For one thing, although all males register, those to be called up are chosen by a national lottery, the rest are exempted; thus a person has at least a 50-50 chance of not being called up. Moreover, if selected, he can be rejected on physical grounds, and local Chinese claim that Thai army doctors co-operate willingly, for a price, in finding reasons for rejecting certain draftees. Or, if finally selected for service, through a judiciously placed request to the proper official a soldier can be transferred almost at once to the Reserves, or discharged on physical or other grounds. Furthermore, university students are exempt from military service, and studies show that more and more local-born children of Chinese parents are attending the universities in Bangkok.

## CITIZENSHIP BY NATURALIZATION

Until recent years, the requirements that any alien had to meet when applying for naturalization as a Thai citizen were relatively easy to fulfil, on the surface at least. The Nationality Act of 1911, in effect until 1952, for example, set forth the following conditions:

SECTION 3. Any alien who complies with the conditions required by Sections 7 and 6 may apply to be naturalized as a Thai subject. . . .

SECTION 6. No naturalization may be granted unless:

*i.* The applicant be of full age, both according to the Thai law and to the law of his nationality; and

*ii.* The applicant shall be residing in Thailand at the time of his application; and *iii.* The applicant has resided in Thailand for not less than five years; and

*iv.* The applicant be a person of good character and in possession of sufficient means of support.

SECTION 7. The five years' residence in Thailand is not required in the following cases:

*i.* If the applicant has rendered service of an exceptional nature to the Thai Governmentr; or

*ii.* If the applicant was originally a Thai subject who has been naturalized abroad with the sanction of the Thai Government and who now desires to resume his Thai nationality; or

*iii.* If the applicant is a child of an alien who was naturalized as a Thai subject and if, at the time of the naturalization of such alien, he was of full age, both according to the Thai law and the law of his nationality.

The Nationality Act of B.E. 2495 (1952), which repealed the 1911 law, cited above, raised considerably the requirements for naturalization, as the following quotation shows:

SECTION 9. Any alien may apply for naturalization who:

*i.* has become *sui juris* under the Thai law and his own law;

*ii.* is of good conduct and is substantially occupied;

*iii.* *has taken up residence within the Kingdom for an uninterrupted period of not less than ten years to the date of applying for naturalization;*

*iv.* *has such knowledge of the Thai language as prescribed by Ministerial Regulations.*

But here again we find a liberalization of the requirements in the most recent law. The Nationality Act of B.E. 2499 (1956 sets forth the following provisions for naturalization:

SECTION 5. The provisions of Section 9 of the Nationality Act B.E. 2499 are repealed and replaced by the following:

SECTION 9. Any person may apply for naturalization who:

*i.* has become *sui juris* under the Thai law and his own law;

*ii.* is of good conduct and is substantially occupied;

*iii.* *has taken up residence within the Kingdom for an uninterrupted period of not less than five years to the date of applying for naturalization; and*

*iv.* *has such knowledge of Thai language as prescribed by Ministerial Regulations.*

SECTION 10. The provisions of Section 9 *iii.* and *iv.* shall not apply if the applicant:

*a.* has performed distinguished services to Thailand or has been of value to the government service in Thailand as the Minister may find appropriate;

*b.* is a child of a naturalized Thai subject or of a person who has reacquired Thai nationality and is *sui juris* at the time when either of his parents becomes so naturalized or reacquires Thai nationality;

*c.* is a former Thai subject.

The requirements concerning residence and fluency in the Thai language do not appear to be unreasonable—America's demands on aliens seeking naturalization are more stringent in fact. However, it should be noted that the provisions of the law requiring a knowledge of the Thai language is an exceedingly flexible one; the requirement can be raised or lowered by Ministerial Regulation alone; thus, at any time without a change in the basic law, the number of naturalizations can be quickly and easily limited. The Ministerial Regulation issued under the Nationality Act of 1952, and still in effect, set a standard which presumably could be easily met, requiring only that 'aliens applying for naturalization must be able to read and write the Thai language'.

In both the old and the new nationality laws, the decision to grant or refuse the application lies entirely with the government; even when all the provisions of the law have been fully satisfied, an alien may have his application rejected. That the government has not always been anxious to encourage the naturalization of the Chinese is evident from the statistics to be cited below. The Chinese in Thailand confirm this conclusion. Few Chinese, they report, can obtain Thai nationality, and then only after considerable difficulty; the obstacles are reduced, however, if one has good government connections and, moreover, is willing to pay a price which is said to be ten times the official fees (these have ranged in recent years from 2,000 baht, or US$100 to 4,000 baht, or US$200).

Statistics on the number of Chinese aliens actually naturalized are difficult to obtain. Only for recent years have such figures been published. However, through informal government channels the author obtained data on the total number of persons who applied for Thai citizenship and the number who were actually naturalized in the twenty-four year period between 1935 and 1958.

The figures given in Table 11, over page, indicate the operation of two complementary attitudes. Basically the Chinese, until very recent times, have not wanted to become citizens, except during the War years when by acquiring Thai nationality they could escape restrictions imposed on aliens. Thus out of a total of about half a million Chinese aliens, only some 9,300 actually applied for naturalization during this twenty-four year period. There could be no more telling evidence of the unwillingness of the Chinese minority to identify with the land in which they live. On the other side, the Thai government showed itself to be increasingly reluctant to grant citizenship even to the relatively few persons who applied, probably realizing the opportunistic intentions behind many applications. Both attitudes worked to keep down the number of persons naturalized as Thai citizens to the insignificant figure of only 4,650 in this twenty-four year period, less than one

11. CHINESE APPLICATIONS FOR THAI CITIZENSHIP AND NATURALIZATION

| *Year* | *Number of Applications for Citizenship* | *Number of Persons Naturalized* |
|---|---|---|
| 1935 | 22 | 22 |
| 1936 | 33 | 33 |
| 1937 | 83 | 80 |
| 1938 | 109 | 109 |
| 1939 | 192 | 170 |
| 1940 | 131 | 124 |
| 1941 | 646 | 589 |
| 1942 | 134 | 100 |
| 1943 | 6,086 | 2,761 |
| 1944 | 789 | 175 |
| 1945 | 47 | 11 |
| 1946 | 6 | 4 |
| 1947 | 13 | 10 |
| 1948 | 43 | 11* |
| 1949 | 104 | —* |
| 1950 | 118 | 3* |
| 1951 | 97 | 1 |
| 1952 | 29 | 13 |
| 1953 | 54 | 38 |
| 1954 | 47 | 30 |
| 1955 | 92 | 61 |
| 1956 | 118 | 96 |
| 1957 | 196 | 163 |
| 1958 | 104 | 48 |
| Total | 9,302 | 4,652 |

* No naturalization was permitted between November 1948 and April 1950.

person out of every 100 aliens if we accept the lowest estimate of the number of Chinese aliens, and less than one in every 200 if a more reasonable estimate is used.

There is a belief in Thailand that in recent years the number of naturalized Chinese has increased markedly, and collusion with corrupt officials who allegedly will sell naturalization certificates is widely suspected. But the figures cited above do not bear this out. Naturalization may have a price, but no substantially greater number of aliens than formerly is paying it. Naturalization continues to be useful for Chinese business men; as we shall see in the subsequent section, it does not always give them full citizenship rights but it does at least entitle them to a Thai passport which permits travel without restriction. This is not true for holders of either a Chinese Nationalist passport or a passport of the Communist Government of China; with the Nationalist passport a traveller cannot get into Indonesia, Burma or Cambodia; with a Communist China passport he cannot enter Singapore, Malaya, British Borneo, Laos, South Vietnam and the Philippines, or do more than transit Hong Kong. In these days of a divided China and a divided world, it pays to be a Thai citizen.

## RIGHTS AS CITIZENS

Thai citizens of Chinese descent are wont to claim they are in effect only 'second-class' citizens of Thailand. This is not entirely accurate. Actually in so far as rights and privileges are concerned, the Thai government seems to recognize not two but three 'classes' of citizens: native-born citizens of Thai parentage, or so-called 'pure Thai'; native-born citizens of alien (i.e. Chinese) parentage; and naturalized citizens, or former aliens. The simple fact of having Thai nationality does not by itself entitle a person to all the rights of citizenship, even such fundamental rights as voting and standing for public office. Only native-born citizens with Thai forbears are accorded full citizenship rights without limitations. Moreover, only these 'pure Thai' are certain of retaining their Thai nationality.

Thailand's first election laws, following the inauguration of the constitutional government in 1932, established a fundamental distinction between citizens of Thai parentage and all other citizens, and this legal distinction has persisted to the present time. The Amendment of B.E. 2476 (1933–34) to the Act on Elections of B.E. 2475 (1932–33), Article 6, granted the right to vote in elections for local government *(tambon)* and national parliament representatives to Thai citizens but for those citizens whose fathers were aliens additional requirements had to be satisfied:

> *a.* If his father was a foreigner, whether legally married to the mother or not, he must be a person who has studied the Thai language until he has obtained a certificate of a middle school, third year, or have served the state according to the Act on Military Conscription, or have served the state in other departments not less than five years.
>
> *b.* If he is a person who has been naturalized as a Thai, he must have one of the qualifications required in (a), or have lived in the Kingdom of Thailand since being naturalized for not less than 10 years.

This law stipulated that candidates standing for election had also to fulfil the requirements cited above.

A 1936 amendment to this Election Act repeated without change these restrictions on voting and candidacy rights of citizens with alien fathers. Naturalized citizens met additional hurdles, however —according to this amendment, they were now required to have lived in Thailand *continuously* for ten years since the date of their naturalization before being permitted to vote or to stand for public office. For many former Chinese this would be a difficult provision to fulfil, because as merchants they would probably have travelled outside the Kingdom fairly frequently. Any who had returned to China for visits could be denied the right to vote in any election in Thailand.

The most recent election laws, promulgated in 1951 and 1956, raised the requirements for native-born citizens of alien fathers. These latter now, in the absence of having performed military service or served the government in other ways for at least five years, must have obtained a certificate of proficiency in the Thai language equal to the sixth year of middle school before being eligible to vote. This is equivalent to denying voting and candidacy rights to every citizen of alien parentage who has not attended a Thai secondary school. A great number of second-generation Chinese who have attended only Chinese schools either in Thailand or abroad, would have difficulty in passing such a literacy test. Nor have these persons ordinarily performed military service or worked for the government. Given these considerations, it is likely that up to the present time the majority of second-generation Chinese, even those possessing Thai citizenship, cannot qualify to vote in any election in Thailand under the present laws.

Naturalized citizens must satisfy even more difficult conditions. They must not only have lived in the Kingdom continuously for ten years since the date of naturalization but, in addition, fulfil the same requirements as for native-born citizens of alien fathers regarding military service and proficiency in the Thai language or have served as a government official for five years (Election Act of 1956, Section 17). So few naturalized citizens could fulfil these requirements that we are justified in concluding that this group is denied any voting or candidacy rights whatsoever.

By contrast to the limitations placed on citizens of alien parentage and on naturalized citizens, the government has consistently granted Thai citizens whose fathers were also Thai nationals the right to vote without being required to fulfil any literary or educational qualifications. In fact the only persons in this latter group specifically denied the franchise are the feeble-minded, physically handicapped, persons unable to read or write, criminals and the like who are deprived of their voting rights by court order, and Buddhist monks and novices who are for the period of their monastic service considered to be above politics.

Similar distinctions between classes of citizens have been made for local elections. The Municipal Elections Act of B.E. 2482 (1939–1940), which governs elections for the Municipal Council of Bangkok, requires citizens whose fathers were aliens to have completed the third year of middle school, or to have served in the central or municipal government or army for a period of at least five years before being allowed to vote or to stand for a municipal office. A naturalized citizen likewise must fulfil these requirements, and have been domiciled in Thailand for at least ten years since the date of his naturalization. On the other hand, citizens whose fathers were Thai may vote and stand for office without fulfilling any of these requirements.

In addition to such limitations on the rights of certain citizens with alien forbears, the Nationality Act of 1952 introduced broad prohibitions on the actions of certain citizens which in effect gave the government justification to strip anyone of his Thai nationality and all rights as a citizen. First, native-born citizens of alien parentage:

> SECTION 16. When any person having Thai nationality for the reason of being born within the Kingdom but having an alien father has taken up residence in his father's country for an uninterrupted period of over ten years from the date of his becoming *sui juris* or is proved to retain his father's nationality or has done anything which is detrimental to the safety, interests or right of Thailand or the welfare or prosperity of the public, the Court may, upon the application of the Public Prosecutor, make an order denaturalizing such a person. The said order shall be published in the Government *Gazette*.

Secondly, naturalized citizens, according to SECTION 18 of this law, may be denaturalized if:

> *i.* Fraud or concealment of facts was practised in applying for naturalization.
> *ii.* There are evidences to prove that he still retains his former nationality.
> *iii.* He has done anything which is detrimental to the safety, interests, rights or honour of Thailand.
> *iv.* He has done anything which is detrimental to the welfare or prosperity of the public.
> *v.* He has left his domicile in Thailand and has taken up residence abroad for a period of not less than seven years.
> *vi.* He retains the nationality of any State at war with Thailand.

Again, attention is called to the imprecise wording of this law, particularly the omnibus phrase 'anything which is detrimental to the safety, interest, or right of Thailand', which would cover a very broad range of behaviour.

For some time, even before the 1952 Nationality Act, native-born citizens of alien fathers who refused to perform their required military service might be deprived of their Thai citizenship. Thus two editors of a Chinese Communist newspaper in Bangkok, both native-born citizens of Chinese parents, were denaturalized and deported to China in 1951 on the grounds that by failure to perform their military service some years before they had lost all rights to Thai citizenship. More recently, another ground for denaturalization was briefly specified. As indicated earlier, it is fairly common to find local-born offspring of Chinese parents registered with the authorities as Chinese citizens. In the past this was done sometimes to avoid military service, or to facilitate travel to China, or simply out of an unwillingness to accept status as a Thai citizen. The Thai government has been aware of this opportunistic stratagem; in the Nationality Act of B.E. 2496 (1953) it took steps to deprive these native-born citizens of their Thai nationality. SECTION 5 of this law states:

> The following statement shall be added as subsection 16 of the 1952 Nationality Act: Subsection 16. Any person of Thai nationality born inside the Kingdom of an alien father who obtained an alien certificate of registration in accordance with the provisions of the Alien Certificate of Registration Law prior to or following the promulgation of this Act shall no longer be considered a Thai national.

Attention is directed particularly to the *post facto* character of this provision—in short, any second-generation Chinese who at any time obtained, or presumably whose parents obtained for him—registration as other than a Thai citizen was automatically denaturalized under this law. Fortunately for the sake of justice, this reason for loss of citizenship was specifically repealed by the 1956 Nationality Act.

These several laws have been quoted in detail to illustrate one central point already made, that in so far as the rights and privileges of citizenship are concerned, the government tacitly recognizes three classes of citizens—native-born citizens of Thai parentage, native-born citizens of alien parentage and naturalized citizens. Of these, only native-born citizens of Thai fathers are granted full rights without qualification or restriction.

What are the justifications for this policy? In making these distinctions among its citizens the Thai government is for the most part merely taking cognizance of reality. Naturalized Chinese and native-born citizens of Chinese parentage all too frequently have stronger emotional, social and even political attachments to China than to Thailand. All these persons have dual nationality, being Chinese citizens by the laws of China, and few indeed take any overt action to divest themselves of their Chinese citizenship. Both Chinese governments, Nationalist and Communist, regard these persons as essentially Chinese still, regardless of their actual nationality status. According to information furnished the author, the Nationalist Chinese Embassy in Bangkok followed the practice immediately after the war of counting all China-born persons, as well as the sons and grandsons of such persons, as Chinese citizens, in the event they wished to travel to China. Thai passports presented to the Chinese Consulate by these persons were not visé'd for China but a certificate of dual nationality was issued instead which entitled the holder to the rights and privileges of a Chinese citizen.

More often than not, persons two and even three generations removed from China describe themselves as 'Chinese', even when actually Thai citizens. With so many of these persons reluctant to assume the responsibilities of citizenship, possessing sometimes a weak grasp of the Thai vernacular or, more serious, an incomplete understanding and acceptance of Thai cultural values, lacking any identification with the government as their own, Thai officials feel fully justified in making distinctions, so far as rights and privileges of citizenship are concerned, between 'pure' Thai and those persons of alien descent.

## CHINESE POLITICAL INTERESTS

Unfortunately those who sincerely desire to take an active interest in the country's political life have few opportunities to do so. Since the 1932 Revolution, the Kingdom has been run by a handful of military men operating behind an elaborate facade of parliament, constitutions and periodic elections. Except for brief periods this group has never sanctioned the formation of *bona fide* political parties. Because of the distrust of the Chinese minority, any organized Chinese interest in Thai politics has been especially discouraged. Whenever the political situation becomes tense—because of an impending *coup d'état* or differences with Thailand's neighbouring States—the Chinese are ordinarily among the first to be warned to keep out of politics. Recently they were forbidden even to discuss political matters in any group, under threat of immediate deportation. In issuing this warning the government undoubtedly was motivated by its fears of Communism, but the Chinese know by experience that communism has often been defined simply as opposition to the existing regime. Politically, the Thai and Chinese groups are seldom drawn together. For a long period even the Communist Party organization of each has been distinct, there being a Thai Communist Party and a Chinese Communist Party operating clandestinely but separately in the Kingdom—certainly the ultimate in political separation!

It is not Thai society, then, but the Chinese community itself which provides the Chinese minority with opportunities for a limited kind of political expression. First there are the many Chinese associations whose directors, chairmen and committee heads must be chosen every two years. Not much attention is paid to the contests themselves—for the most part new leaders are not so much elected as picked by powerful groups and influential personages in the community, and the deciding criteria in the large organizations are not a man's abilities but his usefulness to the association and community *vis-à-vis* Thai authorities. However, a great deal of prestige attaches to leadership of the various associations. To become the chairman of the Chinese Chamber of Commerce, the president of a dialect association, or a director of any of the large benevolent organizations is both an honour and a reward, proof to the entire community that a man has reached the apogee of both financial and social success. The Chinese associations thus give to the individual Chinese a social and political position within his own ethnic group, and a position, incidentally, which is recognized and respected by the Thai government. The rank and file Chinese in a place like Bangkok where the associations are exceedingly active is more concerned with the leadership of his own dialect association than with his district's representatives in the national parliament.

In addition to these local community associations, Chinese throughout Thailand are constantly encouraged by both Chinese governments to take an active interest in developments either in Taiwan or on the Mainland. The Chinese Communists and the Chinese Nationalists have officially declared in the postwar years that the overseas Chinese should be 'good citizens' of the countries in which they dwell, yet neither has fully accepted the severance of ties with China. Branches of both the Kuomintang Party and the Chinese Communist Party have been formed in Thailand, both clandestine organizations in which Chinese participated at some risk, depending on the temper of local police. At the moment Communist cells are vigorously suppressed but the Kuomintang organizations are tolerated.

Overseas Chinese, including those from Thailand, have elected representation in the Nationalist Government on Taiwan, and since the War, especially following the Communist success on the Mainland, the Chinese Nationalist Embassy in Bangkok has worked zealously to stimulate closer ties with Nationalist China—groups of Chinese leaders are periodically invited to tour Taiwan as guests of the Nationalist government, handsomely printed magazines circulate among Thailand's Chinese picturing the strength of the Nationalists' army and the social advances made under the Taiwan government, and an untold amount of money is spent locally in the sponsorship of pro-Kuomintang schools, newspapers and organizations. The Peking government has been no less active. From the moment of their domination of the China Mainland, the Chinese Communists set up a comprehensive organization to work with the overseas Chinese. Article 98 of their Constitution states: 'The People's Republic of China shall protect the acquired rights and interests of the Overseas Chinese', and the range of their organizations, from the central government down to the local communities, gives an idea of the importance attached to this objective. Within the Communist Party's Central Committee, three organizations take responsibility for the overseas Chinese. The first is the Commission for Overseas Work, the function of which is to plan and direct propaganda activities among overseas Chinese; the second is the Third Office of the Bureau of United Front Work which has responsibility for organizing overseas Chinese participation in 'democratic movement'; and the third is the Social Department of the Chinese Communist Party's Central Committee, which has a general intelligence gathering mission. In addition to these, a Commission of Overseas Chinese Affairs has been established in Peking under the Government Administration Council with the same rank as a ministry. This Commission has major responsibilities for handling the thousands of overseas Chinese—visitors, students, and refugees (deported from places like Malaya, Thailand and the Philippines)—who each year return to China.

At each main port such as Amoy, Swatow, Canton and Foochow, a Bureau of Overseas Chinese Affairs provides special assistance and services for these returning from abroad. In provinces and municipalities where returnees and the families of Chinese living abroad are numerous, there are branch offices of the Commission for Overseas Chinese Affairs; those *hsien* with exceptionally large numbers of such persons have either an office of the Commission or a special branch concerned with overseas Chinese matters in the Civil Affairs Office of the *hsien* government. In the local governments *(ch'ü)* of these districts one or two 'managers of overseas Chinese affairs', appointed by the local government, handle problems concerning these persons. 'Returned Overseas Chinese Friendship Societies' are active in Peking, Canton, Foochow, Amoy, Swatow, Kunming, Hoikow and Chuen-kiang, as well as in other emigrant municipalities, districts, and villages. These societies organize returnees for study and indoctrination purposes, and encourage them to buy government bonds and otherwise invest capital in various government-sponsored enterprises (Lu Yu-sun 1956: 13–14).

Chinese Communist policy toward overseas Chinese can be divided into two stages. Before 1954, when the land-reform programme was being implemented, the Communists confiscated the lands and estates owned by overseas Chinese and others, and resorted to blackmail to extort money from Chinese living abroad. Beginning in the spring of 1955, however, a lenient policy was adopted. Wealthy overseas Chinese, formerly looked upon as 'class enemies', were now called 'nearest relatives and good friends'. Overseas landlords were granted preferential terms and exempted from the punishing 'labour education' meted out to other landlords. Restrictions on the exit of overseas Chinese and their relatives were relaxed and by reducing to a minimum the requirements for entry into China, the overseas Chinese were encouraged to return to the motherland for visits and for study. Toward persons of little means the Communists are usually cold and strict; but toward those possessing wealth and influence abroad, exceptional measures are taken to insure their comfort and pleasure while travelling in China (Union Research Institute *1956:* 213; *1957:* 195–196).

Thus while the Thai government, justifiably or not, has actively discouraged the political integration of the overseas Chinese, their own governments have stepped up efforts to secure their allegiance. Neither government loses an opportunity actively to champion the overseas Chinese in disputes with the Thai government. For example, when the alien registration fee was increased from 20 baht to 400 baht in 1952 Taiwan lodged a vigorous protest through its Embassy in Bangkok and tried unsuccessfully to effect an immediate reduction in this tax. At the same time the Chinese Communist Government, unfettered by the niceties of diplomacy, denounced the increase as a 'form of extortion' and called on the Thai government to rescind its action 'as well as other acts of persecution against Chinese' in Thailand (*Bangkok Post*, March 13, 1952). The Communists have made clever use of these incidents to propagandize their support of the overseas Chinese, in their cataloguing of alleged persecution is a veiled threat of 'grave consequence'. Peking Radio, late in 1952, broadcast the following statement of the Chairman of the Overseas Affairs Commission, after that the Thai Government had banned two Chinese Communist newspapers in Bangkok.

> The Phibun Songgram Government has been consistently undermining the interests of Chinese residing in Thailand. Instead of bringing an end to such measures, it has further enlarged and intensified them. The increase made in the fee for alien registration certificates in February of this year is an example of the intensified measures it has taken to undermine the interests of several million Chinese residing in Thailand. The wanton and unreasonable closure of *Chuan-min-pao* and *Nan-chen-pao* is an act which deprives our Overseas Chinese of their legitimate rights and, as such, is intolerable to the Chinese residing in Thailand.

The statement said in conclusion:

> The Overseas Chinese Affairs Commission of the Central People's Government hereby warns the Phibun Songgram Government that it must immediately stop undermining the interests of Overseas Chinese in Thailand, release all Overseas Chinese that have been illegally detained, and lift the ban on *Chuan-min-pao* and *Nan-chen-pao* so that they can resume publication. Failing this, the Phibun Songgram Government will be held responsible for the grave consequences.

Again, in late 1958, following the *coup d'état* by Marshal Sarit Thanarat and emergency measures against various leftist elements in Thailand, the Committee of Overseas Chinese Affairs of the Chinese Communist government issued a protest 'against the persecution of overseas Chinese by the Thailand authorities', parts of which follow:

> Recently, under the pretext that the overseas Chinese in Thailand are engaged in 'Communist subversive activities, the Thailand authorities have persistently arrested overseas Chinese on a large scale in Bangkok and other places, searched stores and schools of the overseas Chinese and closed down their newspaper offices. Such serious persecutions have aroused indignation and disquiet among the overseas Chinese in Thailand. We cannot refrain from expressing our concern and paying serious attention to this development. . . . This is an unfriendly act toward China. The Thailand authorities should immediately stop their persecution of the overseas Chinese, release the arrested overseas Chinese and allow the closed newspaper offices of the overseas Chinese to reopen. Otherwise, the Thailand authorities will have to take all the consequences.
>
> (Broadcast in English, Peking, Nov. 3, 1958)

One might well ask what lies behind the concern of both the Nationalists and Communists for the overseas Chinese. In formulating an answer one should not overlook the economic potential of the Chinese living outside of China. Traditionally the overseas Chinese have sent back remittances to their relatives still living in China. Such funds often formed the principal means of their support but they also have served to offset the deficit in China's balance of international payments. The individual amounts remitted may seem insignificant, but the total of these small amounts from millions of people made a huge figure every year. For instance, in 1935, when there was a trade deficit of over US$116 million, remittances from overseas Chinese amounted to almost US$94, about 80 per cent of the deficit. The 1956 trade deficit of US$79 million was more than offset by overseas Chinese remittances amounting to US$106 million. Remittances now are estimated to amount to from US$110 to 140 million yearly. The Chinese Communists must have this rich source of foreign exchange as well as other capital from the overseas Chinese, and are hurt economically to the extent the Nationalist Government can check its flow and divert it to Taiwan (Lu Yu-sun 1956: 3).

Before and during the War Thailand's Chinese, like the overseas Chinese everywhere, united to support the Nationalist government against the Japanese. Some of the most violent terrorism ever seen among the normally peaceful Chinese occurred in the late 1930's against merchants who refused to support the Chinese boycott of Japanese goods (Landon 1939: 289). During this period many Chinese youth joined the Nationalist Army—in Thailand today one is occasionally shown pictures of some of these young men who were killed fighting for China. The Nationalist cause was given a tremendous boost by the final Allied victory over Japan, but with the outbreak of warfare between the Nationalists and Communists, and particularly upon the domination of the entire Mainland by Communist armies, the Chinese minority split apart. On the one side are those supporting the Kuomintang, and on the other the Communists and pro-Communists. Although the cleavage is bitter and community-wide, so far terrorism has been conspicuously absent. Instead each side is content to establish its own schools and newspapers, disseminate its own brand of propaganda, attempt to collect funds, and vilify the other group.

The disruptive effect of all this on the Chinese community is apparent on every hand. One finds Chinese openly accusing other

Chinese of illegal and criminal activities in Thailand. Thus a pro-Nationalist newspaper reports that Chinese are engaged in arms-running in South Thailand. A Communist newspaper retorts with a story of Chinese Kuomintang troops in Burma about to attack Thailand. Each faction accuses the other of collecting money for political purposes, an open violation of Thai laws. The Communists charge the Kuomintang group in Bangkok with secretly recruiting troops for the Nationalist forces in northern Burma and of practising extortion and blackmail against other Chinese. The Kuomintang newspaper declares that Chinese Communists have orders to create riots, commit arson and murder, and disrupt Southeast Asian governments by any possible means.

The Thai government must wonder how much truth is contained in such charges. In any event charges like these inevitably worsen relations with the Chinese minority. The war in Korea, the revolt of the Chinese in Malaya, and the jingoism concerning overseas Chinese coming from Chinese Communist leaders in Peking—these things would scarcely serve to bring the Thai any closer to the Chinese in their own country. Vilification and the ominous threat of terrorism can only confirm conclusions held by many Thai: that the Chinese are a dangerous element, ruled by alien ideologies, unreliable and potentially treasonable. In these circumstances the extension of further political rights to the Chinese minority is not likely.

CHAPTER IX

# RETROSPECT AND PROSPECTS

## MISCONCEPTIONS

VARIOUS misconceptions about the Chinese minority in Thailand have gained popular acceptance as fact, often by way of serious and scholarly studies. In so far as these myths are believed, they impede a true assessment of the present situation and future prospects of the Chinese minority. Some of these we have discussed earlier in this study, but let us review a few briefly.

It is often implied, if not stated explicitly, that the Chinese group is principally alien, that is, that the three million Chinese in the Kingdom are foreigners living in a 'host' country. This three million figure itself is little better than a guess and a doubtful guess at that because decade after decade it seems neither to increase nor to decrease. Apart from the accuracy of the count, however, available evidence indicates that less than a third of the so-called Chinese are aliens, the majority being native-born citizens of Thailand. This therefore, is not an outside alien group but for the most part indigenous and entitled to all the usual rights and privileges that citizenship ordinarily confers. Viewed in this light, the Chinese problem takes on a different aspect; it is a problem of Thai acceptance of China as much as one of assimilation.

Another notion—that the Chinese group is culturally and socially homogeneous—must be heavily qualified by recognizing speech-group differences, occupational diversity, varying socio-economic levels, differences between the immigrant and succeeding generations with regard to the acquisition of Thai culture and retention of Chinese patterns, regional variations, especially the contrast between the Chinese in the southern provinces and the central plain, political differences, and even religious differences. Any policy decision concerning the overseas Chinese should take into consideration these differences. It is true that the trend seems to be from dialectual diversity to class diversity, toward cultural uniformity within socio-economic groupings; but whatever the trend the fact of difference remains. The need in treating with this minority is to identify the significant differences and the influential factors. Little along this line has thus far been achieved. Despite the fact that dialect group differences have been the most obvious demarcation among the Chinese group, no study has ever been made of contrasting patterns of acculturation or assimilation among the various dialect groups, or even between the Bangkok Chinese and those up-country, nor between those in the capital and those in the southern provinces, or between the Christianized Chinese and the non-Christian.

We have also called attention earlier to the fact that, contrary to popular notions, the Chinese do not monopolize commerce in Thailand; rather, important segments are firmly held by Thai people themselves and by Westerners; and observers note a steady movement of Thai into occupations formerly dominated entirely by the Chinese. We wish now to discuss in some detail two additional beliefs regarding cultural and social changes among the Chinese minority.

One of the oldest and most persistent myths is about the 'unchanging Chinese'. These people, it is said, show no desire to assimilate into the society to which they have migrated; rather, they remain aloof, perpetuating themselves as a distinct social and cultural entity within the Kingdom, drawing upon Thai society for their livelihood but otherwise maintaining their own way of life virtually unchanged from that of China. One of the most graphic statements of the plural society in this region of Asia comes from J. S. Furnivall in his *Colonial Policy and Practice* (1956: 304):

> . . . probably the first thing that strikes the visitor is the medley of peoples—European, Chinese, Indian and native. It is in the strictest sense a medley, for they mix but do not combine. Each group holds by its own religion, its own culture and language, its own ideas and ways. As individuals they meet, but only in the market-place, in buying and selling. There is a plural society, with different sections of the community living side by side, but separately, within the same political unit.

Statements such as this have some validity. The overseas Chinese certainly wish to retain their cultural identity in what is for many of them an alien land. But to regard this minority as unchanged and unchangeable is to ignore quite obvious signs. As this study has shown, the typical overseas Chinese has altered his way of life, culturally and socially, to such an extent often that much of his behaviour is no longer compatible with patterns of people still living in the rural areas of China. Changes are particularly noticeable among the second-generation Chinese who would indeed be misfits in the social structure of the South China village whence their parents have come.

### THREE SPHERES OF INLFUENCE

All Chinese, whether born in Thailand or entering as immigrants, are influenced by three socio-cultural spheres: the Chinese community already established in Thailand; Thai society itself; and finally, the Western world which is represented most directly by the small group of European and American diplomats, business men, professional people and missionaries in Thailand. The local Chinese community undoubtedly exerts one of the strongest influences on the arriving immigrant and its ways soon mould his patterns of behaviour. For example, he learns the Teochiu dialect, the language of the community's most numerous component; often his occupation shifts to some trade or specialty emphasized by the community; he adopts religious practices followed by the overseas Chinese which are different in many respects from those found in the villages and towns in South China; his patterns of work and leisure change, and his aspirations for social mobility are remodeled to conform to existing opportunities and social organizations of the local Chinese community. The list of changes produced by this community are extensive and profound; no individual loses completely his rural China ways and values, still participation in this urban overseas Chinese society produces an unmistakable hiatus between the present and the former way of life. The changes are by no means skin deep.

This minority has not been untouched by Thai culture, as some ardent Thai nationalists profess to believe. The overseas Chinese community itself is an instrument for acculturation, a kind of cultural decompression chamber in which the immigrant is prepared for a new way of life. Most Chinese learn to speak Thai, and the second generation become so proficient in this language and other aspects of Thai culture that one detects signs of a distinct cultural estrangement from the parental generation. Curiously perhaps, the Chinese school must be credited with this Thaiification process during the present generation. These schools have more Thai instructors than Chinese, devote three times as much time to the teaching of Thai as Chinese, send increasing numbers of their students on to entirely Thai secondary schools and universities, and more than any other single institution prepare the youth for life in a Thai cultural setting.

While many institutions of the Thai and Chinese are distinct and separate, innumerable opportunities occur daily for the two people to mingle and mix; from these contacts have come an awareness and an appreciation of the cultural and social characteristics of the other. The items readily accepted by the Chinese cover a wide range: certain Thai dishes, such as curries, find a place in the Chinese diet; the comfortable *sarong*-type skirt is worn by both men and women; Chinese names are Thai-ized; an increasing number voluntarily acquire Thai nationality; the worship of Thai gods and belief in Thai magic is widespread among the Chinese. We should not want to over-estimate the amount or the depth of the cultural transfer that has occurred, but one would be mistaken to deny it altogether or to slight its importance. Integration of two peoples is a gradual process which begins with changes which are in themselves apparently ephemeral or capricious.

The assimilation situation of the Chinese in Thailand and of minorities in the United States, including the Chinese, has been different in one noteworthy respect: in the United States, minorities have often been pulled by the attractions of a more highly specialized and materially superior national culture from their attachments to traditional ways; the government has played a minor or neutral role. In Thailand, on the other hand, the strongest single force for assimilation has come from the government through its various laws regarding education, citizenship, vocations, and land ownership; the fact that this push has not been matched by an attraction from Thai society would seem to make the push the more essential in this situation.

On the other hand, there is no denying the persistent and pervasive attraction of Western culture for the overseas Chinese. The pull is unmistakeable. Indeed, the Chinese minority as a group is probably one of the most westernized elements in the population of Thailand, and the most receptive to further change in this direction. In so far as dress is concerned, interest in popular music, dancing, films, fads, and fashions, the typical Chinese youth is not greatly different from his western counterpart; but this can be said of many people in Asia for whom Westernization has been a shallow experience. For the typical overseas Chinese, however, deeper similarities exist. His notions of responsibility, of the intrinsic value of work, of contractual obligation, his drive and industry—all these qualities are the ones extolled by Western culture and have consistently excited the admiration of Westerners, perhaps because they seem lacking in other Asians. One reason why Western business men prefer to deal with Chinese—and the typical European business house employs whenever possible Chinese clerks—is that both are sure of each other, which is another way of saying that for both the rules as they see them are the same. More so than other groups in the population, the Chinese minority, particularly the younger generation, is more fluent in English, more adept at Western commercial skills, more eager to adopt Western methods of business and finance, and above all more ready to acquire the material culture of the West as symbols of social position. The earliest Christian missionaries in Thailand found it easier to work among the Chinese, and today a large proportion of the Christians in the country are Chinese—indeed American missionaries have found it more useful from a proselytizing viewpoint to speak Chinese rather than Thai because their congregations and converts are more likely than not to be Chinese.

The combined influence of these three culture spheres, Chinese, Thai and Western, has produced a minority which is different from the original immigrant stock and different certainly from the rural peasantry of South China from which the overseas Chinese derived. Although by no means completely integrated into Thai society, the overseas Chinese group is culturally alienated from China, and the differences between the local community and the homeland grow with each generation. Recent efforts by the Chinese Communist government to destroy the traditional Chinese family, to communize the country, and to introduce what amounts to a new written language will, if successful, make overseas Chinese culture and society anachronistic so far as the homeland is concerned. The Thai may derive some measure of hope from this unfortunate circumstance, for as the Chinese lose a sense of identity with China, they may acquire a sense of belonging in Thailand and other nations of Southeast Asia.

## THE ASSIMILATION QUESTION

Another notion commonly held by Chinese as well as many Thai, is that the Chinese minority has not been and indeed cannot be assimilated. 'Assimilation' is a slippery term. If we define it as the social mixing of the two peoples, and see it as the process by which Chinese persons become members of Thai social groupings and Thai persons join Chinese groups, or both belong to a third-party group, then without question there has been assimilation. We find on different social levels a common sharing of membership in the same groups. Some examples can be cited. Both become part of the typical Western business organization, although often in different capacities; in an effort to trade wealth for political influence, many leading Chinese companies have welcomed Thai politico-militarists onto their boards of directors; young persons from each group enter the same schools established by Western missionaries in Thailand; moreover, a definite integration is found in Thai secondary schools and universities; Chinese and Thai worship the same animistic shrines, participate in Buddhist observances at Thai temples, and as co-religionists make up groups of travellers to journeying to various holy places within the Kingdom. To think of the two peoples as being socially distinct, mingling only in the market place, as Furnivall has suggested, is not quite accurate. We do not wish to claim more for these situations than actually occurs; contacts may be fleeting and superficial, but daily, in a hundred different ways, assimilation constantly goes on. It goes on in the schools beyond primary levels, on religious festivals which give occasion for social integration, and no less in business with its demands for recreative gatherings and relaxation after hard bargaining.

Certain institutions, on the other hand, with members drawn exclusively from one or the other ethnic group, remain separate and distinct. Both the Thai and Chinese nowadays tend to be endogamous. Moreover, the typical Chinese association, the Thai Buddhist monkhood, the small Chinese business organization, the government bureaucracy all tend to be exclusive ethnic groupings. In general, the assimilation found is dictated by the demands of public life and one's livelihood—what might be called 'assimilation for convenience'; a voluntary desire for more thorough integration is lacking. If the children of Chinese parents are to get a higher education in Thailand, they must attend a Thai university and they do so; on the other hand, they are ordinarily under no pressure to intermarry with Thai, and show no desire to. Many of the changes one notices among the Chinese are changes of convenience which have not greatly disturbed pivotal overseas Chinese institutions.

One must remember that the Chinese are a very flexible people whose main concern is self-interest 'in compensation for the hardships of living so far away from our native places,' to cite a familiar phrase often heard in overseas Chinese communities. Their degree of Thai-ness or of Chinese-ness varies from time to time, from situation to situation; depending on the way they interpret their interests.

In this fluid situation, however, certain objective indices of the persistence of Chinese cultural elements and interests can be recognized. First, the unremitting demand among the Chinese (including those who are Thai citizens) for a Chinese education. This demand has kept Chinese primary schools alive and has given rise to tutoring classes, evening schools, and various sorts of illegal schools designed to give Chinese-language instruction beyond the elementary level. Secondly, the total circulation of Chinese newspapers in Thailand and of imported Chinese publications during the last decade and more has been stable, indeed, in the opinion of some, on the increase. Thirdly, the membership of Chinese ethnic organizations, such as the dialect associations, the trade guilds, and the Chamber of Commerce, has not fallen off, despite the increasing numbers of second- and third-generation persons in the community.

A number of conditions can be cited as having hindered a greater depth of integration of the Chinese minority into Thai society. Large scale immigration in the recent past has been of particular importance. The thousands of Chinese immigrants who annually flowed into the country during the past forty years placed an intolerable burden on the assimilative powers of Thai society. Most of the immigrants concentrated heavily in cities and towns where they formed tight ethnic communities. These centres of Chinese culture in turn were continually revitalized by the uninterrupted arrival of fresh immigrants, and only in recent years have Thai laws and conditions on the China Mainland combined to reduce the flow, thereby giving Thailand its first chance in almost half a century to begin to absorb this minority. There are now at least one million alien Chinese living in Thailand and another two million persons who are culturally Chinese—in all, one-sixth of the total population. If Thailand is even to begin to absorb these millions already in the Kingdom, immigration must be maintained at its present low level.

Another factor hindering assimilation has been the nature of the Thai economy. Thailand is a predominately agricultural country with very few industries. There is a division of labour along ethnic lines, with the Thai as farmers, fishermen, and employees of the government, and the Chinese by and large as traders and shopkeepers. The standard of living of Thai farmers and fishermen, while not desperate by any means, is not one to attract immigrants who themselves have come from a sub-standard agricultural economy. The Thai government's elaborate bureaucracy offers few opportunities for the average immigrant, who lacks the nationality status and skills demanded for such work, and the immediate descendants of immigrants are not in a much more favourable position. Thus, in contrast to the situation which might obtain were Thailand an industrialized country, the average Chinese has little likelihood of becoming a part of a predominantly Thai work group, which might serve as the first step in a continuing process of assimilation.

On the other hand, he has every chance of entering a Chinese work group or organization. The Chinese community has consistently provided almost unlimited economic opportunities for immigrants and their descendants. By contrast with farming and the bureaucracy, commerce pays handsomely and as for advancement and wealth, the sky is literally the limit. These life chances offered by the community are so superior to all others that few Chinese would think twice when mapping out his own or his son's future. Drawn into the Chinese community by basic economic considerations, the typical Chinese becomes part of its institutions, accepts its values, and in so doing is removed from the institutions and values of Thai society.

The Chinese community, particularly the one in Bangkok, is so self-sufficient that by becoming a part of its life, the individual is relieved of making more than a superficial compromise with the demands of Thai society. All social needs can be satisfied through community agencies—work, proper education, social status and recognition, protection and social security. Chinese who gravitate to the community initially are likely to remain a part of it and to identify themselves with its institutions; the community does not act as a corridor to complete integration. The unwillingness of the second- and even the third-generation persons to disassociate themselves from this community is in marked contrast to the experience of comparable groups in the United States, and has given the impression that Thailand's Chinese are in fact impossible to assimilate. It is not so much a will to resist assimilation as lack of opportunities and economically profitable reasons to enter into a closer relationship with Thai society.

The absence of protective and social services must be regarded as another obstacle to assimilation. The onset of ordinary misfortunes like unemployment, sickness, disability, and death leaves the individual in Thailand relying largely on his own and his family resources. In the event of strikes and labour disputes, or catastrophes like fires and floods, the affected persons can expect little immediate help from public or private agencies, except for those which they themselves have organized. Furthermore, in the case of the Chinese there must also be added the hazards to liberty and property at the hands of an imperious government and at times quixotic officials.

Such circumstances place a premium on the development of organizations which can provide the needed relief and protection of the individual and the group. Chinese associations established with these aims in mind have at the same time become the principal means for the unification of the entire minority, for propagating separatist sentiments, financing minority institutions like schools, and for perpetuating Chinese cultural values and patterns. It seems obvious, therefore, that if the Chinese minority is ever to be assimilated, there must be an extensive development of social services and democratic processes. Ethnic associations, now the individual's main defence, must be replaced by an efficient and effective system of law and order on which all persons can rely regardless of their ethnic origins.

Feelings of fear and persecution have also hindered a closer integration of the two peoples. Thai leaders fear the economic power of the Chinese minority, and to the simmering resentment of the rank and file over alleged exploitation there has been added in recent years the threat of Communism and internal subversion. The politically conscious Thai sees Red Chinese waiting close to Thailand's northern border; from the south in Malaya whence the Chinese Communist revolt has from time to time spilled over into Thailand, comes another threat, while to the east in Cambodia there are signs of growing Communist influence. All these events seem to point up the dangerous explosive potential of the large, concentrated Chinese minority. It can be argued that such fears are illusory and the actual threat exaggerated, but the situation has not helped the Chinese. Rather, it serves to justify further restrictions and a sterner use of police power with regard to arrest, imprisonment and deportation. The summary execution in late 1958 of several Chinese accused of being Communist arsonists illustrates the stern attitude not infrequently seen in official quarters.

Chinese reactions are to be expected: fear for their security, resentment of arbitrary police action, uneasiness about the intentions of the government, and a strengthening of those in-group ties which in the past have spelled protection. This is not an atmosphere conducive to assimilation.

## VALUES: CHINESE AND THAI

The values emphasized by Chinese society in Thailand are in many instances the direct opposites of those stressed by the Thai people, and these must be regarded as a fundamental barrier to assimilation. The following chart sets forth the major differences:

| *Chinese* | *Thai* |
|---|---|
| Materialistic, concerned principally with the acquisition of wealth as an end in itself or as a means to social position. The successful business man typifies the principal values of the overseas Chinese. | Hinayana Buddhist values emphasize the spiritual development of the individual, rather than the acquisition of wealth as such, and the Buddhist monk who leads a life of poverty epitomizes this nonmaterialistic ideal of Thai society. |
| Social status defined largely in terms of wealth and business leadership. | Social prestige and position gained through relationship to royalty and landed wealth for the upper classes; for the great bulk of the population by bureaucratic position, family membership, and by faithfulness to Buddhist principles, particularly by service in the Order and donations to *wat* (temples). |
| Family regarded as keystone of society; strong family ties emphasized; separation or dissolution of the family strongly opposed. | Other groups in society, notably the Monastic Order and the bureaucracy, regarded as of greater value than family ties; divorce and separation of common occurrence. |
| Confucian organization of the family with roles and statuses based on generation, sex and age; restricted role and status of women. Family is patriarchial and patrilocal. | A loosely-structured family organization with considerable variation of individual behaviour permitted; women are particularly given freedom of movement and expression both inside and outside the home. Husband recognized as family head, but no clear cut patriarchal authority. Residence after marriage usually with bride's parents. |

On the other hand, certain similarities have also bred separation. Both peoples share a disinterest and inexperience in national politics and with democratic procedures in general. The Chinese have not wanted to get into Thai politics and there is little about Thailand's political ethic which would encourage them to do so. Other examples of this phenomenon can be cited. Thai support of private schools has coincided with the Chinese desire to maintain their own schools. The value of arranged marriages is accepted by both people, thereby helping to perpetuate ethnic endogamy. Both people exhibit a certain flexibility and tolerance toward the practices of the other group, a kind of cultural permissiveness which permits the persistence of difference. Neither the Thai nor the Chinese support or encourage religious proselytism, but both are content to worship in their own way and permit others to do as they wish. This spirit of permissiveness may also be seen in the enforcement of laws regarding the Chinese; a more intransigent application of laws might well force a faster rate of change among the Chinese.

Perhaps the root of many difficulties involving the Chinese minority is a conflicting concept of what assimilation means. Thailand since the revolution has expected of the Chinese not merely obedience to its laws and the negative virtue of keeping out of trouble, but also true identification with the political, social and economic interests of the Kingdom. As evidence of this identification, the government expects fundamental changes in the overseas Chinese way of life and voluntary participation in Thai institutions. Recent naturalization laws provide an illustration of the government's point of view. These laws declare in effect that the mere fact of acquiring Thai nationality, even by birth in Thailand, is not in itself sufficient proof that a person has truly identified himself with the interests of the Kingdom. Thus it demands further evidence of *bona fides* of both former aliens and second-generation Chinese in the form of government employment, education according to Thai standards, and honourable military service, before granting such persons the full rights of citizenship.

Complete integration, to the extent of losing their Chinese identity, is obviously further than many Chinese wish to go, or think it necessary to go. One must admit that to make a living, gain response, or even win social recognition, the degree of acculturation and assimilation expected by the Thai government and people is unnecessary. The Chinese believe they have fulfilled all reasonable expectations if they obey the law, work hard, and co-operate when possible in the development of public institutions and activities. But they insist on the right to maintain their own temples, schools, businesses, associations, and families free from interference. By their own standards of peacefulness and public service, the Chinese make excellent citizens. Moreover, they regard themselves as having a culture superior to the Thai, and higher ethical standards. It is therefore a difficult matter to convince them that complete assimilation is desirable. The basic grievance of the Chinese minority is not that they are denied access to Thai society—Chinese do not complain that they are unable to marry Thai girls, or get jobs with the government, or enter the universities, or join Thai clubs—but rather that they are not permitted freedom to run their own schools, businesses and associations as they wish.

## RAPPROCHEMENT

To find grounds for a substantial *rapprochement* between the Thai and the Chinese we must look beyond the two cultures and peoples so intimately involved, to the penetrating and pervasive cultural influences coming from the Western world. Both the Thai and the overseas Chinese have readily accepted the technology and material culture of the West without realizing that the effect of this change will not be confined to the technological surface of life but will gradually work its way down to the depths until the whole traditional culture has been penetrated. This process takes time, but even now we can see changes in traditional Thai and Chinese values under the continual bombardment of Western material culture and its concepts. Let us cite a few widely separated examples of the kind of changes that Westernization has produced. The introduction of a modern educational system, Western in style, content, and scope, and the establishment of a modern conscript army dependent for its effectiveness on Western-educated military specialists, helped to undermine the old order, finally in 1932 removing the royalty from the centre of political power and installing instead the intellectual and the professional soldier; in this process many traditional usages and ideas relating to social position and mobility were broken up, to be replaced by a more fluid and 'democratic' social system. In a different sphere the introduction and widespread use of pedicabs in Bangkok has stimulated a migration of young men in search of remunerative seasonal work from the agriculturally poor northeastern provinces. These 'samlor' drivers not only help to raise the living standards of their native villages, through remittances sent back to parents, but on their return they act as a progressive influence in the development of the northeastern area, opening the way for the wider acceptance of Western innovations in farming, sanitation, health and recreation. The widespread use in Bangkok today of Western-style dresses, high-heeled shoes, permanent-wave preparations and lipstick have changed the traditional Thai concept of feminine beauty, while at the same time the acquisition of such modern skills as typing and shorthand by thousands of Thai girls has not only altered the composition of the civil service but has encouraged Thai women to re-evaluate their position in society and in the family. Religious institutions, probably Thailand's strongest link with tradition, have not been without change, small in themselves but indicative of more to come. Buddhist monks who are supposed to renounce the joys and desires of the material world are commonly seen accepting rides in comfortable automobiles or riding in buses, rather than walking. Certainly the government's notions of police power have changed considerably as the Thai police have been equipped with such modern weapons as armoured cars, tanks, artillery, and airplanes; and in turn the police organization has become to many Thai the fastest avenue to higher social and economic position.

Changes in traditional Chinese values are also apparent, small and seemingly insignificant, but important as precursors of trends. Second-generation Chinese youths object to working as hard or as long as the immigrant generation—they want more leisure, more enjoyment than the task of making money affords. The second- and third-generation Chinese are the inheritors of wealth rather than its creators, and behaviour has changed due to this very fact. Chinese parents complain that Western movies serve to weaken traditional family discipline, 'to put ideas' in the minds of their sons and daughters. What we are witnessing in this situation is the gradual alteration of the host society and the minority group by the technology of the West welcomed and readily accepted almost by all. Whether changes in the superficial aspects of culture will be followed at once by the adoption of the whole body of Western materialism and values seems unlikely; institutional controls in both Thai and Chinese society are too strong for any quick collapse of traditional values. Yet the experience of other non-Western societies—Japan, sections of China, India, Turkey—shows conclusively that the innovation of Western technology leads inevitably to revolutionary changes in all parts of culture and society. As Toynbee writes, 'In a cultural encounter, one thing inexorably goes on leading to another when once the smallest breach has been made in the assaulted society's defences' (Toynbee 1951: 81).

Thus, although there are conflicts in fundamental values and patterns between the Thai and the overseas Chinese, the two peoples are attracted by similar aspects of Western culture, and their common acquisition of Western material culture, techniques, practices and values enlarge the basis for eventual social integration. It is said that the Western-educated élites of Southeast Asia have more in common with each other, because of their unique Western experiences, than each has with other groups in its own country. [The increasing westernization of Southeast Asia in the future will not only draw all the countries of this region closer together but will also serve to reduce the cultural and social differences which up to now have separated minority groups within these countries.]

The situation of the Chinese in Thailand will be influenced in the future, as it has been in the past, by events occurring in the world beyond the Kingdom, particularly as these affect the Far East. Two major trends are discernible in this region, both of which have implications for them. The first is the rise of strong Asian governments, united at home and influential in world affairs. Prewar Japan was one such state, postwar India is another, and Communist China is still another. The second trend, both the cause and the result of the first, is the decline of direct Western power and influence in the Far East. This trend was marked initially by the defeat of Russia by Japan in 1904, and more recently by the withdrawal of Western colonial powers from Southeast Asia after World War II.

That the rise of Communist China as a world power would have the most telling influence on the future position of the overseas Chinese one might readily guess. From the beginning this minority has lacked one advantage possessed by other foreigners—the direct support and protection of a strong home, or colonial government. During the nineteenth and twentieth centuries all other nationalities were represented in Thailand by embassies and consulates, some enjoyed the protection of special courts and the advantage of very favourable commercial treaties. [The Chinese, on the other hand, were very much on their own, for not until 1946 did China open an embassy and consulates in Thailand. Without help from their government, the overseas Chinese developed their own protective associations and devices, but these are now a thin defence against unfriendly policies of the Thai nationalists.]

A powerful China introduces a new element to the situation, and this the overseas Chinese know full well. Part of the overseas enthusiasm for Red China comes from pride in the homeland, but deal also comes from the expectation that a strong Chinese ment will champion their cause abroad. What Thailand ars is indeed that China will seize this opportunity to play on the minority's frustrations and hopes, and deliberately fan Chinese nationalism—smoldering in these overseas communities—into a hot flame, binding the overseas people more closely than ever to China.

But if we are to judge by the present actions of Peking, these fears are exaggerated. China has espoused overseas Chinese interests, but not to the point of exacerbating relations with Southeast Asian governments. With the exception of South Vietnam and Laos, threats and denunciations and incitements to subversion are being replaced by the exchange of trade missions, by the visits of cultural delegations, and by economic assistance—curiously, at a time when the overseas Chinese are being hard pressed by local governments—the air is heavy with good-will from China. We can expect that this minority will still be courted by China because of its wealth and useful commercial position. But when Peking will have to make a decisive choice, the interests of this overseas minority will be sacrificed for the larger objective of winning over the region itself, not simply one relatively small minority group there. The first trend, therefore, the rise of a strong China, will not materially or immediately help the Chinese in Thailand.

## WESTERN INFLUENCE

The decline of direct Western political influence in the internal affairs of Asia has led to the gradual weakening and withdrawal of Western business interests in the area. In newly independent countries the state has simply nationalized enterprises formerly run by Westerners, or has insisted they be turned over to local personnel to manage. In Thailand such nationalization has coincided with the Government's determined efforts to restrict Chinese influence in domestic trade and commerce so that Thai nationals might take over this field. No group is ever willingly deprived of its status, the Chinese in Thailand least of all, and, partly in reaction to governmental restrictions, partly in response to growing commercial opportunities, they have already begun to move on to different, and larger, commercial activities.

As noted earlier, the Chinese in the course of the last two decades have gotten well established in banking, export-import trade, insurance, and shipping, all enterprises formerly monopolized by Westerns. If the Western sun is setting in the Far East, as many observers believe, then the overseas Chinese are best qualified by previous experience and commercial acumen to take the Westerners' place, particularly in Thailand where they have a running start over the indigenous people. The main obstacle to this is the Thai Government. Though concerned with restricting the commercial position of the Chinese, the government may yet at the same time countenance the expansion of their wealth and influence. To gain their advantageous economic position Westerners first sought political protection *vis-à-vis* Asian governments through treaties which granted them extra-territoriality privileges and in effect put them beyond local control. Such treaties are of the past and are not likely to be renewed now for Chinese merchants. The rising Chinese big-business group in Thailand must by necessity protect its rights and investments in a different manner. Two ways suggest themselves. One is to enter politics directly; the other is to support leaders or groups already in politics who are amenable to direction by Chinese capitalists. In both cases the goal would be the same: to secure some measure of political power and through it protection for Chinese business interests. A new political power élite in Thailand in the form of wealthy Chinese business men seems already to be forming. In the southern provinces, particularly in the major towns such as Haadyai and Phuket, Thai who are ethnically Chinese have entered local politics directly, with considerable popular support; in the Bangkok area wealthy merchants have formed business alliances with leading Thai politicians and military men and gained thereby the protection of these strong men in the national government.

## CHINA'S MARCH SOUTH

Both of these trends must be evaluated against two demographic factors in the Far East. The first concerns the position of the overseas Chinese *vis-à-vi* other Southeast Asian peoples. In all countries of this region, except Singapore, the Chinese are now a minority. They are moreover a predominantly urban group, and it can be assumed—in the absence of contrary evidence—that like other urban peoples they are characterized by relatively low-death and low-birth rates, as compared to the mass of rural indigenous peoples. Demographers see in Asia the beginnings of a great population explosion; by the end of this century Thailand for one is likely to double its population. But to such an increase, the rural areas of the country will contribute most, for their present relatively high-death rates, will drop as sanitation and health conditions improve, while their relatively high-birth rates may be expected to remain high for some time. Although the Chinese urban groups in the population may also increase in size, their growth rate will be much less, and thus, in the future the proportion of Chinese to Thai will be smaller than it is at the present time. In short, the Chinese will become over the years more of a minority, if given no greater immigration than at the moment. On demographic grounds alone, therefore, conditions will favour the integrating of the Chinese minority during the next generation.

The second dynamic factor is the growth of population in China itself, now numbering some 650 million people. Rapidly industrializing, China is likely to turn to Southeast Asia for living space, for markets, and for raw materials and food as several hundred millions are added to its population, whose yearly increase now nearly equals the total population of Thailand. In a decade more new people will be added to China's population than the present total population of the entire Southeast Asian region. Historically, the lands south of China have served as outlets for China's population. As floods, droughts and famines have intensified the precariousness of livelihood in South China, an irresistible tide of Chinese people has flowed into Southeast Asia. There is no reason to believe that this centuries old movement has now run its course. Indeed one recent writer concludes (Wiens 1952: 199):

> Regardless of the political systems that develop in China, or of the present geographical and biographical obstacles presently obstructing development of the southern tropical frontiers, historical indications point to the ultimate engulfment of Southeast Asia within the . . . Chinese cultural fold.

Because of their fear of overseas Chinese economic and political influences, all Southeast Asian governments, Thailand included, have erected immigration barriers against the Chinese. None welcomes the revitalization of its Chinese communities by a new wave of immigration. But one must ask whether small nations like Thailand can resist the tremendous pressures exerted by China's expanding population, and if that, whether they can also resist the extraordinary cultural dynamic that China represents in Asia today. We have been so conditioned to think of the inevitable assimilation of an immigrant minority group by the host society that we overlook too easily the likelihood of the host society itself being overwhelmed, demographically and culturally, by its giant neighbour. Perhaps it is more realistic to think of China assimilating all the lands to the south, with a gradual, but determined penetration, the first stage of which is now taking place. The overseas Chinese have a double identity, both Chinese and Southeast Asian; rather than a withering ethnic group, they may in fact be the present-day image of the future Southeast Asian.

# NOTES

## Chapter I. Dimensions of the Problem

p. 5 [1] The 1947 census does cite a total of 618,791 persons of Chinese 'race' as living in Thailand—in the absence of an explanation in the census statistics it can only be assumed that this category includes both immigrants and persons whose fathers at least were Chinese aliens. In 1950 a total of 1,099,084 Chinese aliens were registered with the police, as required by law (*Statistical Year Book* 1952). These totals are more meaningful than the 1947 census count of Chinese aliens alone.

p. 5 [2] Skinner (1957) has provided the most recent and probably the most systematic estimate of Thailand's Chinese population. By 1955 there were, he estimates, 2,315,000 Chinese in Thailand, of whom 696,000 were Chinese-born and 1,619,000 local-born. While these figures are plausible, they like other estimates lack the substantiation of official census counts.

p. 7 [3] Inasmuch as the term 'dialect' is so commonly used to designate these overseas Chinese languages, it seems sensible to retain its use here, with the understanding of course that in a strictly linquistic sense, these speech groups are languages (i.e. mutually unintelligible to native speakers) rather than dialects.

## Chapter II. Immigration

p. 19 [1] In 1949 a group of these Western-educated Shanghai business men, one the son of Dr Wellington Koo, with the assistance of the Thai government, established a cotton-yarn manufacturing plant in Bangkok. Machinery was brought directly from Shanghai, rushed out before that city fell to the Communists, and the initial workers were Chinese, also brought from China and Hong Kong for this purpose. These have now been replaced by Thai women. In 1951 this factory employed a total of 1,100 women working in three shifts and constituted the largest single private enterprise in Thailand. This is one illustration of the potential economic influence of the 'White Chinese'.

p. 24 [2] B.E. stands for 'Buddhist Era'. Officially dates in Thailand are counted from the death of The Buddha, which occurred 543 years before the birth of Christ, or 543 B.C. Thus, 1957 becomes B.E. 2500. Until 1941 the Thai calendar year began April 1, and bridged two Western years, for example, B.E. 2470 began April 1, 1927 and ended March 31, 1928. When referred to in this study this date is given as B.E. 2470 (1927–28). By government decree B.E. 2484 (1941) and all following years were ordered to commence, like the Western year, on January 1.

p. 25 [3] Thailand's immigration regulations and the immigrant categories they set up are similar to those in the United States. Temporary visitors of any nationality are allowed to enter Thailand in unlimited numbers. However, in the case of Chinese visitors, at least, each must have a sponsor in Bangkok who is held responsible if the visitor fails to depart from the country at the end of his stay or commits an illegal act while in Thailand. Sponsors must be reputable persons of some means, for often a bond is required of them by the immigration authorities, and they are carefully investigated and approved before the persons they wish to sponsor are issued visas by the Thai consuls abroad. This procedure makes it exceedingly difficult for the ordinary poor immigrant from South China to enter the Kingdom under the guise of a temporary visitor. It was much easier, presumably, for the affluent 'White Chinese' to do so. A temporary visitor may remain in the country for 30 days only; in actual practice this period may be extended almost indefinitely, or until the person can be assigned a quota number as an immigrant.

p. 27 [4] The value of the baht fluctuated during the 1930's between US$0.44 and US$0.38. After World War II the baht dropped to US$0.05, where it has remained to the present. The U.S. currency equivalents of the fees given here are approximate only, after taking into consideration the different baht valuations.

p. 28 [5]

| *Year* | *Immigration Fees* | *Total Revenues* |
|---|---|---|
| 1937–38 | 2,931,875 baht | 109,412,311 baht |
| 1938–39 | 2,331,395 baht | 118,233,206 baht |
| 1939 | 2,359,212 baht | 59,611,536 baht |
| 1940 | 2,608,530 baht | 141,330,981 baht |

Source: *Statistical Year-book of Thailand*, 1939–44, p. 386–387.

## Chapter III. Chinese Community Life

p. 47 [1] *Feng-shui* or *fung-shui* 風水 literally means 'wind and water' and refers to the traditional Chinese practice of geomancy for determining the best location for tombs, houses and buildings in general. In deciding on suitable sites the configuration of the land, the courses of running water, surrounding buildings, and the prevailing winds must be considered. If these factors are desirable, evil influences may be counteracted and good fortune obtained. For a grave, a wide river in front, a high cliff behind, with enclosing hills to the right and left, would constitute a good geomatic position. The grave must face the south, or some auspicious landmark, where the beneficial and vivifying influences emanate.

p. 50 [2] The Bangkok Chinese Chamber of Commerce is distinct from the Bangkok Chamber of Commerce. The latter organization has a much smaller membership composed of Europeans and Thai firms, and it has no connection whatever with the Chinese Chamber of Commerce.

p. 57 [3] The Chinese distinguish between their traditional homeopathic treatment of illness and disease and the newer Western medical practices and techniques. Thus clinics are of two kinds: Chinese-medicine clinics in charge of doctors trained in the diagnosis and treatment of illness in the traditional Chinese manner, and Western-medicine clinics where doctors and nurses employ Western medical knowledge and techniques. In the case of the Chinese-medicine clinics, the doctors are always Chinese men; in the Western-medicine clinic, the doctors and nurses may be Chinese but are more often Thai. Some hospitals provide both kinds of medical treatment, Chinese and Western, and permit the patient to make a choice. The Chinese treatment and medicine, being free, are the more popular at all hospitals.

## Chapter IV. Home and Family Life

p. 75 [1] The addition of Chinese 'blood' is popularly supposed by Westerners and by many Thai also to add vigour, industry, and perserverance to the indigenous population—indeed for many Western businessmen and missionaries to have had Chinese antecedents becomes a kind of character recommendation for a Thai.

## Chapter VI. Economic Organization and Interests

p. 125 [1] Government service, or the bureaucracy, includes much more than the administrative offices and departments of the government. The educational system is a national one, with all teachers in government schools on the central government's pay-roll. The police department and the judicial system are likewise national organizations staffed and controlled by the central government. Practically all provincial officers from the governors on down are appointed by the national government. In addition the government runs or controls the railways, the communication system (radio, telegraph and telephone), and a number of industries—the tobacco monopoly, cement factory, distilleries, paper plant, gunny-sack factory, etc. The majority of these organizations are included under the civil service. In Bangkok in addition to the national government there is also the municipal government which has an administration of its own and control of such enterprises as the Bangkok Electric Works, the water works, and bus companies.

p. 132 [2] These occupations included the making, casting, or selling of images of The Buddha; making or selling of bricks, firewood, charcoal, or torches; manufacture of women's hats; cutting or tailoring of women's dresses; weaving wicker, with the exception of mats; manufacture of lacquer or *niello* wares; setting of Siamese printing types; making of fireworks, dolls or toys; manufacture of umbrellas; hair waving or hair cutting; and legal practice. Aliens engaged in hair cutting and legal practice were given one year to stop their work. Those engaged in other occupations listed were given but ninety days.

p. 132 [3] The following occupations were reserved for Thai nationals: the making and casting of images of The Buddha; lacquer and *niello* work; driving-for-hire tricycles, motor cycles and public motor vehicles; rice farming; salt farming; hair cutting; and Siamese type setting. Non-nationals engaged in any of these occupations were given one year to find other employment. It was reported that many more occupations had originally been listed in this bill at the insistence of members of the National Assembly, but that the Government is considering the abilities and experience of the Thai had wisely decided to drop most of these from the legislation.

Chapter VII: CHINESE SCHOOLS AND EDUCATION

p. 144 [1] No overall organization pulls the Chinese community together except in times of crisis. Chinese schools, even more than other institutions, are separate entities, often competing with each other for pupils. No organization holds them together in a 'system'; there is no common director or supervisor of education. All schools are under the direct control and supervision of the Ministry of Education of the Thai government and answerable solely to that office.

p. 147 [2] These statistics are for the private schools of the Chinese and 'other nationalities'. Inasmuch as Thai, Islamic, American, and European schools are listed separately, it can be assumed that these figures are almost entirely for Chinese schools.

p. 164 [3] By 1954 Thailand had 1,809 private schools with 370,446 pupils.

p. 164 [4] The percentage of the national budget devoted to education in Thailand is unusually low compared with other countries with adequate educational systems:

| | |
|---|---|
| Philippines (1949) ... ... ... | 35·7 per cent |
| United States (1934) ... ... ... | 25·2 per cent |
| Japan (1934) ... ... ... ... | 24·7 per cent |
| Canada (1933) ... ... ... ... | 23·2 per cent |

(United Nations 1950: 20)

# REFERENCES

CARTER, A. CECIL, editor, *The Kingdom of Siam*, Putnam Sons, New York, 1904.

CHEN SU-CHING, *China and Southeastern Asia*, China Institute of Pacific Relations, Chungking, 1945.

COUGHLIN, RICHARD J., 'The Chinese in Bangkok', *American Sociological Review*, *20*, No. 3 (June 1955).

*Directory for Bangkok and Siam*, 1933.

EMBREE, JOHN F., 'Thailand: a loosely structured social system', *American Anthropologist*, *52*, No. 2 (April–June 1950)

FURNIVALL, J. S., *Colonial Policy and Practice*, a comparative study of Burma and Netherlands India, N. Y. University Press, 1956.

GRAHAM, W. A., *Siam: A Handbook of Practical, Commercial, and Political Information*, Alexander Morning, London, 1890.

HALL, D. G. E., *A History of South-East Asia*, Macmillan, London, 1955.

HALLETT, H. S., *A Thousand Miles on an Elephant in the Shan States*, W. Blackwood and Sons, Edinburgh & London, 1890.

HRAF, *Thailand Handbook*, Human Relations Area Files, New Haven, Conn., 1956.

INGRAM JAMES C., *Economic Change in Thailand since 1850*, issued under the Auspices of the Institute of Pacific Relations, Stanford University Press, 1955.

KULP, DANIEL HARRISON, *Country Life in South China: The Sociology of Familism.* Teachers College, Columbia University, 1925.

LANDON, KENNETH PERRY, *Thailand in Transition*, University of Chicago Press, 1939.

——*The Chinese in Thailand*, Oxford University Press, London & New York, 1941.

LANG, OLGA, *Chinese Family and Society*, Yale University Press, New Haven, 1946.

LU YU-SUN, *Programs of Communist China for Overseas Chinese*, Communist China Problems Research Series, Union Research Institute, Union Press, Kowloon, Hong Kong, 1956.

MACDONALD, ALEXANDER, *Bangkok Editor*, The Macmillan Company, 1949.

PURCELL, VICTOR, *The Chinese in Southeast Asia*, Oxford University Press, London and New York, 1951.

SKINNER, G. WILLIAM, *Report on the Chinese in Southeast Asia* (mimeographed), Southeast Asia Program, Cornell University, 1950.

——*Chinese Society in Thailand: An Analytical History*, Cornell University Press, Ithaca, New York, 1957.

——*Leadership and Power in the Chinese Community* in Thailand, Cornell University Press, N.Y., 1958.

*Statistical Year-book of Thailand* (Siam), Central Service of Statistics, 1935–37; 1939–44; 1952.

THOMPSON, VIRGINIA, *Thailand, The New Siam*, The Macmillan Co., New York, 1941.

——*Labor Problems in Southeast Asia*, Yale University Press, New Haven, 1947.

THOMPSON, VIRGINIA and RICHARD ADLOFF, *Minority Problems in Southeast Asia*, Stanford University Press, 1955.

TOYNBEE, ARNOLD: *The World and the West*, Oxford University Press, London and New York, 1951.

UNION RESEARCH INSTITUTE, *Communist China 1956*, Union Press, Hong Kong, 1957.

——*Communist China 1957*, Union Press, Hong Kong, 1958.

UNESCO (United National Educational, Scientific, and Cultural Organization) *Report on the (Educational) Mission to Thailand*, Imprimerie Union, Paris, 1950.

WINES, HAROLD J.: *China's March into the Tropics*, a study of the culture and historic geography of South China. Office of Naval Research, United States Navy, Washington, 1952.

# INDEX

*v.* vide, *f* following page(s), *n* note page


acculturation 67, 71-74, 77, 87, 88, 92, 104-105, 114-115, 121, 168, 188, 190, 198, *v.* culture
Aerated Waters Bill 50*f*
agricultural economy of Thai 194
peasantry 117, 118
Alien Registration Certificates and Fees 27-28, 53, 65, 83, 90, 154, 172, 180, 184*f*, 207*n*
'aliens' 135, census (1947) 136
American Presbytherian Mission School 146
Americans *v.* U.S.A.
Amoy 厦門 xiii, 7, 18, 184
ancestral halls, in China 36-38, 44-46, in Thailand 66, 100
animism 84, shrines 193
anti-Chinese/Sinicism 28, 127, 128, 132, 136*f*
anti-Semitism (Chinese as Jews of the Orient) 2, 128
army, armed forces 28, conscript 199
Westernization 199, *v.* military
arsonists, execution of Chinese 196
*a-sia* 阿少 (playboy) 73, 87
assimilation 12, 30, 32, 66, 76, 79, 91, 116, 158, 164, 168, 172, 189-201, 203-4, *v.* integration
and acceptance 188*f*
hindering factors 194
meaning of 198
associations *v.* benevolent, Chinese Chamber of Commerce, Chinese organizations, dialectical groups
functions 60-66
occupational 47, 55, *v.* trade guilds
open membership 60
Assumption Commercial College 166
attitudes, Thai towards Chinese 2, 6, 10*f*, 24, 25, 51, 59, 61-62, 81-83, 116, 128, 137, 138, 143, 146, 148-149, 152, 167, 175, 176, 181, 182-183, 187, 196, 209*n*.
Australian companies 119
avoidance of Thai controls 152
*v.* bribery, conscription
Ayuthia 14, 81, 116, destruction 117

B.E., Buddha Era 207*n*
baht, inflation 126, value 208*n*
Bangkok xii, 13, 195, *v.* Chinese community, Chinese organizations
Chamber of Commerce 208*n*
Chinese business area 1, 32
Chinese Chamber of Commerce 50*f*
Chinese concentration 6, 15-16, 32, 140
election laws 179
immigration figures 17*f*
occupations 116-119
pedicabs 199, *v.* tricycles
population 14
residence restrictions 142-143
urban districts 32, 52
Bangkok Commercial School 159
*Bangkok Post* 25, 81, 137, 185
Bangrok 32
bankrupts and creditors 45, 123
banks, banking 3, 41, 202
barbers 137
benevolent associations (*shang-t'ang* 善堂) 33, 36*f*, 39, 42, 55-60, 63, 66, 90, 99, 182
*Bibliography of Thailand* x
references 211-212
'big business' 120, 203
bird's-nest concession 129
blackmail 123, 187
blind, school for 56
blood, Chinese 75, 91, 209*n*
relatives 36
Bombay Burma Trading Co 4
bookkeeping in Chinese 122, in Thai 128
Borneo (British) 177
Bowring Treaty (1855) 16
boycott of Japanese goods (1930) and riots 186
Brahmanism 84
bribery 2, 82, 136, 173
British advisors 127
Buddhism 93*f*
and slaughtering industry 130
Hīnayāna 92*f*, 104, 114, 197
Mahāyāna 92*f*, 96, 104
monastic order 126, *v.* monks
monastery schools 144
Theravada 11
bureaucracy 16, 118*f*, 195, 197
*v.* Thai government
burial practices *v.* death rites
Burma ix, 12, 18, 139, 177, 187
Burmese destruction of Ayuthia (A.D. 1568) 117
business acumen of Chinese 124
business associations, Chinese 47-55, 121-127, *v.* trade guilds
changes in 4-5, 121-127, 200, 202

business assns. Chinese—*(continued)*
co-operation with Thai 72-78, 88, 121, 138, 193, 203, 208*n*
disputes 45, 63, *v.* political
employees 49, 70, 107, 108, 124-125
exclusion of Thai 49-50, 83, 121-127, 193
extent 1-2, 121
location of shops 68-70
restrictions on 127-138
businesses, nationalization of foreign 202
butchers 130, 137

Cambodia 12, 177
Canada 210*n*
canals 17, 117
Canton 廣州 xiii, 7, 18, 184
Cantonese 7, 8, 67, 99, 111, 146, 158
(speaking) association 40, 42-43, 46
Carter A. Cecil 14, 211
Catholic schools 166
cemeteries *v.* death rites
censuses, Thai 5, 14, 17, 23, 76-77, 136, 158, 159
Central Plains 6
certificates of residence 27, *v.* Alien Registration
Chainat dam 141
Chamber of Commerce, Bangkok 208*n*, *v.* Chinese
Chang Lan-ch'en 張蘭臣 52
changes, myth of 'unchanging Chinese' patterns 86*f* 189
socio-cultural 190
Ch'ao-chou hui-kuan 潮州會館 *v.* Teochiu Assn
Chao Phraya (Menam) river 6
*Chao Thai* (newspaper) 143
Chao-Yang Assn 潮陽 42, 66
charms 84-85 temple 100
Chekiang Province xiii, 43
Ch'en Chia She 陳家社 38
Chen Su-ching 5, 211*n*
Chen Te 振德 No. 2 School *v.* Ching Da
Chevrolet trucks 4
Chi-sheng Book Co 集成圖書公司 (Hong Kong) 155
Chiang-che hui-kuan 江浙會館 (Kiangsu-Chekiang Provincial Assn) 43
Chiengmai xii, 2
'China Town' 32, 143
Chinese Chamber of Commerce 32-33, 34, 35, 42, 47, 50-55, 59, 60, 63, 64, 65, 66, 128, 138, 157, 182, 194, 208*n*
Chinese Communist Party Government 19, 31, 53, 65, 114, 136, 142, 156, 164, 165, 166, 177, 181, 192, 196, 201-202
Overseas Chinese 183-185
Chinese community 6, 7-8, 32-66
economic power 116*f*, 195
*v.* monopolies
importance 63, 106, 108, 141, 182, 186, 190, 195
locus of power in 36, 87, 89, 116
organization 33, 210*n*
political factions 8, 43, 63, 65, 186*f*
recognition of beneficence 58
Chinese, definition of 5
Chinese economic position 1-5, 16-17, 21, 32, 137, 166, 189
opportunities 195
Chinese embassy and consulates 201
consular tasks 54
Chinese hospitals and clinics 34, 39, 41, 55, 57-59, 90, 126, 209*n*
*Chinese in Bangkok* vii, 211
'Chinese Language Schools' 145
Chinese minority *v.* dialect groups, immigration
attitude toward Thai 10, 28, 56, 59, 71, 83-86, 114, 122-123, 132, 136, 139, 160, 172, 176, 181, 191, 194, 196, 198
characteristics 10*f*, 21*f*, 32, 71, 82, 87, 114-115, 118, 143, 159, 191-192
classes 8, 62, 188
contributions 3, 117-118
definition 5-6
demographic position 5-6, 14-15, 17, 188, 194, 207*n*
distribution 6, 7, 32, 116
future of 126
misconceptions about 188*f*
occupations 1-2, 17, 71, 116-143, 188, 190
political interests 169, 181*f*
residence 139-143
sex ratio 23-24, 30
significant differences 188
South Thailand 6, 43, 94, 131, 165, 187, 188, 189, 203
sphere of influence 190-192
unity and disunity 6, 7-8, 22, 32, 33, 34, 36, 39, 43, 45, 49, 56, 59-66, 115, 138, 139, 144, 187-189, 190, 196
Chinese Nationalist Government (Kuomintang, in Formosa since 1949) 5, 54, 65, 81, 114, 136, 139, 154, 156, 165, 166, 177, 181, 183-187
Chinese organization 32-66, 159, 168, 183, *v.* dialect assns, *tsu*, etc.
activities and functions 33-35, 38-39, 40-41, 44-47, 49, 50-55, 59, 60-65, 87, 88, 89, 161, 196
composition 34, 59, 194
contributions to assn 42
headquarters 35

Chinese organization—*(continued)*
illegal organizations 36, 40
leadership 34, 39, 45, 50, 53, 63-64, [182-183
no Thai counterpart 35
origins 35
personnel 34, premises 35
ranking 40, 42, 43, 46, 48-49, 50, 55, 63-64, 99
support 34, 42, 55, 57-58, 62, 66, 95, 145, 155, 196
Chinese Republic (founded 1912) 20, Revolution 22
Chinese schools and Thaiification 190
Chinese view of the Thai 83, 85, 122, 172
Chinese village organization 20, 35, 36
Ching Da No. 2 School 振德 42
Ch'ing-ming 清明 festival 39, 103, 109
Chou Ts'ang 周倉 (black-face god with sword) 102
Christianized Chinese 189, 192
*ch'ü* 區 (district) 184
*Chuan-min-pao* 全民報 (Communist [paper) 185
Chuen-kiang 晋江 (Chinkiang) 184
Chulalongkorn (King Rama V, 1864-1910) 75
Chung-hua Fo-hsüeh she 中華佛學社 (Buddh. assn) 98
Chung-hwa Book Co 155
Chung-yüan festival 中元節 39, 103, [111
*Chung-yüan wan-pao* 中原晚報 52, 56, 142 [177
citizens or aliens 188*f*, second class
citizenship 134, 135, 136, 169, 170, 191, 194-195, 198, *v.* naturalization and denaturalization
by birth 170-173, by naturalization [173
categories of 177, 181
desire for 171-173, 177
fair-weather citizens 11
full 198
right to 168, 169*f*
rights of 140-141, 177-181, 187
three classes of 177, 180
Civil Service and Pensions Act 127, *v.* bureaucracy
discharge of aliens from C. S. 133
clan system *v. tzu* 族
Clark, Graham x
'class enemies' but wealthy 184
Coca-cola *vs* Seven-up 51
cohesion of Chinese 138, and schools 144, frustration 202 *v.* Chinese minorities—unity
*Colonial Policy and Practice* (Furnivall) 189, 193, 211
colonialism 11, extraterritorial privi- [ledges 203
commerce *v.* business, Chinese, Chinese minority, Chinese organizations, Chinese Chamber of Commerce
Commercial Press 155
Communism 10, 43, 48, 49, 54, 55, 62, 65, 114, 141, 152, 165, 182-187, 196, *v.* Chinese C. Party
textbooks 150, 151, 155
communities in China 189, 190
*v.* ancestral halls, *tsu*
description 19-20
institutions of 35, 36
life of 32-66
compradores *v.* middlemen
concentration of Chinese 6, 15-16, 32, 140, 194
concubines (second wives) 67, 70, 71, 73 [197
Confucian gentleman 10, organization
conscription 171*f*, 173, 178*f*, 180*f*, 199
Chinese evasion 172
consular tasks 54, *v.* Chinese Chamber of Commerce
co-operatives, Thai 131
Cornell University x
cost of living 2, 83, 133
cotton-spinning factories 120, 207*n*
*coup d'état* 9, 48, 51, 81, 142, 143, 182
craftsmen, Chinese 2, 117 [186
crime 82, 85, 179, 186-187
culture, change 86-91, 189-192, 199-
group 5 [201
similarities 79, 84, 92, 197-198
Culture, Chinese 5, 144, 150, 158, 160, [165, 188, 192, 197
dynamism 204
feeling of superiority 10, 198
refugee elements 19 [197
Sino-Thai differences 78-79, 80, 92,
Sino-Western similarities 191-192
Culture, Thai 30, 190, 197

Danish East Asiatic Company 4
Davie, Maurice R., x
death rites
ancestor tablets 36-37, 38-39, 100*f*, 103, 159, *v.* ancestral halls
burial in China 46, 111
changes 71, 100, 109, 111, 115
Chinese cemeteries 34, 39*f*, 43, 46-47, 56, 64, 109-110
funerals 98, 105, 115, 159
decorations 58, 63, *v.* titles
demographic movement 5*f*, 14, 17, [203*f*
denaturalization 177, 170-181
deportation 52, 53, 182, 183, 196
dialect (speech) groups 6-8, 75, 86, 122, 158, 161, 188, 207*n*

dialect (speech) groups—*(continued)*
associations 33, 36, 40-47, 57, 59, 63, 66, 95, 107, 138, 182*f*, 194
description 6-7
distinctions 7-8, 67, 103, 106, 111, [189
percentage 7
*v.* Cantonese, Hainanese, Hakka, Hokkien, Ningpo, Shanghai, Taiwanese groups
diligence, Chinese 137, drive 191
*Directory for Bangkok and Siam* 4, 211
divorce 197, *v.* marriage
dress, Chinese 8, 71, 74
Westernization 87, 199
dual nationality 181, 183
dualism, sources of 11

*Economic Change in Thailand since 1850*, x, 211
economic domination of Chinese 1*f*, *v.* monopolies
organization 116, 209*n*
problem of Chinese minority 2
education and schools 210*n*
education, Chinese 24, 33*f*, 39, 41*f*, 52*f*, 59, 65*f*, 71, 83, 89, 183, 187, 190, 194, 196*f*, 210*n*
changes 153-157
content of instruction 150
future 164-168
kindergarten 152
language instruction 41, 144, 145, 151, 153, 157, 165
hours of 149, 151, 155, 159
offensive against 149, 151, 152, 154
Penang 165
persistence of 157-164
rise and decline 145*f*
student numbers 164
teachers 26, 97, 124, 147, 152, 153-155, 158, 164, 165
licensing 149, 151, 153
registered 153, revoked 157
Thai subsidy 146, 161*f*
education, government budget 162, [210*n*
in Communist China 165
in Malaya 157, 165
in Taiwan 165
private schools 145, 148, 150, 152, 157, 161*f*, 164, 197, 210*n*
salaries 154, 161*f*
school enrollment 147-150, 151, 154, 165
textbooks 150, 152, 155*f*, 165*f*, 167
Thai education 112, 126-127, 129, 130, 144, 152, 160, 166, 178, 190, 193
universities 89, 124, 144, 165, 167, 173, 190, 193, 198
Western 89, 167
elders 37, *v.* leaders
election laws 177-179, 181, vote 9
Embrée, John F. 79, 211
emigration 15, Communist restrictions 31, *v.* immigration
and floods 20, 31
English language instruction 157, 166, fluency 87, 192
entertainment 32*f*, 42, 44, 66, 73, 87, 106*f*, 110, 190, 199, 200
entrepreneurs, Chinese 118, 123, *v.* middlemen
Er Siak Hong (Mr) x
ethnic affiliation in business 4
associations 196
endogamy 77, 160
group of future 205
prejudice 80-86
standards 198
tight community 194
Europe 3, 89
European circles 190, *v.* Westerners
import-export houses 117, 123, 135
preference for Chinese 191 [202
export-import companies 3, 43, 135,
exservicemen 141 [ism
extraterritorial priviledges *v.* colonial-

family, Chinese 35, 45, 58, 62-63, 86, 103, 113, 125, 130, 137, 144, 165, [192, 200
enterprise 121
home 68-74, 101, 105, 121*f*, 159
plan 69
marriage 39, 72*f*, 74-76, 78-80, 88, 105, 115, 159, 198
traditions and the Communists 192
*vs.* Thai values 78, 80-1, 197
family, Thai 72, 78-79, 197, 200
fears, Thai of Chinese 116, 196
festivals and holidays, Buddhist 126
Chinese 39, 71, 73, 92*f*, 99*f*, 103*f*, [106-115
Thai 71, 92*f*
flexibility of Chinese 11, 193
floods 56, 196, and emigration 20, 31
fires 56, Bangkok (1932) 68
firms, ethnic affiliations 4
Fishing Act (1939) 131
Foochow xiii, 19, 184
food, Thai 191
food vendors 3, restrictions on Chinese 130, 133, 137
Formosa xiii, *v.* Taiwan
friction, sources of 116,167

Fukien hui-kuan 福建會館 *v.* Hokkien Assn [36
Fukien Province 建省 xiii, 7, 13, 18,
*fung-shui* 風水 (geomancy) 47, 208*n*
Furnivall, J. S. 189, 193, 211

gasoline, Liquid Fuel Act 131
Gedney, William (Dr) x
go-betweens x, Western firms and *v.* middlemen [Thai 2, 12, 88
gods, Chinese 101
government service 124*f*, 137
*v.* bureaucracy
Graham. W. A. 146, 211
'Group of Kind Persons' 59
guided democracy 9

HRAF (Human Relations Area Files)
Haadyai 203 [x, 79, 211
Hainan Island xiii, 6, 13, 18, 38
Hainanese (Hailam) 6-7, 38, 146, 158
association (Hainan hui-kuan 海南
Hakka 6-7, 67, 146, 158 [會館) 43
association (Ko-shu hui-kuan 客屬
hospital 58-59 [會館) 42, 45
Hall, D. G. E., x, 211
Hallett, H. S., 14, 211
Han River 韓江 delta 6, 19
hawkers *v.* food vendors
Hing-min School 醒民 146
Hīnayāna *v.* Buddhism [Hall) x, 211
*History of Southeast Asia* (D. G. E.
Hoikow 海口 184, *v.* Hainan
Hokkien, Fukienese 7, 8, 146, 158
association (Fu-kien hui-kuan 福建會館) 43, 58-59
holidays, official Thai 125, *v.* festivals
home and family life 67*f*
and business 121
Chinese home 68*f*, plan of 69
sources of change in 86*f*
homeopathic treatment 209
homogeneity of Chinese group 6, 188
*v.* Ch. minority—unity, ethnic group
Hong Kong xiii, 4, 7, 13, 19, 86, 177,
horoscopes 74 [207*n*
hospitals 57*f*
hotels, Chinese 1, call house 83
*hsien* 縣 (county) 184
*Hsin-pao* 新報 52, 143
Hsing-min 醒民 *v.* Hin-ming School
Hua-chiao Hospital (of overseas
Hua-yi school 146 [Chinese) 57

illiterate aliens in Thai language 158
immigration 10, 13-31
Act (First) 24, (1950) 25, 26, 27
assistance of dialect group 44-5
changes in 29-30
compared with Japanese and Indians
control 24-29 [18
effects 194
fees 27-28, 208*n*
history of 13, 14-18, 22-23, 30
illegal 27
occupations 21-22, 28, 71
quota 24*f*, 29
reasons for 20-21, 203
restrictions by China 15-16, 31
restrictions by Thailand 24-29, 31, 158, 203-204, 208*n*
sex composition 22-24, 30, 76
sources 18-20
sourthward drive 204
statistics 13-14, 23
trends and volume 14-18
volume 17-18, 25, 27, 28, 29, 194
income tax 129, evasion 122*f*, 125
India, Indians 18, 56, 58, 104, 159,
Anglo-Indians 90 [183, 189, 200*f*
Chinese preference for 83
firms 4
minority in Burma 139
Indo-China ix, 18
Indonesia 12, 90, 177
intolerance towards Chinese 167
*peranakan* Chinese 90
industrialization, penetrative effect 12
*v.* Westernization
Ingram, James C. 211
insurance 5
integration 9, 11, 24, 30, 49-50, 59*f*, 77, 91*f*, 99, 104, 115*f*, 134-135, 144, 158, 164, 166, 168, 170, 172, 190-201, *v.* acculturation, assimilation, culture, marriage, plural society
intermarriage *v.* marriage, women

Japan, Japanese 18, 48, 86, 150, 200,
education figures 210*n* [201
military occupation 132, 141, 186
Jews of the Orient *v.* anti-Semitism, anti-Chinese
jingoism, chauvinism, nationalists
*jus soli* 170 [(ultra) 82, 187

Kiangsu Province 江蘇省 xiii, 43
*Kiattisak* (Honour) 52
Koo, Wellington (son of) 207*n*
Korea 187
Kra Isthmus 6
Kuan Kung 關公 (God of War) 102
Kuan P'ing 關平 (adopted son of Kuan Kung) 102
Kulp, D. H. 19, 20, 36, 211

*kung-hui* 公會 *v.* trade organizations
Kunming (Yünnan) 184
Kuomintang (KMT 國民黨)
*v.* Chinese Nationalist Government
*kuo-yü* 國語 (mandarin or official speech of the Chinese) 8, 41, 158
Kwang Chao hui-kuan 廣(州)肇(慶府)會館 Cantonese Speaking Assn 40, 42-43, 46
Kwang-chiao school 154
Kwangsi Province 7
Kwangtung Province (capital city, Canton) xiii, 7, 13, 18, 36

labour, Central Labour Union (CLU) 47-49
disputes 45, 49, 196
force, Chinese 1, skilled 117, 120
Free Workers Assn. 48
law, defeated 61
organizations 47*f*, 195, membership 47
Overseas Chinese L. Union 48-49
Thai Labour Union (Thai National TU Congress) 47-48
Lak Muang ('Stone of the City') 104
landlords, Communist policy and overseas Chinese 184
land-ownership restrictions 138*f*, 191
Land pertaining to Aliens Act (1943) 139
Landon, K. P., ix, 4, 21, 24, 26, 28, 76*f*, 94, 118, 128, 134, 146*f*, 149, 157, 159, 163, 211
Lang, Olga 37, 211
Laos 12, 177, 202
lay worshippers 95, 97*f*
leaders, leadership (Chinese), elders 34, 37, 39, 41, 88, 182*f*
social rating 64
legal associations 36
legislation to protect Thai interests 2
*v.* occupations (Thai)
Lien-hua nien-Fo she 蓮華念佛社 94
Liquid Fuels Act 131
love philters 84*f*
Lu Yu-sun 184, 186, 211
*luk-chin* (child) 89, *v.* Sino-Thai

MacDonald, Alexander 25, 81, 211
Mahāyāna *v.* Buddhism
mandarin (*kuo-yü* 國語) or official Chinese language 8, 158, 159, 161
marriage and intermarriage 24, 74-80, 90, 160, 193, 199, *v.* family
dialectual exogamy 8
expenses 80
Sino-Thai 72
matrilocal residence 79
Mei-Kwai School 166
memorial tablets 36, 38, *v.* ancestral halls
Menam ('The River') delta 14
*v.* Chao Phraya
middlemen, compradores, Chinese as 2, 12, 16, 88, 117
military politicians, army officers 9, 51, 121, 138, 181, *v. coup d'état*
military service 135, 171, 173
*v.* conscription
and nationalization 177, 180, 198
avoiding m. s. 173
military specialization (Western) 199
minorities ('foreign') 11, *v.* assimilation, Chinese minorities
missionaries (Christian) 146, 157, 190, 192*f*, 209*n*
schools 89, 166
monastic order 193, laity 95, 97*f*
*v.* monks
money for political purposes 187
Mongkut (King Rama IV, 1851-1868) 75
monks 94*f*, 105, 144, 197, 200
and politics 179, *v.* military
monopoly, exaggerated view of Chinese 3, 189
Chinese middlemen 117
occupations 2
opportunities 137
tobacco 130
'moral training' (Chinese) 160
and military life 171
mortgages, land 139*f*, *v.* landownership
movies 200
Municipal Election Act (1939-40) 178
mutual aid (Chinese) 35, 56, 60*f*

*Nan-chen-pao* 南辰報 (Communist paper) 185
Nan-Yang 南洋 (South Ocean Region) 16, 19
National Assembly (Parliament) 9, 50, 61, 75, 90, 141, 169, 178, 181
members banquetted by Chinese 51
nationalists, ultra 9, *v.* jingoism, military politicians
Nationality Acts (1911) 173
(1952) 170*f*, 174*f*, 179
(1953) 171*f*, 180
(1956) 172*f*, 180
nationality laws 107*f*, *v.* citizenship
nationality (Thai), deprivation 179
nationalization of industries 129, 202
naturalization 135*f*, 171, 173*f*
Chinese with Thai nationality 175*f*
Chinese opportunists 175
economic advantages 135, 175
fees 175, bribery 176
Navigation Act (1939) 131
Near East 12, firms 4
New Year festival 106, 124
New York 32

newspapers 81*f*, 85, 122, 140, 160
anti-Chinese reporting 132*f*
sensationalism 85, 142
Chinese 53, 59, 65, 83, 132-3, 141-2, 169, 187, 194
Communist editors 180
pro-Kuomintang 183
Ningpo 寧波 xiii, 7, 44
speech groups 7, 43-44
Northeast Thailand 3
nuns 98, 99, *v.* monks

occupational associations 47-48, [*v.* Chinese
categories 119
dialect group 7
diversity (Chinese) 188
patterns 116-121
separation 116
occupations, Thai reserved 2, 132*f*, 210
low paid 120
officialdom (Thai) 117, *v.* bureaucracy, military, Thai government
Omega watches 4
Opium War (1842) 15
Overseas Chinese, Hua-chiao 華僑
*v.* Chinese

Parliament (Thai) *v.* National Assembly
patriots, 'summer', 'fair weather' 11
*v.* jingoism
peasantry (Thai) 1, 117, 118
Pei-ming Middle School 146
Peking (seat of Communist government, 1949-) 183*f*, 185, 187, 202
Penang 165
People's Republic of China and Overseas Chinese 183
persecution, Chinese fear and integration 196
personnel, Thai in foreign firms 134
Pethai Amatavakul, Nai 51
Phao Sriyanon (Sriyanod), General 51, 52, 142
Phenix Village 19-20, *v.* Kulp
Phibun Songgram 25, 47*f*, 51, 75, 81*f*, 129*f*, 134, 143, 186
philanthropy 58
*v.* benevolent Assn, mutual aid
Philippine Is. 12, 143, 167, 177, 183, 210*n*
Phrabat 104
Phuket (South Thailand) xii, 8, 58, 203
physicians, Chinese P. Assn 49
pirates 15
plural society 189
Poh Tek Assn (報德善堂 Pao-te shang-t'ang) 55-57, 62, 64
*v.* benevolent assn
political factions in Chinese community 8, 43, 63, 65, 186*f*
*v.* Communist, Kuomintang
politicians, militarists (Thai) 169, 193
Chinese alliance with 10, 203
politics, Chinese and Thai 10, 181
Pomprap 32
population and Chinese emigration 20, 203
fluctuation 24
*v.* census, demography
*Prachathipatai* (Democracy) 50, 51
Prachinburi 142
Prajadhipok (King Rama VII, 1926-1935) 75, 127, 148
Pratumwan 32
Presbytherian Hospital of N.Y., x
Press Guild (Chinese) 49
*v.* newspapers
Pridi, Phanomyong 25, 75, 81, 128
Primary School Law (1921) 144, 163
Private School Act (1918) 148, 149, 168
professional assn 36
(occupation) 19, 22, 26, 89
*v.* 'White Chinese'
profiteering 2, *v.* cost of living
prostitution 83, call houses 83
protection, buying 9, 121, 138
*v.* bribery
Purcell, V., 5, 212
'pure' Thai 135, 141, 177, 181

quarrels, disputes *v.* political conflicts
quota *v.* immigration

racial affinities of Chinese and Thai 11
railways 117*f*, 127
alien restrictions on employment 133
construction labour 16
Rama VI (1910-1925), King Vajiravudh 75, 128
recreation *v.* entertainment, festivals
Red China, Chinese 19, 201, 202
*v.* Chinese Communist
march South 203-205
Reed, Stephen W., x
refugees from Communist China 19, 26, 71, *v.* 'White Chinese'
religion, Chinese assns 33, 63*f*, 95, 96-99, 105
differences with Thai 84*f*, 188
practices 74, 92-115, 159, 189, 190
temples 34, 39*f*, 42*f*, 48, 93-100, 106, 108-109, 110, 113, 159, 198
*v.* ancestral halls, death rites
religion, Thai 60, 73, 84-85, 92, 97, 104-105, 114, 126, 130, 133, 144, 163, 179, 191*f*, 197, 198, 200,
*v. wat*
remittances 2, 186, 199
renting to aliens 140
residence, continuity and naturalization 174*f*, 177*f*
restrictions 138*f*, areas 141*f*

residence—*(continued)*
temporary 26
Thai matrilocal 79
restrictions, limitations on alien occupations 127*f*, 169
effect 135*f*, self defeating 143
retailers of Western goods 4
*v.* middlemen
Returned Overseas Chinese Friendship Societies 184
Revolution (June 24, 1932) 8-9, 75, 125, 128, 148*f*, 169, 181, 199
rice 6, 16, 43, 119-120, 125
Chinese R. Merchants Assn 49
export xi, 3, 4
growing ix, 1, 118*f*
low price 2, 128
mills 17, 116, 136, coolies 47, processing 117 [131
Thai R. Co 129, 133, co-operatives
rickshaw pullers, pedicabs, *samlor* 52, [86, 120, 133, 199
riots 86, 187
*Royal Gazette* 25
rubber ix, x, 1, 3*f*, 6, 43, 119-120, 125, [131
plantation labour 16
prices 128
Russia 201

salaries, government and Chinese business 124
Salt and Tobacco Act (1939) 130
Sam Kuo Khoon (Buddhist statue) 104
*samlor* (tricycle 三輪車, pedicabs) 86, 120, 133, 199
Sampang 32, old maids 76
San Francisco 32
Sangnan Sirisawang, Nai 51
Saowapa, Queen 75 [185
Sarit Thanarat, Marshall 47, 51, 133,
saw-mills 135, 136, *v.* teak wood
schools *v.* education
girl 146
missionary 87
revenue 145
secret assns, societies 36
self-sufficiency of the Chinese 195
'Seven-up' and Coca-cola 51
sex ratio, Chinese 76*f*
Shanghai 7, 26, 50, 43
'Chinese' 19, 207*n*
Shanghai Book Co 155*f*
Shell Company 131
shellac 3, 4, 16
*shen-k'an* 神龕 (shrine) 101
*Shih-chieh* newspaper 世界日報 52, [143
Shih-dai School 116
shipping 3, 17, 203
Navigation Act 131
shops, Chinese 1, 194, signs 159
and home life 68*f*
*Siam Mai* (New Siam) 82
*Siam Nikorn* (Thai People) 143
*Siam Radt* (Siam State) 29, 51, 143
Siamese Red Cross 61
Siamese Vessel Act (1939) 131
*Sian Lua Hua Ch'iao Pao Teh Shan T'ang* 暹邏華僑報德善堂 (Siamese Overseas Chinese Repay Virtue Benevolent Assn) *v.* Poh Tek
Singapore 1, 4, 86, 177, 203
Sino-Thai 23, 53, 72-3, 75*f*, 89-91, 146, 148, 155
rapprochement 199-200
*v.* intermarriage, *luk-chin*
Skinner, G. Wm. 5, 118, 147, 150, 154, 207*n*, 212
slaughtering animals 130
social mobility 190, 199, status 195, 197, *v.* leaders
Social Science Research Council xi
social welfare service 60*f*, absence 195*f*
solidarity, Chinese 139, *v.* Chinese [minority—unity
Somsakdi, Nai 51
Songkhla (S. Thailand) xii, 2
Soo, Linda xi
South America 12 [36*f*, 192, 204, 208*n*
South China 6, 13, 15*f*, 18, 20, 31, village 189, 190, *v.* Phenix Village
'South China Republic' 81
South Vietnam 12
speech-group differences 6, 188
*v.* dialect groups
spirits 59, 94, 101, 103, *v.* animism
Standard Oil Co 131
*Statistical Year Book of Thailand* 17*f*, 21, 23, 147, 207*n*, 208*n*
stratification, social 11, 16, 48-49, 50, 53, 63*f*, 89-99, 116-119, 120, 124-127, 182-183
Sun Yat-sen (1866-1925) 146
Suraphong Trirat, Nai 143
surnames, Chinese S. Assns 33, 36, 38-40, 64*f*, 159
introduction of Thai 78
Thai s. adopted by Chinese 71, 191
Swatow 汕頭 xiii, 6, 18, 19, 22, 184
Teochiu dialect 146

tablets, ancestral 38, 159
Taiwan 7, 19, 54, 184, 186
assn (台灣會館 Taiwan hui-kuan) [43-44
*tambon* (Thai commune) 177
taxation 63, evasion 52
teachers *v.* education
teak wood ix, x, 3, 4, price 128
*v.* saw-mills

technology and revolution 200
v. Westernization [*wat*
temples 46, *v.* ancestral halls, religion,
Teochiu 潮州 (Tiochiu, Twechew, Chaochow) 6-7, 8, 19, 41-42, 60, 71, 98*f*, 111, 146, 158, 161, 190
assn 41-42, 46, 64, 66, 100, 111, 159
terrorism 186, *v.* blackmail, riots
Thai Cement Co 89
Thai Chamber of Commerce 128, Bangkok 208*n*, clubs 199
Thai government 8, 9 [159, 161-164
aid to schools 145, 151, 154-155,
and Communism 114
characteristics 8-9, 169, 182
civil service 125, 126-127, 133, 210*n*
decorations to Chinese 58, 88, titles
educational policies 144*f*, 165 [125
employment 118*f*, 124-127, 128, 133, 193, 198, 209*n*
labour relations 47-48, 61
relations with China 54
religious tolerance 92
restrictions on Chinese 11, 65, 83, 107, 127-143, 144-145, 147-153, 158, 169, 182, 185, 191, 196, 202, 209*n*
welfare and medical care 60*f*, 195*f*
*v.* citizenship, election laws, naturalization
Thai language 71, 86, 129-130, 144*f*, 148*f*, 151, 153*f*, 156-157, 158, 167, 172, 174-175, 178*f*, 190
and naturalization 25, 201
*Thai Mai* (Thai State) 51
Thai-ness of the Chinese 194*f*
Thai Rice Company 129, 133 [194
Thai society 116-117, 125-127, 138, view of Chinese 2, 81, 82*f*, 116
*v.* culture, religion, family and women
Thai vocations 3, 16, 23, 82, 117-120, 127*f*, 133, 134-135, 137-138, 189
reserved occupations 132, 209*n*, 210*n*
Thanom (Premier) 143
Thien Na Songkla, Nai 52
Thompson, Virginia 5, 61, 127, 212
Thonburi 143, 150, temple 99, 104
thrift of the Chinese 1, *v.* economy
Tien Hua Hospital 57
tin industry ix, x, 1, 4, 6*f*, 43, 58, mine labour 16 [119-120, 131
prices 128
titles 88, 125, *v.* decorations
tobacco monopoly 130
Toynbee Arnold 200, 212
trade guilds, organizations (*kung-hui* 公會) 32, 47, 49-50, 59, 63*f*, 66, 82, 138, 194 [202
trade missions (Chinese Communist)
traders, Chinese 2, *v.* middlemen
transport 1, 203, *v.* canals, railways, rickshaws, shipping
vehicles for hire law 131
Triad (Heavenly) 102
*tzu* 族 (clanship) 36-40, 44-47, 100
Turkey 200

Ubon xii, 2
Union Research Institute 184, 212
United Front Work, Bureau of 中共中央統一戰線工作部 183
United Nations 161, 210*n*
urban concentration of Chinese 203
*v.* residence
U.S.A., Americans 4, 31, 62, 89, 132, 143, 174, 190, 191, 208*n*, 210*n*
quota system 25, 30 [tion xi
U.S. Education (Fullbright) Founda-

Vajiravudh (King Rama VI, 1910-1925) 75, 128 [78, 197*f*
values, Chinese and Thai compared
Vegetable Merchants Assn 49
Vietnam, South 177, 202 [35, 36
village, South China organization 20,
violence 86, terrorism 186
Vocational Assistance to Thai (Act, 1956) 134
vocational schools, Thai 129
vote 9, *v.* election

Wan, Prince 143
*wan-phra* (holidays) 104
*wat* (Buddhist temple) 60, 93, 104, 163, 192*f*, 197
wealthy overseas Chinese 8, 27, 62, 88
alliance with Thai politicians 203
as class enemies to be conciliated
Sampang 76 [184
weddings, Chinese *v.* family
West Indies 12
Westerners, 84*f*, 89, 104, 108, 114, 119, 123, 127-128, 130*f*, 135, 137, 139, 145*f*, 157-158, 167, 189*f*, 193, 201-203, 208*n*, 209*n*
commercial interests 3-4, 16-17, 117
number 4
Westernization, 30-31, 86*f*, 88-89, 114, 121, 144, 157, 166 [16, 31
effect of industrial penetration 12,
of overseas Chinese 191*f*, 199*f*
'White Chinese' 19, 26, 50, 71, 207*n*

'White Paper' 81
'Who's Who' among Chinese leaders [64
Williams, Robert L. xi
Wines, Harold J. 204, 212
wolfram 3, 4
women (Chinese) 13-14, 22-4, 30, 33, 40, 44, 58, 64, 67, 93, 95, 97, 98-9, 100, 103, 109, 110-11, 112-3, 121, 146, 155, 197
conservatism 86*f*, changing modes [87
numbers 76*f*, *v*. sex ratio
occupation 72, 73-4
women (Thai) 3, 73, 77-8, 79, 83, 84-5, 197, 199-200, 207*n*
and hospitals 59
in business 118
Thai by marriage 170
wives 22*f*
working conditions 120
World Federation of Trade Unions (WFTU) 48

Yale University x
Yat Waidi, Nai 51

泰國華僑之雙重身份



著者　高國麟
出版者　香港大學出版社
承印者　國泰印刷所
定價　港幣弍拾伍圓
出版日期　一九六〇年四月